DEVELOPMENT STRATEGIES RECONSIDERED

John P. Lewis and
Valeriana Kallab, Editors

Irma Adelman
John W. Mellor
Jagdish N. Bhagwati
Leopoldo Solis
Aurelio Montemayor
Colin I. Bradford, Jr.
Alex Duncan
Atul Kohli

Series Editors:
Richard E. Feinberg and
Valeriana Kallab

 Transaction Books
New Brunswick (USA) and Oxford (UK)

Library of Congress Catalog Number: 86-24582
ISBN: 0-88738-044-1 (cloth)
ISBN: 0-87855-991-4 (paper)
Printed in the United States of America

Library of Congress Cataloging-in-Publication Data
Main entry under title:

Development strategies reconsidered.
    1. Developing countries—Economic policy—Addresses, essays, lectures.
2. Developing countries—Commercial policy—Addresses, essays, lectures.
3. Industrial promotion—Developing countries—Addresses, Essays, lectures.
I. Lewis, John Prior.
HC59.7.D482   1986   338.9'009172'4   86-24582
ISBN 0-88738-044-1
ISBN 0-87855-991-4 (pbk.)

Development
Strategies
Reconsidered

Acknowledgments

Guest Editor:
John P. Lewis

Series Editors:
Richard E. Feinberg
Valeriana Kallab

The Overseas Development Council gratefully acknowledges the help of the Ford, William and Flora Hewlett, and Rockefeller Foundations, whose financial support contributes to the preparation and widespread dissemination of the policy analysis presented in the ODC's U.S.-Third World Policy Perspectives series. The Council's special thanks for support and encouragement of this volume in the Policy Perspectives series go to the Johnson Foundation and to the International Development Research Centre (IDRC).

On behalf of the ODC and the contributing authors, the editors wish to express special thanks to members of the ODC Program Advisory Committee and others who participated in the discussion of early versions of the papers included in this volume at the conference on "Development Strategies: A Synthesis," sponsored by the ODC and the Johnson Foundation, with assistance from the IDRC.

Special thanks for their respective roles in the editorial preparation and production of this volume are due to Patricia A. Masters, Linda Starke, Carol J. Cramer, Lisa M. Cannon, and Robin E. Ward.

Contents

Foreword

When the Overseas Development Council launched its U.S.-Third World Policy Perspectives series in 1984, firm criteria were established that each issue should analyze different facets of a major U.S.-Third World policy issue on the current agenda of decision makers. The initial volumes in the series thus were devoted to the debt crisis, the role of the commercial banks in financing development, and U.S.-Third World trade issues relating to a new round of international trade negotiations.

Development Strategies Reconsidered departs from that pattern. We asked John P. Lewis, Senior Advisor to ODC and Chairman of its Program Advisory Committee, to take on a more difficult task: to set out, for non-specialists, an overview of current thinking among development strategists on the broad issue of how best to promote development in the economic and political environment of the mid-1980s. That task seemed urgent for three reasons. First, while development as an international policy goal is only about four decades old, a great deal has been accomplished; in fact, the record of both economic growth and human improvement in the developing countries has been nothing short of spectacular (albeit very uneven between and within countries). Second, there currently is a pervasive feeling that somehow development has "failed"—a feeling reinforced, at the extremes, by the food and environmental problems of Sub-Saharan Africa and by the debt crises of the more advanced developing countries. Third, there is no agreement among policymakers as to the "correct" development strategy for Third World governments or aid agencies.

This volume of Policy Perspectives was deliberately designed not to recommend one correct development strategy—whether for aid agencies or Third World governments; rather, it was designed to analyze what has been learned from nearly 40 years of development cooperation in terms of economic growth, societal equity, and political participation. The reader will then be in a much better position to participate in what we hope will be the coming debate over how U.S. policy can best support both legitimate U.S. interests in the Third World and the developing countries' own hopes and aspirations for economic progress and improved human wellbeing.

No one is better qualified for this task than John P. Lewis. During a distinguished and productive career, Dr. Lewis has served in the Council of Economic Advisers under President Kennedy, as head of the U.S. Aid mission in India, and as Chairman of the OECD's Development Assistance Committee. For many years, he has alternated between government posts and academia; he is Dean and professor of economics and international affairs at Princeton University's Woodrow Wilson School of Public and International Affairs. He has been an active participant in the evolution of development theory, policy, and practice that is analyzed in this policy volume.

On behalf of the Overseas Development Council, I would like to express special thanks to the Johnson Foundation of Racine, Wisconsin, and particularly to its President and Vice President, William Boyd and Rita Goodman, for their support and encouragement of this project.

John W. Sewell, *President*
Overseas Development Council

February 1986

Development Strategies Reconsidered:

Overview and Summaries of Recommendations

Development Promotion: A Time for Regrouping

John P. Lewis

The promotion of Third World development, both as a subject for study and as a realm of public policy, is about thirty-five years old. In this comparatively short period, both the practical and academic sides of the field have had star-studded histories. Currently, however, both are in the doldrums.

In the U.S. case, references to "aid fatigue" have become commonplace. Compared with twenty years ago, the study of development has lost standing in the universities. Whether or not the appeal of careers as development practitioners has diminished for young Americans (some of them, certainly, are as eager as ever) there are fewer jobs for them. We are into the second term of an administration that has reduced the official focus on North-South economic matters, especially on those which are not country- or region-specific.

Moreover, the sag in pro-development energies and efforts is not uniquely American. It is evident in a number of other developed countries. One cannot attribute quite the same policy lapse to the developing countries themselves; clearly, their interest in their own development has not flagged. Yet distracting circumstances have mounted, and in many, not all, developing countries, the resources assignable to development have thinned and expectations have diminished. In this sense, the current wilting of development effort and analysis is a global, not just a "North-Western," phenomenon.[1]

This situation and mood provide the occasion for this book. The authors are all adherents to what might be called mainstream development doctrine (although some of them are not entirely happy with the label). By "mainstream" doctrines I here mean those which broadly reflect the views of most influential North-Western analysts and policy advisers, and which typically are widely shared by (indeed, often are derived from) counterparts in the South.[2] By "doctrine" I mean theories about how public policies, both in the Third World itself and in the international community, can promote Third World economic development. Such policies of course include development assistance, or aid, but they include as well a whole array of other policies—mainly in the developing countries themselves but also in the industrialized world—that shape the environment for development both indirectly and directly.

The contributors to this volume agree that this is a "down" time, a period of slack, in development thought and efforts. To them, this is no surprise—in that development doctrine has evolved in a series of revisionist surges throughout its thirty-five-year history. The process has been roughly dialectical: In a particular period, an effective majority of theorists and policy makers has pursued one theme to the partial neglect of one or more others; then has overcorrected; and then perhaps has achieved a synthesis that itself becomes an input to further zigzagging forward.

And right now, most of the authors and most (although, as I shall be emphasizing, not all) mainstream analysts agree, we are between conventional wisdoms. This is not because some disembodied cycle or rhythm is at work, but because, just as happened when mainstream doctrines reached turning points in the past, events have forced shifts in the dominant beliefs. In the present case, as my sketch of the sequence of mainstream strategies will try to indicate, the critical events prompting such a shift have been the pre-emptive claims of the adjustment and debt crises that since 1979 have been preoccupying North-South attention—and, indeed, the attention of the Overseas Development Council in its own analyses.[3]

Those of us writing in this volume share this concern with the adjustment and debt crises as well as with the overlapping but distinguishable trauma afflicting much of Sub-Saharan Africa in these years. But we attempt to look through and beyond these immediate crises to the resumption of more effective long-term development promotion. How, we ask, can the lessons that have been learned now be put to work? Can a reasonably coherent set of strategies be articulated? What should be the thrust of the next revision of development doctrine?

The first half of this overview chapter introduces the authors' responses to these questions. The second half takes on the quite different task of establishing the *relevance* of their reflections for policy, and for development itself—attempting to address the views of those observers who assert that the whole development promotion effort, past and prospective, is a waste of time.

I. Looking to the Next Round of Development Strategies

In this section, I first briefly trace the path that dominant ideas concerning development have taken from the 1950s down to the present. Thereafter, I characterize today's "mainstreamers"—noting those whom the category leaves out, noting that all of those whom it includes are proponents of active development promotion, but noting also a present cleavage within the mainstream set. One faction (probably a minority, but it has the louder voice) preaches what I am calling the new orthodoxy; the ideas of the others are more heterodox, but no less positive as to the feasibility of development promotion. At the end of the section, I turn to our own particular authors and their topics.

Past Development Strategy Fashions in Quick Review

In the 1950s, mainstream development strategists—adopting the new neo-Keynesian growth model of Roy Harrod and Evsey Domar and following the intellectual lead of such Third Worlders as Arthur Lewis, Raul Prebisch, and P. C. Mahalanobis—were preoccupied with industrialization and with lifting the capital constraints on development. There was pessimism about the ability of developing countries to increase their earnings from exports fast enough to keep pace with import requirements. Accordingly, two measures were emphasized for helping countries gear themselves up onto paths of self-sustaining growth: They needed net inward transfers of preferably concessional capital (i.e., aid), and they needed to encourage import substitution.

At that time, in the aftermath of the 1930s and of World War II, many theorists as well as policy designers were less than awed by the magic of the market. In the poor countries—the older ones of Latin America, those newly independent in Asia, and others yet to achieve independence in Africa—there was need, it was felt, for massive, restructuring interventions by governments that could be adequately knit together only by comprehensive economic planning. The planning pressed upon clients by the U.S. and other bilateral aid programs and by the World Bank was inspired at least as much by the models of U.S. and British World War II economic mobilization as it was by the Soviet example that the literature now so typically cites. And planning in most developing countries—under circumstances of thin, imperfect, slow-acting markets and import-substitution-induced imbalances—tended to be coupled (although the linkage was not logically essential) with proliferating direct controls and proliferating bureaucracies to administer them.

Although it is customary these days to ridicule the kind of 1950s conventional wisdom I have just sketched, one of the lessons our story tells is that one set of mainstream doctrines is never totally abandoned. Elements are sloughed off or revised, but others are retained. Nevertheless, there plainly was a major reaction, a change of course, in mainstream circles in the 1960s. The virtues of the market as an instrument of social control were rediscovered. In the estimates of development analysts, the importance of policies and needed policy changes began to dominate the importance of quantitative planning. There were related efforts to unshackle economies from direct controls internally, liberalize their trade regimes, rationalize their exchange rates, and thereby shift toward export-promotion strategies. Both the focus on agriculture, which had suffered from the emphasis on industrialization, and the effectiveness of strategies for agricultural expansion were greatly enhanced. At the same time, the commitment to aid slowly gathered strength and coherence, in part because of the priority that some major donors assigned to agricultural development.

The conventional wisdom about conventional wisdoms has it that then—at the beginning of the 1970s—the emphasis shifted from growth to equity. Many Indian economists, including Jagdish Bhagwati, rightly argue that the issue of poverty was discovered long before the 1970s—that growth was not pursued as an end in itself in the 1950s and 1960s. They note that from 1961 onward, the Indian Planning Commission was defining and trying to implement minimum-needs programs as a way of contending with domestic poverty.

Nevertheless, the folklore is mostly right. It *is* true that in India and in much of the rest of the developing world, as well as in much of the development cooperation community, a kind of double-take occurred at the very end of the 1960s. There was a sense that development professionals had become so operationally preoccupied with growth promotion that they had lost sight of poverty. Much more attention was addressed to intra-national distributional questions—in particular to low-end, "absolute" poverty, but also to inequalities up and down the income scale. The pejorative "trickle-down growth" entered the mainstream vocabulary. There was renewed concern with the problems of unemployment and underemployment, which in poor countries were seen to merge with the problem of poverty. Direct attacks on the latter, along with growth promotion, were needed. Meeting "basic human needs" became a target, if not the primary target, of development promotion. However, most analysts and policy makers (if not publicists) argued that basic needs had to be met mainly by raising the productivity and therefore the earned incomes of the poor, not via handouts. Yet it is also true that much of the basic-needsmanship of the 1970s was closely associated with an array of social-sector or human-resource issues (health, nutrition, population, education), as well as with a variety of innovative but complex integrated-rural-development ventures.

This new shift in conventional wisdom—some, perhaps speaking pejoratively themselves, called it "populism"—spread, and quickly, to most of the development promotion community in the early and mid-1970s. Robert McNamara became the school's most prominent spokesman, but he did not invent it or set its boundaries. Anti-poverty cum basic needs was particularly a donor fashion. It was favored by various multilateral agencies, and nearly every bilateral aid donor represented in the Development Assistance Committee (DAC) of the Organisation for Economic Co-operation and Development (OECD) adopted the nomenclature and reformed its operations in some of the directions indicated. But most developing countries also went along for a while. The populist movement reached its crest in the remarkably substantive Declaration of Principles and Programme of Action adopted with very few reservations by all the developed- and developing-country delegations to the International Labour Office's (ILO) World Employment Conference of June 1976.[4]

Thus by the middle 1970s, we had been through two versions—that of the 1950s, then that of the 1960s—of how to accelerate growth, followed by a heavy pro-equity shift in mainstream development policy. It would appear the time was ripe for a tidy growth-cum-equity synthesis. But from here on things became more complicated. The model of successive fashions and reactions continued to serve reasonably well, but the dialectics started fragmenting and overlapping.

For one thing, if John Mellor is right in his chapter in this volume, the basic-needs, integrated-rural-development thrust fell partly of its own weight. It gave too low a priority to aggregate agricultural output as well as to building human and institutional infrastructure for development. Beyond this, developing-country tolerance for intrusions into various internal distributional issues was short-lived. The conciliatory tones of basic-needs dialoguing were soon overtaken by the harsh cadences of "NIEO" dialoguing,[5] wherein the developing countries of the "Group of 77," emboldened by the newly evident muscle of their oil-exporting members, demanded faster reductions in inter-country inequalities while asserting sovereign prerogatives to deal with their own internal equity issues as they saw fit.

This last, however, suggests an overlapping 1970s phenomenon whose impact was far more direct and profound than were the effects of any shifts in North-South, inter-bloc diplomacy. I refer to the effects of the oil shocks—first in 1973–74, then in 1979–80. The first shock (in ways that have been described in various ODC publications[6] among others) established the context in which the newly industrializing countries (NICs) and some of the middle-income countries pressed ahead with the export-oriented growth strategies they had adopted in the 1960s. In continuing their productive expansions, some of these countries made more, some made less, precarious use of the temporarily cheap, variable-rate credit that was available. The production and income advances of all of them, however, contributed to the widening differentiation of development performances that characterized the 1970s. With many low-income countries (especially in Africa) not sharing these advances and even in economic retreat, it became clearer than ever that in the future even the broadest development strategies would need to be country-group specific.

The second oil shock (along lines also reviewed in other ODC publications,[7] including two earlier volumes of the Policy Perspectives series) pushed us into the present era of adjustment. The oil-price jump triggered a set of macro policy decisions, especially in the United States, that in turn triggered financial crises—not only in the most heavily indebted Latin American countries but also in much of Africa and parts of Asia. Arguments over the appropriate goals of development strategy—growth or equity? or what balance between them?—were pre-empted. Both goals had to yield priority to adjustment. The inescapable, non-postponable need of any country not prepared to retreat into complete economic isolation is to "adjust"—that is, to bring the excess of its imports over its exports into line with the maximum inflow of capital (concessional or otherwise) it is willing and able to obtain.

Plainly, giving priority to adjustment does not mean forgetting about either growth or equity. The goal is a type of adjustment—and adjustment-facilitating finance—that slows growth as little as possible. Likewise, there is great concern—it is voiced constantly with respect to the programs of the International Monetary Fund (IMF)—to cushion the impact of adjustment on the poorest, most disadvantaged, developing-country constituencies. But the adjustment priority has remained in the fore of mainstream thinking for the past half-dozen years.

The New Orthodoxy and the Mainstream State of Play

The kind of adjustment now being favored goes beyond austere demand management. The mood is to press for greater efficiency—to give precedence to optimal uses of scarce resources—throughout the economic system. As indicated, those who advance this "new orthodoxy" do not feel they are fresh out of conventional wisdoms. On the contrary, they are surer of themselves than ever. Their "orthodoxy" is, as to economics, neoclassical. It carries forward with redoubled vigor the liberalizing, pro-market strains of the thinking of the 1960s and 1970s. It is very mindful of the limits of governments. It is emphatic in advocating export-oriented growth to virtually all comers. And it places heavier-than-ever reliance on policy dialoguing, especially between aid donors and recipients.

The new orthodoxy characterizes the macro-economic thinking of those factions of the Reagan administration that stand for a positive approach to development promotion. It is also currently identified with a number of other bilateral donors as well. But the new orthodoxy is headquartered at the World Bank, which has not so much changed its views on this matter (one can find antecedents as far back as one wishes to look in the Bank's history) as it has sharpened and hardened them.[8]

There is, however, currently a fair amount of disarray in the ranks of mainstream development strategists. The orthodox ones are sure of their heading. But many of the rest of us—and, as noted, I think we account for a majority of all the mainstreamers—sense a good deal of unsettled and/or unfinished business.

We question which revised brand of long-term development strategy will best suit different portions of the Third World if and as they surmount the current adjustment crisis. We are mindful that there needs to be more differentiation of strategies to match the differentiation of developing countries and groups of countries. We wonder whether a standardized prescription of export-led growth will meet the needs of big low-income countries in the latter 1980s as well as it did those of small and medium size middle-income countries in the 1960s and 1970s. We are concerned about the special needs of low-income Africa and, in particular, about how aid programs can help the other-than-capital needs that seem to dominate development problems in that beleaguered continent. We have a sense that in the sequences of development thought and practice in the 1950s and 1960s, the relationship between agriculture and industry never got adequately sorted out—nor, more recently, has the balance to be sought between export expansion and some version of internal agro-industrial expansion as engines of growth. We see a great deal of unfinished business under the heading of poverty and equity. That some of the policy experiments of the 1970s were misdesigned or did not work, or work fast enough, obviously does not diminish the importance of the poverty issue; we have learned some lessons here that need assimilation. Finally, most of us who look at development primarily through *economic* lenses also are curious about the *political* dimensions of the process. We prefer democratic modes of governance. But there are claims to be answered that more authoritarian political models are better suited to growth and equity promotion.

Issues Debated by the Contributors

It was with all these questions in mind that the Overseas Development Council gathered together the contributors to this study, joined also by group of able discussants, to review some major issues in the development promotion debate at a conference at the Wingspread headquarters of the Johnson Foundation in Racine, Wisconsin, in January 1985.

In my lexicon—although, as I say, one or two do not accept the label cheerfully—the authors are all "mainstreamers" who have been in or close to development policy-making agencies and institutions. They have experience with development policy change and are interested in further change—but change of an evolutionary, incremental character. Thus, one parochial characteristic of these writers (for which, as editor, I accept responsibility) is that they do

not include analysts or advocates advertised as radicals by themselves or others. Another limiting trait is that, as to disciplines,
they incline toward economics. They are mainly economists because
development strategies are public policy designs, and mainstream
development promotion policies have been concerned largely with
national and international measures to alter economic performance
at the country level. Atul Kohli is a political scientist, but of the
subset of that discipline that is highly concerned with political
economy.

The tilt toward national policies implies another limiting characteristic of the papers in this book. They touch very little on an
important aspect of development promotion activity that dates back
at least to the early days of India's community development movement in the 1950s but that acquired a broader new impetus in the
1970s. This is development promotion "from the bottom up"—involving highly decentralized, localized initiatives that mobilize the
energies of local citizens in improving the quality of their lives
while at the same time empowering them with more command over
the direction of the changes in which they become involved.

With respect to social science disciplines, those currently active
in this bottom-up kind of approach to development—both in developing countries and in the North-West—probably have stronger
links to sociology, anthropology, and (public and private sector)
management than to economics. But much of the intellectual energy and illumination in the field is being generated by creative
practitioners in both non-governmental and public agencies (indigenous and expatriate alike) whose writings reflect more their experience than their disciplinary roots.

The papers gathered in this volume do not, however, entirely
ignore the bottom-up approaches to development. Irma Adelman
devotes attention to some of the dynamics of inequalities between
castes and classes at the local level, and John Mellor gives considerable emphasis to the "spatial" dimensions of development—that is,
to the deployment of activities across the array of small to large
settlements (villages to metropolises). Settlement patterns and the
extent to which they can be steered constitute one of the issues
linking micro and macro strategies. Nevertheless, we cannot give
enough attention to bottom-up development in this slim volume; it
deserves one of its own. Meanwhile, having dwelled on what our
invited incrementalists do not do, it remains for me to summarize
briefly what they do.

Being seasoned, engaged people, the authors do not come up
with any "eureka" visions of brand-new development departures;
but they address a representative majority of the mainstream de-

velopment issues. They were not asked to, and do not, adopt a single, homogenized stance. Indeed they voice a few strong differences, but for the most part their contributions are complementary rather than conflicting. Some interesting linkages develop between particular chapters. And together, the chapters provide a state-of-the-art review of mainstream development strategy that is couched essentially in non-technical terms.

Irma Adelman returns to the unfinished poverty and equity business of the 1970s with the authority of one who has done a great deal of seminal statistical and technical as well as conceptual work in the field. She argues that, thanks to various policy experiments, we do indeed know more than we used to about how to target direct attacks on poverty. She herself would favor a more radical strategy of *first* redistribution, *then* growth rather than the redistribution-*with*-growth strategy that became identified with Hollis Chenery, the World Bank, and many others in the middle 1970s.

But the novel thing about Adelman's chapter, as an anti-poverty piece, is the degree to which she finds anti-poverty outcomes to be determined by the *kind* of growth strategy a country adopts. Broadly, the more successful a country is in choosing efficient, labor-intensive patterns of products and production processes, the smaller its income inequalities will be. And here Adelman supplies explicit links with the four chapters that follow hers. For there are, she says, two alternative growth strategies that are both relatively pro-egalitarian: on the one hand, the kind of agriculture-led industrialization advocated by Mellor; on the other, the new orthodoxy of export-led growth articulated in this volume by one of its creators, Jagdish Bhagwati, as well as by Leopoldo Solis and Aurelio Montemayor, and given a more skeptical reading by Colin Bradford.

Interestingly, both Mellor and Bhagwati emphasize that their alternative prescriptions are complementary, not competitive. But plainly each has his allegiance. **John Mellor** is an agricultural economist who is not bounded by his subdiscipline. He has written and directed official policy analysis with respect to the whole span of economic development; yet he has long bridled at what he has seen as the failure of a succession of mainstream development doctrines to assign a sufficiently central and dynamic role to agricultural expansion. He recognizes that there are natural limits that keep agriculture by itself from being an adequate engine of growth in most developing countries. But with respect to populous countries where most of the people still live in the countryside and where, for purposes of employment and spreading the benefits of expansion, the need is for labor-intensive development, Mellor for a dozen years has been perfecting a model of agriculture-led industrialization. He sees a progressive agriculture (requiring active government promotion) providing supplies and wage goods as well as markets to a complementary industrial expansion, which itself is kept labor-intensive, thanks to the market's rationing of scarce capital.

What makes Mellor's current rendering of this thesis particularly salient is that many will judge it to be very timely in view of the present obstacles they see to orthodox export promotion. Mellor himself, as noted, sees his focus on internal market interactions as complementary to, not competitive with, the new orthodoxy. But, as to growth engineering, his model has great appeal in a period when China and India have displaced the likes of Taiwan and South Korea as the test countries for determining whether a strategy works or not, and when the economic environment is characterized by scarce transfers and sluggish OECD growth.

Let me say in passing, however, that Mellor seems to me to remain somewhat exposed to the criticism that another broad-based agricultural economist, Vijay Vias, leveled at him at ODC's Wingspread conference: His prescription probably does not sufficiently meet the needs of the landless and the other most disadvantaged members of peasant economies. If their disadvantages cannot be dealt with at their roots by the kind of (politically difficult) land reform advocated by Adelman—and by Bhagwati—then in a "Mellor world," there would remain need for more *direct* antipoverty measures than Mellor suggests.

Jagdish Bhagwati, one of the founders of the (outward-oriented) new orthodoxy, was asked to stand off a bit and consider whether there is anything about his progeny that should be judged less robust for the 1980s than it was for the 1970s. Bhagwati is not one who would have hesitated to declare doubts if, on reconsideration, he had encountered them. In our chapter, he first establishes some terminology (e.g., "export promotion" does not necessarily mean tilting incentives *toward* exporting; it means only *not* tilting them *against* it) and summarizes the findings of the great analytical exercises of the late 1960s and the 1970s that so strongly supported outward-oriented strategies.

Then, one by one, Bhagwati considers four new kinds of doubt that are being cast on the current appropriateness of the export promotion prescription—1) that past export promoters are now paying a heavy price for past successes as they struggle under present debt burdens; 2) that export promotion is less promising in a world of slower growth and rising protectionism—wherein not everyone, especially the giant countries, can expect to find as much market room as did the "gang of four" (Taiwan, Korea, Hong Kong, Singapore) in the recent past; 3) that other, would-be export promoters are likely to be harried by wage indiscipline; and 4) that effective outward orientation may depend on authoritarian politics. Bhagwati considers each of these arguments. He is not persuaded by any of them. He notes, for example, that, even with completely open, distortion-free markets, the ratio of a large country's trade to its GNP would be expected to be smaller than that of a small country. He does, however, make an interesting concession: To graduate from the import-substitution phase that characterized nearly all early industrializations probably has been harder for a democratic country like India than for the more authoritarian countries of East Asia "simply because pluralistic democracies may find it much harder to dismantle the controls, protection, etc., that inevitably accompany the import-substitution strategy."

But as to the new orthodoxy, Jagdish Bhagwati, after careful reflection, finds no reason to turn to apostasy. At least as interesting is the fact that **Leopoldo Solis** and **Aurelio Montemayor**, two Mexican economists who write from a depth of highly placed and respected official experience, strongly second the outward-oriented view. They draw a sharp and detailed contrast between the comparative adjustment experiences—both in the 1970s and since 1979—of the outward-oriented, middle-income, Asian countries and the predominantly inward-oriented, larger, Latin American countries. They spell out the somewhat paradoxical case that export dependency rendered the Asian set of countries capable of quicker adjustment. And while they cast a resounding vote for outwardness—demonstrating that orthodoxy by no means is confined to such corners of the world as the World Bank and the University of Chicago—they do not imply a bright or easy prognosis for economies, such as their own, that are struggling with the accumulated problems of delayed adjustment.

Colin Bradford, on the other hand, does raise some questions about the confidence with which orthodox policy-medicine is being dispensed in all directions these days. He starts with some interesting reflections on the general state of development thought and policy—reflections roughly congruent with my own in this chapter but different enough to be abundantly worth including. Bradford then homes in on two issues that bear pointedly on the Bhagwati and Solis-Montemayor chapters preceding: *First,* he casts quite detailed doubt both on the representativeness of the "gang of four" cases on which so much of the export-promotion advocacy tends to rest—and on the conventional interpretations being placed on those cases (e.g., that they involved minimal roles for government). *Second*, he makes a more general methodological point. Referring to the major trade and industrialization studies that Bhagwati mentions, Bradford notes that policy stances, when they rest on careful, scientifically assembled, empirical findings, almost invariably tend to reflect situations of ten or fifteen years earlier, which by now may have changed profoundly.

With the paper by **Alex Duncan**, we move to a different, albeit closely related, quadrant of development strategy. It will be remembered that in the 1950s, mainstream growth theory, and therefore development strategy, was heavily *capital*-centered. Without denigrating the importance of capital inputs for development, successive phases in the evolution of strategy have given increasing attention to other contributions to the development process. In particular, at present, such contributions include (in the eyes of many analysts) a developing country's managerial and institutional capacities; its capacities for developing effective—including trained—human resources; and its ability to acquire, adapt, and/or develop improved and appropriate technologies. These are the strategic dimensions that Duncan tackles from the viewpoint of his hands-on experience in East Africa. But in light of that experience as well as work he has done for the World Bank/IMF Development Committee's Task Force on Concessional Flows, he examines these issues mainly in a context or setting of foreign assistance: How—or how well—can aid help build institutions, develop human resources, and facilitate technological transfer and improvement? He thus gives to our discussion a twist that happens to be responsive to what still are the proclivities of a North-Western readership: say "development strategy," and many people still think "aid." They narrow the subject, but they make a kind of sense, since aid, although it is a minor determinant of developmental outcomes is a significant one, and since aid is usually the determinant over which expatriate actors such as the U.S. government have the greatest influence.

In the final chapter, **Atul Kohli's** analysis turns up two rather unexpected responses to the familiar complaint of democrats that authoritarian regimes are much the better promoters of development. On the contrary, says Kohli, the development record of such on-balance democracies as India, Malaysia, Sri Lanka, Venezuela, and Costa Rica is really quite good: 1) the growth record is not as flashy as that of some of the dictatorships, but it is substantial and comparatively steady; and 2) the equity record is distinctly better.

But if this is so, why does the democratic mode not have wider incidence and a better survival rate in the Third World? Kohli's second point is that an array of structural obstacles inhibit democracy's spread in developing countries. In particular, especially when resources are scarce, the intensity of competition among elites reduces the chances for establishing and sustaining democratic rule.

II. Is Development Promotion a Lost Cause?

Before we proceed to the rest of this book, some would argue that a prior question must be addressed. The authors of the following chapters, not questioning the validity of development promotion itself, consider how to reformulate future efforts—present efforts being in a period of disarray under the onslaught of the adjustment crisis. There are others, however, who subscribe to an alternative, bleaker explanation for the current disarray: Most simply put, the development effort has failed. It is in decline because it is "over the hill." It is not going to be revived, because deliberate, purposeful, policy-led acceleration of development does not work as a practical matter—at least it will not work in the future. Historically, the development policy effort is nearly finished.

There is a great deal of this basic pessimism, disillusionment, anomie in the air these days about the very do-ability of development promotion. If the pessimists are right, they undercut the whole development-strategy question, for whereas the latter asks how to play the development-promotion game more effectively, the disillusioned pessimist answers that the game is unplayable. As the recruiter of views focusing on the "how to" issue, I have an obligation to establish their relevance by first attempting to cut this "can't be done" pessimism down to size.

Sources of Disillusionment

It is easy to catalogue the factors currently contributing to a depressed view of development promotion possibilities. Even where these are inconsistent among themselves, they do not cancel each other out: The several pessimistic views of development prospects to which they contribute get aggregated uncritically. Nor does the fact that some of them are only perceptions, even mistaken ones, automatically eliminate the effects of these negatives. It is perceptions, not facts, that actuate decision. The perceptions are harder to dislodge when they are grounded in fact. But even when they are wrong, they may begin to reorder the facts if enough people believe them.

Collapse in Africa

For several years now, much of the international community's time for the discussion of development has been preempted by Sub-Saharan Africa. The news there is nearly all bad. In a region where independent governments have been pursuing explicit, often formally planned, development efforts for a quarter-century, where dozens of aid donors have been at work for much of that time, and where both investment and aid per capita have been fairly high by Third World standards for many years, average per capita incomes are actually lower than they were fifteen years ago. Per capita food production is down sharply. Many of the poorest of the poor have been hurt grievously. Moreover, while the rains have been worse than average over much of the region during the past dozen years, most of the problem cannot be blamed on the weather. By and large, the continent has become one great composite case of development not working.

The Debt Crisis

Until three or four years ago, a number of the larger Latin American countries were near the other end of the Third World spectrum. Most of them had been and/or were suffering political turbulence and repression—raising grave doubts about the predictability of the interplay between political and economic development. But the latter-day economic performance of the larger Latin American countries was quite striking. Except in cases of gross political mismanagement, such as Argentina, their growth rates were high. They were achieving strong export expansion, especially in manufactured and processed goods. Several were dubbed "newly industrializing countries." And those that were afflicted with hyperinflation seemed to have found means, never wholly understood by persons from jurisdictions not similarly afflicted, for coping with the phenomenon.

But then the roof fell in on these quasi-success stories. As a result of the size of their borrowings, of variable interest rates, and of rate rises triggered in the North-West, their debt burdens ballooned. North-Western markets for their products became softer and more inclined toward protection. Fresh lending to these countries by the commercial banks that during the 1970s had been their main source of external transfers diminished radically; much of what continued reflected pressure from the IMF and from the central banks of OECD countries; much of the rest bespoke the concern of the commercial banks to sustain borrowers' incentives not to default.

By dint of a good deal of skill and effort in many quarters of the financial establishment, including the on-balance determination of debtor-country governments to meet their obligations, major default and financial collapse have been avoided thus far. But the cost has been high in terms of sharp economic contractions, explosive inflations, and prolonged declines in per capita income in the more advanced Latin American countries. The pain almost surely has been concentrated particularly on poorer, disadvantaged groups. One wonders how much more adjustment therapy these countries—several of them moving into a more democratic mode—can stand, especially when the apparent needs for continuing austerity stretch far into the future.

All of this gives the development policy record another large negative to set alongside the African negative. In Africa, development has failed in some of the poorest countries. In Latin America, it also seems to have failed, or at least to have suffered a shattering setback, in some of the larger, more advanced, developing countries. The debt crisis, moreover, has spread much farther than to the few Latin American countries in which it first became prominent; it has become serious even in some of those impoverished African nations. By putting the U.S. and European financial systems at risk, the crisis has heightened appreciation of the stake that North-Westerners have in the Third World. But, mainly, it has cast a further pall over the whole development enterprise.

Endless Aid

Yet another set of negative perceptions arises under the rubric of development assistance. These perceptions are inconsistent, but each is discouraging to its own constituency. For one thing, those who had been sold on the temporariness of aid find that it goes on and on. In a number of countries, aid was billed and sold to parliaments and publics as a time-bound exercise. It was administered by temporary agencies. Along with responding to emergencies, it was to give poor countries a head start toward self-reliance and then be done. Clients were to graduate, and in due course the overall aid enterprise was to taper down to a graceful end.

Instead, the demands for this peculiar form of gift-giving keep mounting.[9] Africa is just the latest case of new requirements. Other requirements do not subside to an offsetting degree—there are few "graduations." The demand continues to be for new programs to add to, not replace, the old.

Ineffective Aid

This is a charge that has risen from all sides—especially in the past half-dozen years. Some of those voicing it are people who, for budgetary or other reasons, have been looking for excuses to stop aid. But most of the complaints are genuine: Aid has not solved Africa's problems . . . It did not forestall the debt crisis . . . It is sometimes badly designed. Or it is clumsily implemented . . . It gets tangled with corruption . . . It breeds dependency . . . It does not engineer needed policy changes . . . On the contrary, it is too high-handed and intrusive . . . It encourages capital-intensity and inappropriate technologies. It protects the elites and ill serves the poor . . . Not so! It supports radical transformations and accommodates radical ideologies; It assists statist regimes . . . Rather, on the contrary, aid presses market solutions on reluctant clients.

This discordant chorus reminds anyone in or close to the aid business what a complex, inherently awkward and frustrating endeavor it is. Aid is seldom more than a minor determinant of the outcomes it seeks, and overall, I will be arguing below, it does indeed work reasonably well. But it is hard to prove this conclusively. If one is looking for bad news in the field, it always can be found. Once aid-ineffectiveness suspicions are aroused, it is hard to lay them to rest.

Inadequate Aid

A different kind of aid pessimism afflicts some of those who, while recognizing its flaws, believe in the great usefulness of the aid instrument. This is an apprehension of gradually worsening impotence on the part of donors. The donors collectively, these observers perceive, are becoming less and less capable of meeting legitimate aid needs. All but two of the so-called traditional aid donors (the

OECD member countries belonging to that organization's Development Assistance Committee, or "DAC") have accepted the international aid target, namely, that official development assistance (ODA), which by definition is concessional and excludes military aid, should be at least 0.7 per cent of the donor's GNP. But only four of the smaller DAC countries have attained the target unambiguously; the DAC members collectively are only halfway there; and the ratio of ODA to GNP for the United States, which used to be near the top of the DAC list, is now at the bottom. Whereas overall DAC aid had a real growth rate of about 4 per cent in the 1970s, it is now projected to grow only about half that fast, i.e., slower than the members' collective GNPs, through the balance of the 1980s.

Scanning this scene, it is easy for aid supporters to have a strong sense of powerlessness. In the DAC countries, all the talk is of political limits and budgetary constraints. Countries have let themselves blunder into bizarre government deficits, exchange-rate distortions, and trade imbalances. Given the basic robustness of their real economies, however, it is hard to believe that their underlying ability to sustain relatively small flows of concessional resources to the Third World has diminished. But the OECD governments are acting as if it had. Meanwhile, Arab-OPEC aid, which became very generous after the first oil shock, is down from those peaks and declining, although still high in ODA/GNP terms. Communist economic development assistance is very limited, both in scale and in its number of recipients. Moreover, in the face of ODA scarcity, neither of the two main donor groups, DAC and OPEC, seems politically able—in the interest of channeling more resources to the poorest countries—to allocate less to those middle-income countries that are the donors' strategic, political, historical, and/or commercial favorites.

Limits to Gap Closing

If the last item reflects a comparatively dated, policy-specific constraint on development prospects, there is, lurking behind it, a more fundamental limit binding the development agenda. Until the early 1970s, the happy assumption of most development-promotion efforts was that, while the OECD countries would keep growing, growth in the South would be accelerated enough, and then sustained at that pace long enough, so that the economic welfare gap between North and South would be narrowed and eventually closed. In due course, everyone (if intra-country inequalities in the

South were curtailed) would have an improved U.S.-type living standard.

This vision has been blurred by the widening disparities emerging among countries in the South itself. A few countries may indeed graduate into the OECD circle. But the gap-closing agenda has been confounded by the limits-to-growth case. Even when one makes every allowance for the ways in which buoyant and creative technologies can push back physical resource constraints, it is exceedingly improbable that the finiteness of the planet will ever let all the late starters catch up to the material standards of the early starters, especially if the latter keep growing. Convergence is doubly improbable, given the radically different paces of population growth to which North and South are now committed for many decades.

One route to convergence logically remains: to cut back on, and even reverse, North-Western growth *deliberately*—saving non-renewable resources for the Southern incomes that will be climbing to meet the shrinking per capita availabilities in the North. Although mooted by a few economic philosophers (by Wassily Leontief, for one, in 1980), such a program plainly is a non-starter. Politically, it just is not "on" in the North. And practical Southerners, who prize growing Northern markets, also vehemently reject it. But this implies a long-term prospect of enduring dualism in the world—which may seem badly to blunt the moral thrust of development promotion.

The Wages of Sovereignty

The dilemma posed by Southern versus Northern growth rates is only one of the ways in which development prospects are harried by the most fundamental fact of international politics: namely, that ultimate authority in the world lies, inchoate, with the heads of twelve dozen nation states. Our arrested global political development also means—harking back to the aid issue—that the most straightforward rationale for transferring resources from richer to poorer people and from richer to poorer places within a nation state (it is commonly called the progressive income-tax rationale) is severely weakened in the aid case. Legally, and as a matter of political morality, the duty of governments of nation states is to look out for their own constituents, not to be kind to outsiders. Hence all effective aid rationales must be argued in terms of donors' national interests, and aid programs cannot continue until disparities are eliminated; they must seek to get recipients on tracks of self-reliance after only limited assistance.

The tyranny of sovereignty also thins, inhibits, and intimidates the international public sector. Such as we have of the latter has been patched together with great difficulty and is subject to the recurring suspicions of the multilateral agencies' sovereign masters. Would-be development promoters have prized the comparative advantages of a number of multilaterals—particularly their opportunity to focus on development objectives with fewer distractions, their relative political and commercial neutrality, in many cases their professionalism and melding of national styles and biases. Thus it has been a source of considerable frustration to see the multilaterals, after having gained support for a decade, begin again to lose it relatively. The Reagan administration often has been in the forefront of this paring and eroding of the international public sector, but other OECD governments have joined in.

The by-product of sovereignty that I would particularly emphasize as a source of current development pessimism, however, is the failed dialogue between North and South over the "NIEO," or New International Economic Order. The dialogue was a response to the circumstances of sovereignty. The developing countries became impatient with the pace at which North-Western largesse and/or market adjustments were improving their condition. Emboldened by OPEC's newly discovered oil power and the decision of the oil exporters to maintain solidarity with their oil-importing fellow Southerners, the South as a whole overestimated the scope that U.N. fora offered for reordering international structures by means of official multilateral undertakings. The dialogue from 1974 onward—for more than seven years—was loud, often shrill, boring, and baroque. It was inherently cumbersome because of the bloc-to-bloc negotiating into which the autonomy of 150 sovereign actors forced the proceedings. The South, having struggled mightily to reconcile its intra-bloc differences, wholly misjudged how much the larger OECD powers were prepared to submit to "one-flag, one-vote" majority rule.

In the end, the yield of all the efforts invested in the NIEO dialogue was remarkably small. The experience left the impression that a whole assortment of development-related issues could not be dealt with. This was probably because they had been taken on collectively in an extremely unfavorable setting. A number of them have indeed proved more tractable when tackled one by one in more familiar institutional surroundings, such as the General Agreement on Tariffs and Trade (GATT), the World Bank, or the U.N. Development Programme (UNDP).

The Record: No Grounds for Quitting

Thus the gloom with which some now are viewing development's record and prospects has many sources. Yet a recital of the sort just finished quickly becomes tiresome. So what else is new—in an imperfect world? *Of course* development promotion is a flawed, difficult business. But there is absolutely no sufficient reason to be disheartened about its feasibility. On the contrary, what has been accomplished along these lines, together with what has been learned about ways to improve the performance, is one of mankind's major public-affairs achievements in this half-century.

To rate the efficacy of past development promotion, one must specify the goals that "development" seeks. This becomes a bit tricky if changes in the patterns of the goals being sought are themselves one of the dimensions in which past development strategies have shifted or evolved. Yet the problem is more theoretical than real: Each episode, surge, or chapter of new conventional wisdom about development redefines the tradeoffs among, or the comparative emphasis on, certain goals. The actual range of choice, however, is limited: All of the economic development strategies discussed in this volume pursue the same three goals; only their weightings change. These three goals are: 1) *economic growth*; 2) some form or other of interpersonal *equity*, including, in particular, the reduction or elimination of poverty at the lower end of the income distribution scale; and, 3) *national self-reliance*—in the sense of being able to pay for needed imports by means of exports and/or access to commercial credit. This third concept—that each developing nation should move toward standing on its own legs— would have an intrinsic (although, to many of us, not compelling) appeal even if we all belonged to a single super-state. But, as noted, self-reliance is *forced* into the development equation by the fact that ours is a "system" (a semi-anarchical system) of many sovereign states.

Without attempting a country-by-country or period-by-period review of differences and changes in the patterns of development goals, one nevertheless can make a rough but useful assessment of how the Third World's development has proceeded during the era of active development promotion.

The Growth Record in Most Regions

In the aggregate, Third World growth has been a rousing success, compared with the earlier productive performances of the same areas and with both the earlier and concurrent growth records of

the OECD countries. From 1960, when many of the African countries became independent, through 1982, the gross domestic products of all the low-and middle-income developing countries had an
average annual growth rate (population-weighted) of 4.8 per cent
net of inflation. This was well in excess of the real growth rate for
any sizable group of countries over any equally long period prior to
World War II. The OECD countries collectively did grow somewhat
faster than the developing countries collectively (5.1 per cent annually compared with 4.85 per cent) during the buoyant 1960s. But
take Japan's runaway growth (10.4 per cent a year) out of the OECD
average, and the OECD figure for the 1960s reduces to 4.1 per cent.
For 1970–1982, growth in the OECD countries including Japan was
at an annual rate of only 2.8 per cent. The oil shocks did not slow
the average for the oil-importing developing countries nearly as
much; their growth climbed at a rate of 4.6 per cent a year.

Moreover, these totals of course include all the slowest moving
developing economies. In most Third World regions, growth performance has been substantially better. It has been outstanding in
a number of the East and Southeast Asian countries—Korea, Taiwan; the two city states, Singapore and Hong Kong; Malaysia;
Thailand; the Philippines; and after the late 1960s, Indonesia.
Growth also has been fairly lively in South Asia—in Sri Lanka and
particularly in Pakistan. Even Bangladesh, which inherited the
poorer and more economically problematical part of former, un-
divided Pakistan, has been picking up some momentum and giving
greater promise of viability.

In a sense, the most exciting growth success stories of the
recent past, however, are the two outsize giants of the developing
world, China and India. The two account for two-thirds of the total
population of the entire developing-world. The populations of both
countries still are poor on average, and the growth rates of both
remain modest. But both have been coming out of periods of disloca-
tion and gross inefficiency, realigning policies for greater organizational and allocative effectiveness, pressing ahead in technically
sophisticated sectors, and, in particular, making promising strides
in agriculture. That both of these giants—after a history of
droughts, floods, and food deficits—have become substantially self-
sufficient in food and, economy-wide, seem to be building up a good
deal of productive momentum are matters of great global significance.

Finally, as noted, the larger Latin American countries have
suffered recent dents in their growth records. But be it also noted
that they had records to dent. The weighted average annual growth

rate of the real GDPs of Brazil, Mexico, Argentina, Colombia, Peru, and Chile for the period 1950–1982 was 5.9 per cent. This does not eliminate the pain or the political hazard posed by a rapid shrinkage in per capita welfare, particularly at the lower end of income distributions. But the substantial past development performance of these countries augurs well for their prospects once the current adjustment trauma has been put behind them. Indeed, with Brazil's strong 1984 recovery and Argentina's anti-inflation achievements in 1985, it seems clear that these renewed prospects already have begun to materialize.

These country-by-country comments of course have not exhausted the developing-country list. But the only regional group (the African) in which the record marches in a distinctly different direction than those of the countries mentioned is dealt with separately below.

Before we leave the positive side of the growth story, one qualifying point deserves emphasis. The developing countries' productive performance has been less impressive in per capita terms because of the extent to which in this period (compared with the OECD countries) output expansion has been diluted by population growth. For assessing productive performance, the *total* GDP comparisons we have been making—and not *per capita* GDP comparisons—are the right ones to consider. Output growth has not been determined mainly by population growth. For the most part, output has not been constrained by shortages of unskilled labor. It *has* been constrained by shortages of skilled labor and of savings, but both of these are diminished, not increased, by accelerated population expansion.

On the other hand, GDP per capita is certainly the more relevant indicator of welfare, and here the developing countries have done relatively less well. The problem of soaring fertility has been worst in Africa, but it has been serious in other developing regions. Fertility-restraining policies have made some inroads on the problem in many countries, but, with perhaps the single exception of China, not as much as would have been desirable. In most areas other than Africa, demographic trends have begun to move in favorable directions; and reductions in fertility are being encouraged by the constructive side effects of improved income levels and by such specific advances in welfare as gains in female education and reductions in infant mortality. But these trends will continue for some years to require the support of active population policies.

There would scarcely be need, in a summary discussion for an American audience, to underscore this rather obvious and familiar point if it were not for the pro-natalist directions in which White House thinking about population and development has been veering recently.

Equity

The story of what has happened to within-country income distribution and low-end poverty in the Third World during the past thirty-five years is a mixed one. But for that great majority of countries which have not experienced a revolution from the left, the record is more favorable than any good Marxist would have predicted. Where there have been thoroughgoing revolutions along Marxist lines (China is far and away the leading as well as largest example), there have apparently been sharp reductions in distributional inequalities—at the cost of considerable violence and repression. But the striking thing about the overall record has been the variety of pro-equity changes in the non-revolutionary majority of countries. These have been most impressive where a base had been laid by a major land reform—some of the strongest examples of which, admittedly (Korea, Taiwan) were imposed from outside. But in a far broader array of countries, especially since the late 1960s, there has been much concern with minimum and basic needs and direct attacks on poverty—especially in the countryside, where the majority of the poor live.

And this has been more than just talk. Irma Adelman classifies the approaches, successes, failures, and lessons systematically in her chapter in this volume. There has been a great deal of failure, but also a great deal of learning. I would cite among the broader lessons the following:

We have learned that among Third World elites, government officials and others, there are sizable numbers of persons who, liberated from their own stereotypes, are genuinely concerned to empower the poor and capable of pressing reforms, sometimes shrewdly, against the narrow interests of their own classes. Incrementalism *can* achieve significant reforms.

As Adelman says, we have learned that policy makers need not resign themselves to the probability that she, Simon Kuznets, and others earlier discovered—namely, that, as developing countries grow, inequalities tend to get worse before, further up the growth path, they start diminishing. Well-designed policies can hasten attainment of the second phase.

Quite clearly, we have learned that growth and equity are more complementary than competitive. It is much easier to find disproportionate gains for the poor if national income is rising rather than static. Similarly, for the majority of the poor, the more viable and effective anti-poverty and basic-needs programs are those which raise productivity and therefore earned incomes.

But most of us also have learned that, if one is concerned about poverty, growth is not enough. Growth promotion needs to be coupled with direct attacks on poverty via the kinds of employment programs, targeted transfers, and other policies that Adelman discusses. One can note with her that the opportunity costs of such explicitly anti-poverty efforts, in terms of the extra growth they pass up, seem to be very modest.

Overall, therefore, the equity record is not bad, and there is great intellectual—one might say, technical—wherewithal for improving it. The policy opportunities are enormous.

I would add one further point that is more in the nature of an observation than a lesson: Whenever one ventures a predominantly favorable assessment, such as this, of development promotion's equity record and potential, one can be sure of a chorus of protest from the lower-case left, God bless it. These are the folks who, not particularly actuated by Marxist or other radical doctrine, as a matter of deeply held conviction, simply never stop faulting the establishment for neglecting the least advantaged members of society. In the present instance they complain that all of these anti-poverty efforts fail to provide sufficiently for those who are genuinely the least advanced—the infirm, the incapable, some of the old, some of the young, say, the lowest 10 per cent. Such, tragically, is the case. But it is hard to say that an anti-poverty program that thus far is reaching only the upper three-quarters of the lowest 40 per cent is a failure.

Creditworthiness and Self-Reliance

On this dimension of development performance, in contrast to the growth and equity dimensions, the impact of external development promotion is ambivalent. If there are net concessional transfers inward, these by definition increase the dependence of the recipient country while they are going on. If the recipient were allowed to remain an economic island, it could fail to grow or decline, but it would do so self-reliantly. The object of development promoters, of course, is to help the country, after the needed intervening effort and time, to become self-reliant on an improved performance path.

The record of the past thirty-five years plainly does include cases of counter-developmental aid dependency, where countries have relied heavily on patrons for prolonged periods without building assets that move them toward self-reliance. But, by and large, increased outside support has been associated with increased investment; external support and interaction have helped to develop human resources and to build institutions that have increased countries' capacities for self-reliance; and, despite the impressions of pessimists, large numbers of countries, especially in Asia and Latin America, have in fact already virtually graduated from receiving ODA. This last is impressive, for the whole accelerated development-promotion process is still quite young. Given the depth of the welfare levels from which most of the late starters started, one would have expected comparatively few "graduations" in the first thirty-five years.

As indicated earlier, the shortfalls in self-reliance that have been arousing most concern lately, however, stem not from too much aid, but from what has turned out to be too much non-concessional debt. Creditworthy developing countries had borrowed commercially to supplement their export earnings. Then—as a result of overborrowing and/or escalated interest rates, reduced exports worsened terms of trade—servicing their debt became so much more of a problem that they needed to borrow still more at the same time that their access to credit diminished.

This kind of sequence, as we have seen, has had and is having a painful, disruptive impact on a number of Latin American and other, including African, countries. These debt crises do add up to a development failure—but only a limited failure and one that is not integral or fundamental to the development process. There is nothing unwholesome about developing countries borrowing, or staying in debt, or, indeed, continuing to do some net borrowing over a long period of time. It is likely to be economically optimal for capital-scarce countries to make expanding use of other people's capital.

What brought on the debt *crises*, however, were shocks and jolts and lurches. First came the 1973–74 oil shock, the attendant vast quantities of petro-dollars to be recycled, the eagerness of the banks (while protecting themselves with variable rates arrangements) to peddle this money, the eagerness of the creditworthy developing countries to borrow it at then bargain rates, and the lack of much IMF-type disciplining in this suddenly and highly privatized transfers system. Second came all of the post-1979 shocks that stemmed in considerable part from the unintended effects of the monetary, budgetary, and revenue policy choices made by U.S. administrations.[10]

The lesson to be learned is not that development does not work or is bound to come to grief. It is that the global economy is so intricately and insistently interdependent that the ramifications of particular, including "domestic," events and measures must be much more thoroughly thought through than heretofore. Here again, experience puts us in a position to do better the next time around.

The Role of Indigenous Governments

One idea currently in fashion is that governments can do almost nothing right. Talk of bureaucratic sclerocis, political venality, and governmental overload resonates far beyond the Heritage Foundation. Judiciously couched, it can be found, for example, in many recent documents of the World Bank. Indeed, one has a good deal of sympathy with these stylish views; there are limits to how much most governments can do effectively at a time; many of them need to delegate downward, and most of them need to do more "sideways" delegating, making more use of such labor-saving regulatory mechanisms as appropriately conditioned markets.

But as fads tend to do, this one has gone over the brink with assertions in some quarters that government itself is the main obstacle to development—all that is really needed is to get government off the backs of private agents; that done, development, meaning by that advances on the equity and self-reliance as well as the growth fronts, will surge ahead.

This is utter nonsense. In developing economies, as elsewhere, governments are extremely flawed and fallible. Moves toward liberalization are appropriate in many cases. It is well to get governments out of what others can do so that they can concentrate on what only governments can do. But governments are essential to establish policy environments, develop the physical and human infrastructure for development, and carry forward functions that, although they may eventually submit to private implementation, would never (for reasons of scale or externality) be adequately initiated by the private sector. Agricultural research and extension are two among many examples of this last. The substantial progress that many developing countries have achieved since World War II or since they became independent would never have happened without governmental initiative and continuing and (on the average) improving public development policy. There is no substitute for the continuing lead that governments must supply to development-promotion efforts.

The Role of Aid

It is no accident that the same thirty-five years that have seen the Third World's development performance, for all its warts, outdistance anything that large portions of the world ever had accomplished before, has also seen the invention and propagation of foreign development assistance. Aid, as noted, has been a minor factor in most country-by-country development stories. Indigenous policies and efforts have been the main factors. But aid has been a significant influence in many cases. Sometimes its positive effects have been swamped by more powerful influences; and sometimes, by building dependency unduly or providing a crutch that has allowed elites to postpone reforms, aid has been positively inimical to development. But more often it has served to catalyze the mobilization of indigenous resources more powerful than itself. It has had notable successes in assisting and inducing needed institution-building and development of human resources, perhaps especially in parts of Asia. Particularly in certain of its non-project forms, it has served to encourage constructive policy changes.[11]

In its project form, aid has contributed to a great variety of specific improvements, and—as measured by such donors as the World Bank, the regional development banks, and the U.S., Canadian, and Dutch bilateral aid agencies—its average benefit-cost performance has been quite high. It also has had a number of country and sectoral successes, some of them delayed but nevertheless clear—for example, in Taiwan, in South Korea, and in the "green revolutions" of South and Southeast Asian agriculture.

Finally, there are many ways in which the aid record is being and can be improved. In the case of the "green revolution," for example, the alleged adverse inequality of its impact upon farmers with middle-size and small holdings and on landless farmers has been exaggerated; but policies are in progress to steer second- and third-generation agricultural development more toward small producers, to promote gains for agricultural labor that do not impair efficiency, and to open up more non-agricultural opportunities to the landless. Similarly, there is a great untapped potential for improved inter-donor and donor-recipient aid coordination about which, faced with shortages, both donors and recipients are beginning to get serious.

What About Africa?

As to development performance thus far, Africa is the exception. It is easy enough to see why development there is peculiarly difficult.

Governments are new. Many have jurisdictions too small (eleven have populations of less than one million) to be easily viable economically. Politics are fraught with tribal and other cleavages that cut across arbitrarily drawn national frontiers; a great deal of turbulence and violence still persists. Governments continue to be deeply preoccupied with South Africa. And meanwhile, population growth is explosive, aggravating the region's deficits in both physical and trained human and institutional infrastructure.

African governments often have slighted the development priority. They have let policy errors accumulate in forms such as inadequate agricultural incentives, bloated exchange rates, and bloated bureaucracies and parastatal sectors. Outside interveners, for their part, have been less effective in Africa than in Asia in helping to develop relevant institutions and cadres of expertise. They have not yet responded very effectively to the variety and particularity of the continent's agricultural needs. The numbers of donors and their lack of coordination have overtaxed the capacities of African governments.

These and other weaknesses in the record are now widely recognized, however. Internal and external diagnoses of African development problems coincide more nearly than was the case as recently as 1980–81, when the Organization for African Unity's Lagos Plan of Action and the World Bank's so-called Berg Report were at loggerheads.[12] The dimensions of the problem have grown, and the resource requirements have become formidable. But the nature of needed actions is more nearly understood and agreed.

Net Assessment

The conclusion that emerges from this quick scanning of the record is emphatic: It is ridiculous to be as turned off on development as some of our pessimistic friends are. Development promotion is pulsing with potential right now. We are, it is true, all pinioned in the quasi-anarchy of a sovereign-state world, and this lends particular urgency to the pasting and scrambling together of as much support as can be managed for the more effective multilateral development agencies. But there is nothing new about such challenges. We can live with them as well now as before.

Meanwhile both insiders and outsiders know more about development promotion than they did previously. There can be no reason but a loss of purpose or nerve for either group not to pursue the effort vigorously. This, I would particularly insist, applies to development promotion's budgetary requirements on the donor side. The requirements in fact are small compared with other budget heads. They are, therefore, far more the creature of leaders' priorities than of binding economic or budgetary constraints. In short, development promotion is a feasible undertaking that can be pressed with such vigor as leaders wish. As to the question with which we started: It is entirely appropriate to focus on the issue of strategy— of not *whether*, but *how* to pursue development goals. This is the task taken up in the balance of this volume.

Notes

[1] "North" as in North-South, "West" as in East-West.

[2] I return below to a characterization of "mainstream," particularly in terms of the perspectives it slights—radical analyses, for one, and grass-roots orientations, for another.

[3] On this subject, see in successive ODC publications the treatments by Lewis, Bradford, and Krugman: John P. Lewis, "Can We Escape the Path of Mutual Injury?," in John P. Lewis and Valeriana Kallab, eds., *U.S. Foreign Policy and the Third World: Agenda 1983* (New York: Praeger Publishers, for the Overseas Development Council 1983); Colin I. Bradford, Jr., "The NICs: Confronting U.S. 'Autonomy,'" in Richard E. Feinberg and Valeriana Kallab, eds., *Adjustment Crisis in the Third World* (New Brunswick, N.J.: Transaction Books, for the Overseas Development Council, 1984); and Paul R. Krugman, "U.S. Macro-Economic Policy and the Developing Countries," in John W. Sewell, Richard E. Feinberg, and Valeriana Kallab, eds., *U.S. Foreign Policy and the Third World: Agenda 1985-86* (New Brunswick, N.J.: Transaction Books, for the Overseas Development Council, 1985).

[4] "Declaration of Principles and Programme of Action," World Employment Conference Document WEC/CW/E.I., pp. 189–214, *Employment, Growth, and Basic Needs: A One-World Problem*, the international "basic-needs strategy" against chronic poverty prepared by the International Labour Office (New York, N.Y.: Praeger, for the Overseas Development Council in cooperation with the ILO, 1977).

[5] Concerning the South's demands for the "New International Economic Order."

[6] See Lewis, in *U.S. Foreign Policy and the Third World: Agenda 1983*, op. cit.

[7] Feinberg and Kallab, eds., *Adjustment Crisis*, op. cit.; Richard E. Feinberg and Valeriana Kallab, eds., *Uncertain Future: Commercial Banks and the Third World* (New Brunswick, N.J.: Transaction Books, for the Overseas Development Council, 1984).

[8] It would be offensive to project a dull homogeneity of views onto so large and gifted a staff as the World Bank's. I refer to the net institutional stances taken in the Bank's major publications, such as the last several issues of its annual *World Development Report* and its recent special reports on Africa. On a different point, some would fix orthodoxy's headquarters in the Bank and IMF jointly, the two institutions having been collaborating with particular closeness during their recent phase of complementary structural adjustment lending. However, as to development strategy, it is the Bank which has had the dominant voice.

[9] The "grant element" in concessional transfers, so-called ODA—official development assistance—is indeed an unrequited gift; there is little in political theory that anticipates that one set of nation states will give gifts to a group of their sovereign peers, especially under regular, non-emergency circumstances.

[10] See Lewis, in *U.S. Foreign Policy and the Third World: Agenda 1983*, op. cit; Krugman, in *U.S. Foreign Policy and the Third World: Agenda 1985-86*, op. cit; and Bradford in *Adjustment Crisis in the Third World*, op. cit.

[11] It is inherent to the question of "aid effectiveness," as I explained in a chapter on the subject in my 1980 report as Chairman of DAC (Paris, 1980), that it can never be disposed of definitively. But the question has received a great surge of attention in recent years in DAC meetings and reports, the World Bank's retrospective study of IDA (1982),

and, in particular, in the report and supporting materials of the Development Committee's Task Force on Concessional Flows (1985) and in the work of consultants retained by the Task Force, synthesized into a book by the chief consultant, Robert Cassen, *Does Aid Work?*, to be published in 1986. All of these documents draw on the much livelier cross-referencing of findings among the official evaluation units of bilateral and multilateral aid agencies that has been underway since 1980.

[12] *Lagos Plan of Action for the Implementation of the Monrovia Strategy for the Economic Development of Africa*, adopted by the Second Extra-Ordinary Assembly of Organization of African Unity Heads of State and Government, Devoted to Economic Matters, Meeting in Lagos, Nigeria, from 28–29 April, 1980; *Accelerated Development in Sub-Saharan Africa: An Agenda for Action* (Washington, D.C.: The World Bank, 1981).

Summaries of Recommendations

1. A Poverty-Focused Approach to Development Policy (Irma Adelman)

There can be little argument that a reduction in the number of people living in a state of absolute deprivation should be a major objective of economic development and of development assistance. In this paper, Irma Adelman focuses on what developing countries themselves can and must do to reduce their poverty problems.

In a very basic sense, the poverty problem is one of too small a quantity of assets, too low a volume of market sales, and/or too low a market price. The author's approach to poverty alleviation emphasizes productivity increases and labor-intensive growth; it aims to raise the incomes of the poor by increasing their employment, productivity, and access to productivity-enhancing assets.

The policy recommendations in this paper are based on statistical analyses of forces affecting income distribution and poverty across a sample of developing countries; on simulation experiments with econometric models of various countries; on recent experience with anti-poverty programs; and on comparative analyses of the economic histories of various semi-industrial countries. The author highlights the following "lessons" for the design of effective poverty-focused approaches within developing countries:

1. Validated strategies, policies, and programs for poverty alleviation do exist. Indeed, there has been substantial progress toward the achievement of this goal between 1960 and 1980 in the non-communist developing countries as a group, despite the fact that the distribution of income has become substantially more unequal.

2. Strategies for poverty alleviation are not compatible with just any kind of economic growth. They entail particular kinds of economic growth.

3. Approaches to poverty alleviation require the implementation of mutually consistent and reinforcing multifaceted programs. The most effective approaches entail a combination of several elements: asset-oriented policies that are supported by institutions designed to facilitate the poor's access to jobs; investments that enhance the productivity of assets that the poor possess and can sell; and development strategies that generate a rapid increase in the demand for unskilled labor.

4. More than one method exists to achieve each element of the package described above. The choice among instruments needs to be tailored to each country's particular initial conditions, resource base, size, asset distribution, institutional structure, and socio-political configuration—as well as to the external conditions and trends that the country faces at any point in time.

5. Choices among poverty-alleviation packages and programs are inherently *political*. A critical aspect of the political choice among competing goals and instrumentalities is the time dimension.

6. The sequence in which different policy interventions are taken up is important: The most effective approach to poverty alleviation entails implementing asset-oriented policies and institutional changes designed to give the poor access to high-productivity jobs *before*, not after, shifting development strategies. If that is done, there is no "trade-off" between growth promotion and poverty alleviation. The same development strategy is then optimal for both goals.

7. Which strategy and which set of policies is most effective for a given country is likely to change over time—as changes take place both in the initial conditions within each country and in the economic and political environment in which the country operates.

8. With all of this in view, two strategies appear to promise the poor the most: 1) reliance upon export-oriented growth in labor-intensive manufactures, and 2) reliance upon agricultural-development-led industrialization. During the coming decade—

likely to be one of low growth in world demand for labor-intensive manufactured exports—the agriculture-led approach is likely to deliver more in terms of less inequality and poverty, a higher growth rate, and a better balance of payments.

2. Agriculture on the Road to Industrialization (John W. Mellor)

The technological advances of the green revolution provide a major opportunity for agriculture to play an important positive role in the development of poor countries—that is, in their transformation from dominantly agricultural to dominantly industrial and service economies.

Technological change in agriculture—with its concomitants of research, education, and input supply—is essential to agriculture's playing a positive role in development. This is because of the classical application of diminishing returns and rising costs to the land-based agricultural sector.

Accelerated growth in employment is a necessary complement to an agriculture-based strategy of growth. Although demand for food generally responds only moderately to price, relatively poor people do spend the bulk of additional income from increased employment on food. Thus in developing countries, growth in employment provides the market for increased food supplies. Conversely, if accelerated growth in employment is not accompanied by increased food supplies, it will be choked by rapidly rising food prices.

Rapid growth in employment in developing countries requires that limited available capital be used largely for infrastructure for relatively labor-intensive industries and for investment in the improvement of human capabilities. The rapid growth of income in the massive agricultural sector normally creates a large demand for labor-intensive goods and services, a high proportion of which are produced in the towns of rural regions. Even so, an open trade regime is an important complement to an agriculture- and employment-based development strategy. This is because of the rapid growth in demand for very capital-intensive intermediate products—such as fertilizer, steel, or plastics—which, if imported, avoid capital-intensive domestic production and give an extra boost to the export of labor-intensive commodities in payment. However, an agriculture- and employment-oriented strategy does differ importantly from an export-driven strategy in that the bulk of the market for production will arise from increased domestic incomes—and substantially from the higher incomes of farmers applying improved technology.

Such a strategy is inherently efficient in basing growth on the application of modern science to the initially dominant agricultural sector and in spreading capital thinly to maximize the increase in demand for the relatively abundant labor resource. It is favorable to poverty reduction because it increases the supply and reduces the price of food, the principal consumption item of the poor, and because it increases the demand for labor, their principal means of earning income.

Governments must play a major role in the pursuit of a strategy that is both agriculture- and employment-oriented. If agriculture, for reasons of efficiency as well as equity, is to be developed mainly through smallholders, governments must take the initiative in promoting research, education, and even input supply systems. Moreover, because agriculture is widely dispersed geographically and favors dispersed industry, vast investments are needed in infrastructure. The trade element of the strategy requires a large central infrastructure. And, of course, the overvalued exchange rates and unfavorable agricultural marketing and pricing policies appropriate to quite different strategies must be changed.

Society has chosen alternative development strategies for many reasons, including simply equating modernization with the establishment of large-scale industry. Two relatively recent streams of knowledge that now argue forcibly for a change in strategy are: 1) the already demonstrated potential of major science-based agricultural innovations; and 2) accumulating evidence that the domestic demand that grows out of a modernizing agriculture can go far toward facilitating labor-intensive, capital-stretching employment growth, which in turn creates much of the demand needed to sustain expanding domestic food production.

3. Rethinking Trade Strategy
(Jagdish N. Bhagwati)

The focus of Jagdish Bhagwati's concern is on what he describes as the current "clash of orthodoxies." He acknowledges that the export-promoting (EP) strategy of development, which his own research and writings helped shape, has become the "new orthodoxy" among many economists—and has recently found its way into policy-influencing institutions such as the World Bank. But he carefully distinguishes between orthodoxy among economists and orthodoxy among the clients of their advice: Policy makers in many developing countries remain "unabashed" in their adherence to the old orthodoxy of the import-substitution (IS) strategy of development. Their thinking along these lines has been reinforced—unjustifiably, in the author's view—by the Reaganomics-led worldwide recession; by the subsequent capital-inflow-led "overvaluation" of the dollar; and by the growing threat of protection that these phenomena have spawned in the West.

In arguing for the EP strategy's continuing developmental value, Bhagwati first seeks to clear up three aspects of the strategy that he finds frequently misunderstood: 1) The motivation of EP strategy is to avoid tilting the effective exchange rate against exports—to *eliminate the bias against exports*, so as to restore the incentive to export as much as to produce for the home market. Moreover, within the aggregates of an EP country case, there may well be activities that are being import-substituted. 2) In weighing the costs of an IS strategy, it is important to differentiate among IS regimes that are the inadvertent result of reluctance to correct overvalued exchange rates, and those—like India's, Egypt's, and Ghana's in the past—that have been established deliberately. 3) It is also mistaken to identify EP strategy with laissez faire: An important role of government in the EP strategy is the provision of the kind of supportive environment to exporters that is afforded, for example, by Japan's Ministry of Trade and Industry.

Bhagwati recalls the extent to which many leading development theorists in the 1950s relied critically on the assumption that developing countries had a very limited potential for exports. A set of empirical country and more general studies in the 1960s and 1970s—together, in particular, with the ongoing performance of the Republic of Korea, Taiwan, Hong Kong, and Singapore—showed this export pessimism to have been misplaced and demonstrated EP's efficiency advantages over IS. In Bhagwati's view, other IS claims—that import substitution would nevertheless produce more growth by producing more savings, or lead to more employment, or do more for the poor—were likewise persuasively set aside.

To Bhagwati, recent arguments questioning the suitability of the EP strategy for the environment of the 1980s likewise offer no compelling reasons for reversion to the IS strategy:

1. Have recession, adjustment problems, and accumulated debt made EP less attractive? No, says Bhagwati. The East Asian, highly export-oriented, semi-industrialized countries have led the adjustment pack.

2. Is the case for EP being thwarted by protectionism? Not yet, in any case, Bhagwati maintains. Moreover, countries that are

being squeezed can, instead of closing their own markets, pressure their partners to open theirs. Furthermore, it is a mistake to imagine that a vigorous commitment to EP would yield as high a ratio of exports to GNP in a huge economy like India as it does in a small economy like Taiwan.

3. Is there a case against EP on grounds of wage and labor-market distortion? Bhagwati is unpersuaded by this argument in the Caribbean context in which it has been advanced; being small islands, the Caribbean countries do have a high ratio of trade to income, but it is not at all clear that they are in fact EP economies with trade regimes tilted toward exports.

4. Is EP better suited to implementation by authoritarian than by democratic regimes? Bhagwati finds authoritarianism neither a necessary nor a sufficient condition for EP, pointing out that many totalitarian countries have followed IS, while the degree of authoritarianism varies within the Far Eastern EP economies (and not necessarily in proportion to economic performance). Yet it may well be true, Bhagwati observes, that the political patronage that accompanies the control mechanisms that IS strategies spawn makes liberalization a harder dose to swallow for a pluralistic democracy's bureaucrats and interest groups.

Bhagwati's own sights remain on those policy makers in developing countries who remain entrenched adherents to IS strategy; they, he points out, are more likely to draw political inspiration from the recent lines of EP questioning than they are to be enlightened by economic and other proofs of the weaknesses of these arguments. Bhagwati acknowledges that any development strategy, whatever its economic advantages, must be politically viable. He urges "those who seek to include the EP strategy as a necessary ingredient of conditionality imposed by the World Bank or the IMF (as is the case with many structural adjustment loans from the Bank, for example) . . . to exercise some caution lest their prescriptions become counterproductive because of ignored political prerequisites."

4. A Mexican View of the Choice Between Outward and Inward Orientation (Leopoldo Solis and Aurelio Montemayor)

The authors focus on the contrasting experiences of two sets of economically advanced developing countries in coping with the wrenching adjustments that the world economy demanded in the first half of the 1980s. One group of larger Latin American nations, including Mexico, have been largely inward- or import-substitution-oriented in their policy choices. Another set of countries, especially those of East Asia (the authors give particular attention to the Republic of Korea) have been more or less consistent in their outward orientation. (The authors use the latter term in the same sense as Jagdish Bhagwati: The policies of the countries in question have not tilted producers' incentives against exports relative to indigenous substitutes for imports.)

As experienced Mexican policy economists, Solis and Montemayor emphasize that "semi-industrialized countries attempting to make their economic strategies more outward- oriented cannot rely on any single-track export promotion." But as they see it, the comparison as to success between the mostly outward-and mostly inward-oriented records of recent years is no contest: The externally turned East Asian economies have adjusted far more quickly, with less denting of their growth rates and with smaller accumulations of debt.

5. East Asian "Models": Myths and Lessons (Colin I. Bradford, Jr.)

The new conventional wisdom interprets the success of the East Asian newly industrializing countries (NICs)—the Republic of Korea, Taiwan, Hong Kong, and Singapore—as deriving from the adoption by these countries of outward-looking, market-oriented, open-economy development strategies. The "new orthodoxy" contrasts this interpretation of the East Asian experience with a stylized version of Latin American development as inward-looking and interventionist.

But closer examination of the experiences of three of these NICs—Korea, Taiwan, and Singapore—reveals a more complex picture in which government intervention has played a decisive role in export promotion. Credit allocations and interest rate subsidies in Korea, fiscal subsidies in Taiwan, and tax and regulatory incentives in support of sectoral strategies for industrialization and exports in Singapore have been integral parts of development policy.

What seems to distinguish the East Asian development experiences is not the dominance of market forces, free enterprise, and internal liberalization, but effective, highly interactive relationships between the public and private sector—relationships characterized by shared goals and commitments embodied in the development strategy and economic policy of the government. The dichotomy between market forces and government intervention is not only overdrawn; it misconceives the fundamental dynamic at work. It is the degree of consistency between two sectors—rather than the extent of implicit or explicit conflict—that has been important in the successful development cases. A coherent development strategy was not only formulated but followed by both the government and the private sector in providing an unusual degree of common direction to national energies in these cases. This suggests that the differences between East Asia and Latin America are less ones of development style than of capacity to implement.

To Bradford, recognition of the more *dirigiste* aspects of the development strategy thrust of the three East Asian NICs signals a form of convergence of short- and long-run policy perspectives—one that is quite different from the current fusion of conventional demand management stabilization policies typically advocated by the IMF with the new outward-looking orthodoxy of the World Bank. He argues that the East Asian success model turns out to be a policy package composed of: 1) longer-run structural elements connected with the need to find a niche in world trade and to service external debt with export growth, and 2) supportive macroeconomic policies aimed at both growth enhancement and price- and balance-of-payments stabilization.

The imperatives of longer-term financial planning, sectoral development strategies, and export requirements are today playing a more decisive role in shaping short-run macro-economic policies. These policies in turn have a crucial bearing on the realization of the longer-term goals. The sustainability of short-run macro policies is critical to the viability of the longer-run trajectory—just as the long-run trade and financial requirements shape short-run policies. Hence, achieving a sustainable balance between growth and stabilization in the short run becomes *inseparable* from the longer-term structural dimensions. The policy nexus of growth, stabilization, and restructuring now poses the central challenge for economic policy makers.

If there is a "new synthesis" of development strategies, it is that the confluence of these formerly separate forces and perspectives defining the policy nexus of the 1980s requires a new fusion of structurally oriented development and macro-economic policies. The East Asian success stories provide models of this new synthesis, integrating the multifaceted elements of policy into an effective strategy that eschews one-dimensional solutions instead of enshrining them.

6. Aid Effectiveness in Raising Adapative Capacity in the Low-Income Countries (Alex Duncan)

Alex Duncan is concerned with the prevailing need of developing countries—he chooses to concentrate on the low-income countries other than the two giants, China and India—to adapt "in a process of constant change in which new opportunities and new constraints" keep emerging. His focus and emphasis is on the acquisition of important kinds of capacities for such adaptation: management and institutional capacity, human resources development, and the abilities to acquire, adapt, and/or develop better and appropriate technology.

The author looks at these issues in the context of development assistance—its scale, effectiveness, problems, and potentialities for improvement (on the part of both donors and recipients). It is precisely for the low-income countries, a large majority of which are in Africa, that aid has been particularly important during the past decade and a half. In per capita terms and as a proportion of GNP and investment totals, it seems bound to remain so in the foreseeable future. These same countries are also the ones most in need of the kinds of capacities that concern Duncan; hence the intersection of his two subjects.

In the management and institutional category, the author—drawing both on his own experience in East Africa and a careful reading of the recent development-management and aid-effectiveness literature—highlights such issues as the comparative lack of technical analysis and political will; inadequate recurrent-cost funding and excessively "projectized" aid, and poorly articulated budgeting. He places special emphasis on the centrality of education and human resources development. And he distinguishes the poor countries' policy choices with respect to 1) the inward transfer of technology, 2) local adaptations of such imported technologies, and 3) indigenous innovations—noting the differing requirements of these functions for indigenous research facilities and programs.

As they try to help the low-income countries strengthen this set of developmental capacities, the bilateral aid donors, Duncan notes, seldom can be single-purpose development promoters. They are actuated in part by a variety of political, commercial, and other purposes. Yet many of their efforts, as well as those of their multilateral counterparts, are solidly professional; and aid is, in fact, predominantly effective in advancing its announced (pro-development) objectives. Moreover, the author concludes, there are known ways of improving the process in such realms as donor coordination, management (particularly in the area of recipient-government budgeting, recipient institution-building), and policy analysis.

7. Democracy and Development
(Atul Kohli)

In much of the Third World, democracy has proved to be an elusive goal, and the prospects for its spread and rooting in many more countries in the near future are limited. Yet the validity of the old argument that authoritarianism is a natural alternative to failed democracies is highly questionable today, when many of these authoritarian regimes are themselves failed or faltering experiments.

This study analyzes the impact of democracy on economic development—on growth, income distribution, and debt management—and the conditions under which Third World democracies do, or do not, take root. Atul Kohli argues that:

1. The democratic Third World countries examined—countries as diverse as India, Malaysia, Sri Lanka, Venezuela, and Costa Rica—achieved relatively impressive records over the 1960–1982 period. For the most part, their economies grew at moderate but steady rates. On income distribution, their achievement was striking, with income inequalities either remaining stable or even narrowing. Foreign debts were kept within manageable limits.

2. Over the same twenty-two year period, the group of authoritarian countries examined—including (pre-1982) Argentina, Brazil, the Republic of Korea, Egypt, and Morocco—averaged only a somewhat higher growth rate (compared to the democratic group of countries). Their income inequalities widened, however, and their foreign debts rose to staggering proportions.

3. Thus any justification of non-democratic regimes that relies on their presumed greater development capacities is, at best, weak.

4. Historically, democracies have been born when competing

elites within a society have decided to take a chance on their power prospects by agreeing to follow a set of rules in the conduct of their power struggle.

5. The disintegration of Third World democratic experiments is often traceable less to their economic development performance than to explosive divisiveness among competing elite groups.

6. The focus of many conservative and radical scholars on elite-mass (rather than intra-elite) conflict as the nemesis of democracy is exaggerated. If democracy is to have a chance in the developing world, it is not the masses, but overly ambitious political elites, that need to be tamed.

Democracy in the contemporary Third World faces a number of "structural" obstacles in the form of political and economic conditions that militate against stable democratic regimes. These barriers make democracy an uphill struggle, but not impossible. Third World democratic countries are in fact state-dominated, proto-democratic societies, in which democracy still tends to be an affair of the elites—as it was in some Western democracies in their earlier stages. Elite fragmentation frequently is exacerbated both by the competing goals on which Third World political authorities are expected to deliver and by the intensity of personal political ambitions generated within low-income economies. These characteristics help clarify the importance of elite consensus for the functioning of such regimes. Conditions that help pave the way for democracy by facilitating elite consensus—sketched out by the author in this chapter—need to be better understood and created.

The author concludes that if democracy is a valued goal in the contemporary Third World, it may be necessary to settle for moderate growth. More value may need to be placed on the *political rationality* of economic policies. Nation-building is a long-term process in which the need to create viable political institutions has to be balanced against the demands of economic efficiency. This is not to suggest making a virtue out of economic irrationality. Many Third World democracies, including India, could benefit from a "rational" policy shift toward lesser controls and a more open and competitive economy. However, a Korean or a Brazilian "miracle" is not likely in an India, and the reasons for this are in part the differences in respective political systems. Policy advice that ignores such political realities is likely to be counterproductive.

Also important for Third World democracy is greater outside-world understanding of the real meanings of the ideologies of nationalism and redistribution expressed by Third World democratic leaders. Whatever success these leaders achieve in juggling the competing goals of economic growth, decreasing income inequality, and management of external debt (and other) dependencies, their ideologies tend to be characterized by nationalism—often expressed as "anti-imperialism"—and a commitment to both state intervention in the economy and some redistributive goals—often expressed as "socialism" or "social democracy." Those supportive of democracy in the developing world need to cultivate greater ideological tolerance for such political attitudes. These ideological goals should be understood for what they are: legitimizing devices that are necessary accompaniments for many Third World democratic regimes.

Development
Strategies
Reconsidered

Chapter 1

A Poverty-Focused Approach to Development Policy

Irma Adelman

The definition of poverty adopted in this essay is one of abject poverty—a poverty level so severe that it stunts the attainment of human potential. In 1980, 880 million people (22 per cent of the world population) lived below that level. This estimate of the extent of poverty is based on a poverty line specified in terms of the income level required to purchase a nutritional level minimally adequate for calorie replacement at average levels of activity. The World Bank suggests setting the standard at an annual per capita income of U.S. $50 of 1960 purchasing power. There can be little argument that a reduction in the number of people living in such a state of absolute deprivation should be a major objective of economic development and of development assistance. Indeed, many (including myself) would say that this should be the prime objective of economic development.

In this essay, I shall pretend that the removal of absolute deprivation is the accepted priority goal of economic development and shall summarize my understanding of what the pursuit of this goal implies for the design of development policy within developing countries. I shall here leave aside the political problems associated with the adoption of such an approach as well as its foreign assistance implications. With respect to internal politics, I shall assume that a coalition of interests exists that accords high priority to the goal of eradicating absolute deprivation. With respect to foreign assistance, I shall assume the existence of an international consensus that foreign aid ought to aim at supporting policies, financing programs, and establishing an international environment that will enable developing countries to pursue the goal of poverty alleviation effectively. These assumptions will allow me to concentrate upon *what developing countries themselves can and must do to reduce their poverty problems.*

The approach to poverty alleviation that I shall advocate is a productivity-oriented approach that aims to raise the incomes of the poor by increasing both their productivity and their access to productivity-enhancing assets. I will not advocate an alternative, transfer-oriented approach, whereby the goods and services required for subsistence are delivered to the poor *directly*, for several reasons:

(1) A direct-transfer approach becomes less effective over time, since its benefits, even when the transfer continues unabated, tend to be dissipated into higher prices and into other leakages.[1]

(2) It is beyond the fiscal capacities of virtually all developing countries.

(3) It needs to be maintained forever.

(4) It does not allow for a more differentiated approach to enable the poor to decide on their consumption patterns according to their own priorities as defined by their own circumstances and cultures.

To be appropriate, policy must be rooted in the "stylized facts" of the problem that it seeks to address. Before discussing policy, I shall therefore summarize the stylized facts concerning poverty and income distribution that have been learned from the research of the past decade.

The Theory of Poverty: Lessons of a Decade

The Structure of Poverty

In developing countries, poverty is overwhelmingly a *rural* phenomenon. In most developing countries, the great majority of the poorest 40 per cent of the population is engaged in agricultural pursuits. The landless and the nearly landless are the poorest of the poor. In urban areas, the majority of the poor are unskilled workers in the service sector; but even they are generally richer than the rural poor. Workers in the manufacturing sector, whether skilled or unskilled, are part of the richest 20–40 per cent of the population. Thus unskilled labor is the major asset owned by the poor, and what determines the course of poverty is the state of demand for and the productivity of their labor.

The Course of Income Distribution During the Development Process

What happens to poverty over time is determined by the rate at which total income grows and by changes in the share of the poor in that income. If the share of income accruing to the poor declines more rapidly than overall income rises, the poor lose from growth; otherwise, they gain. Just *how* the income share of the poor changes with economic development is, therefore, critical to understanding the poverty problem and its alleviation.

The initial phases of the development process, during which a mostly agrarian economy starts industrialization, are almost inevitably marked by substantial increases in the inequality of income distribution. The shares of the poorest fifth, two-fifths, and three-fifths of the population all decrease sharply—thanks to the introduction of a small high-income island in a large low-income sea.

Subsequent phases of the development process are marked by an increase in the share of the population involved in the modern high-income sector of the economy, an increase in the income gap between the high-income and the low-income sectors of the economy, and increases in inequality within both the high-income and the low-income sectors. The shift in population from the low- to the high-income sectors is a force working for reductions in inequality; on the other hand, the increases in mean income differentials among sectors and the widening of income dispersion within sectors are factors making for greater inequality. Overall, the tendency is for inequality to increase, at least for a while. Various simulations have suggested that this increase in inequality will tend to continue until at least half of the population is in the high-income sector.

There is no *automatic* tendency for the distribution of income to improve as countries enter the last phase of their transition to the status of industrial countries. Whether inequality does or does not increase depends upon the policies that countries follow. In particular, it depends upon the extent to which the policies adopted narrow the income gap between the sectors, the extent to which they decrease the dispersion of income within the modern sector, and the relative speed of absorption into the modern sector. Thus, the plot of the income share accruing to the poorest, as a function of development, can be either U-shaped, as hypothesized by Simon Kuznets from a comparison of a sample of developed with mid- to high-income developing countries,[2] or J-shaped, depending on the nature of development strategies chosen.[3]

Trends in the Size Distribution of Income and Poverty

The trends in inequality during the past two decades are consistent with the stylized facts described above. Table 1 presents summary data on the course of the concentration of income and on the poverty ratio from 1960 to 1980 in groups of non-communist less developed countries. The figures in the table were calculated by estimating how the shape of the size distributions in the rural and urban sectors of each country varies with the country's structural characteristics and level of development. These rural and urban distributions were aggregated numerically to produce a single size distribution for each country. The individual country distributions were then again aggregated numerically to produce a single distribution for geopolitical regions. Within a given group of countries, each individual was treated as if he were a citizen of that group.[4] The numbers labeled Gini coefficients are measures of the degree of concentration of the size distribution of income. A higher figure indicates greater inequality.

The figures in the table indicate that, between 1960 and 1980, income inequality in the entire group of non-communist developing countries increased substantially; but separate groups of countries were subject to different trends in income concentration. Income concentration increased quite markedly in the group of low-income non-communist countries and in the group of oil-exporting countries, and it decreased significantly in the middle-income, non-oil-exporting countries. As indicated by the poverty-ratio figures, on the other hand, the amount of absolute poverty (defined as previously indicated) declined. Despite the overall increase in inequality, the percentage of population falling below the poverty level (held fixed in real purchasing power) declined by a third between 1960 and 1980.

To see how much of these trends can be attributed to within-country inequality and how much to inter-country inequality, two experiments were performed. In the third and fourth columns of the table, per capita income in each country was set equal to the average income in the world; the only source of inequality in these columns is, therefore, inequality in the size distribution of income *within* each country. In the fifth and sixth columns, the opposite

Table 1. Trends in Income Distribution and Poverty, 1960–1980

	Overall		Eliminating Inter-Country Inequality[a]		Eliminating Within-Country Inequality[a]	
	1960	1980	1960	1980	1960	1980
Income Distribution *(Gini coefficient[b])*						
All non-communist developing countries	.544	.602	.450	.468	.333	.404
Low-income	.407	.450	.383	.427	.113	.118
Middle-income, non-oil	.603	.569	.548	.514	.267	.251
Oil-exporting	.575	.612	.491	.503	.328	.375
Poverty *(poverty ratio[c]—percentages)*						
All non-communist developing countries	46.8	30.1	5.2	0.9	8.8	3.5
World	39.8	22.4	9.9	1.6	6.3	2.0

[a] The sum of the only-within and only-between country inequalities does not add up to the overall total because of inter-correlations between the two.

[b] The numbers labeled Gini coefficients are measures of the degree of concentration of the size distribution of income. A higher figure indicates greater inequality.

[c] Percentage of population falling below the poverty level (held fixed in real purchasing power). The definition of absolute poverty adopted for these calculations is that of the World Bank: an annual per capita income of less than U.S. $50 (1960). National currencies were converted into dollars using the Kravis purchasing power parity index for 1975.

Source: Irma Adelman, "The World Distribution of Income," Working Paper, Department of Agricultural Economics (University of California, Berkeley: August 1984).

experiment was performed; each individual in each country was assumed to have a per capita income equal to the country average. Therefore the only source of inequality in the fifth and sixth columns is inequality among countries. The sum of only within-country and only inter-country inequalities exceeds overall inequality because, in all subgroups, countries at the upper and lower extremes of the group had less inequality than countries in the middle (i.e., within-country inequality was negatively correlated with inter-country inequality).

It is clear from these experiments that both within-country inequality and inter-country inequality are important contributors to overall developing-country inequality. Within-country inequality is more important than inter-country inequality in explaining total developing-country inequality; but reductions in *either* source of inequality can make important contributions to poverty reduction. The poverty-ratio lines of Table 1 show that if either of the two forms of inequality could be eliminated (admittedly an extreme assumption), absolute poverty would virtually disappear.

Both within-country inequality and inter-country inequality in the non-communist developing countries increased between 1960 and 1980, but the greater disparities were those generated *within* countries. The dispersion of growth rates among non-communist developing countries also increased, since the middle-income countries grew considerably more rapidly than the low-income countries, and the dispersion in growth rates among the oil-exporting countries went up as well.

Efforts to reduce developing-country poverty therefore must focus both on more participatory growth processes within developing countries and on accelerating the growth rates of the poorer countries.

Policies and Programs Aimed at Reducing Income Inequality Within Developing Countries

How the poor fare during the course of economic development depends on how the distribution of assets, the institutions for asset accumulation, and the institutions for access to markets by the poor all interact with the development strategies chosen.

Chief among assets whose distribution has a significant impact on income distribution and poverty are land and education. The effects of economic change on the poor are critically dependent on land tenure conditions and the size distribution of landholdings. Poverty is greatest where land is divided into many small holdings and where there is a marked concentration of landownership coupled with cultivation by either landless labor or subsistence tenants. In contrast, where commercial farm owners supply most of their own labor, the rural distribution of income is in general more equal, and productivity increases may well improve the distribution of income. Concentration of landownership under circumstances in which small cultivators and landless workers lack alternative employment opportunities permits large landowners to pay low wages and to charge high rents. In addition, these tenurial conditions also increase the probability that innovations that raise average income and productivity in agriculture will have negative consequences for the poor. The opening up of new commercial or technological opportunities to populations with unequal abilities to respond to them widens inequality. Increasing the productivity of land when subsistence farmers and the landless cannot take advantage of that increasing productivity—because of limited access to credit or technologically superior inputs—tends to make for the marginalization of subsistence farmers and small tenants and may even lead to their eviction and dispossession. (An exception to this generalization occurs in the rare circumstances when the increase in the demand for hired labor is sufficiently large to overcome the fall in net income from farming that arises from the price decreases and rent increases that accompany the rise in productivity on larger farms.)

Turning to education's impact on income distribution, a broader incidence of education and literacy is associated with a larger share of income accruing to the middle group of income recipients but, at least initially, may not help the very poor. Increases in education spread the ownership of human capital and reduce inequalities in wage income. They also increase the rate of rural-urban migration—thereby augmenting the share of population that is employed in the higher-income sector and improving the agricultural terms of trade by raising urban demand for food while reducing its supply.

Institutions in factor and product markets are important determinants of how development affects the poor. Structural change associated with development gives rise to processes that simultaneously increase the absorption of some labor and other factors, displace labor and other factors, and generate geographic and sectoral reallocations of employment of labor and other factors. How these processes of absorption, displacement, and labor-force redistribution "net out" in their effect on the poor depends upon the institutional structure of factor and product markets. Segmentation of markets leaves some regions and sectors with labor gluts and others with shortages. Even without market segmentation, socially induced rigidities, the lack of relevant skills, or the absence of capital and information may in the short- or medium-run prevent the poor from escaping the contractionary influences to which they are exposed and finding expansionary ones elsewhere.

If one takes the initial distribution of assets and the structure of institutions as given, the major determinant of the course of income inequality and poverty becomes the overall development strategy chosen. The development strategy defines the basic thrust of economic policy. It combines a definition of policy targets (e.g., export expansion) with an identification of policy instruments (e.g., devaluation or export subsidies). Each strategy is associated with a specific configuration of the structure of production and a particular pattern of factor use. It is the development strategy that determines the pre-tax, pre-transfer (i.e., the primary) distribution of income. It governs the speed of absorption of labor into the modern sector, the extent of the income gap that develops between the modern and the traditional sectors, and the degree of income inequality within sectors.

The primary policy for helping absorption into the modern sectors is to adopt *labor-intensive* modes of expansion in those sectors. The labor intensity of growth can, in principle, be changed either by expanding the share of labor-intensive products and sectors in total employment or by increasing the labor intensity of production of a given mix of outputs (i.e., by appropriate technology). Of the two, the first process appears to be the more effective. Artificial shifts away from best-practice technology for a given factor mix reduce the amount of output obtainable from a given amount of resources. This approach is therefore less effective than shifting the mix of output toward sectors requiring a mix of resources that corresponds more closely to the basic factor endowments of the labor-abundant economies of the developing countries.

Once the choice of development strategy has jelled, policies and programs aimed at changing the primary distribution of income can accomplish very little.[5] This is true of both transfer programs and poverty-oriented projects. The size distribution of income tends to be quite stable around the trend established by the basic choice of development strategy. Following any intervention, even one sustained over time, the size distribution of income tends to return to the pre-intervention distribution. Only large, well-designed, complementary packages of anti-poverty policies and programs can change the primary distribution of income somewhat; but, to be effective, they must essentially amount to a gradual change in the overall development strategy.

Types of Anti-Poverty Policy

If one includes among the "assets" of the poor their personal capacities, trained or otherwise, their incomes consist of the value of the services of the assets owned by them that are sold on the market. In a very basic sense, then, the poverty problem is one of too small a quantity of assets, too low a volume of market sales, and/or too low a market price.

Poverty-focused approaches to policy therefore consist of measures to accomplish one or more of the following policy targets: 1) increase the quantity of assets owned by the poor, 2) increase the volume of their market sales, and 3) increase the prices of the services they sell. The general approaches that have been advocated to achieve a non-immiserating growth process can be grouped under these three headings.

Asset-Oriented Approaches

The quantity of assets owned by the poor can be increased either by redistributing assets to them (e.g., through land reform) or by creating institutions for their preferential access to opportunities for accumulation of further assets (e.g., through subsidized credit or wider access to primary education). Elsewhere I have argued for redistributing land and for tilting new educational opportunities toward the poor.[6] And in the famous World Bank/Sussex study of the middle 1970s, Hollis Chenery and his colleagues emphasized the second strategy, i.e., of concentrating asset *increments* on the poor—primarily on grounds of political feasibility.[7]

My own position is based on the experiences of the non-communist newly industrializing countries, notably Korea and Taiwan, that have successfully combined no deterioration in the relative incomes of the poor with accelerated growth. These examples lead me to advocate 1) tenurial reform in agriculture *before* implementation of policies designed to improve the productivity of agriculture, and 2) massive investments in education *before* rapid industrialization.

My rationale for this sequence, which I have called "redistribution before growth," is twofold: First, a better distribution of the major asset whose productivity is about to be improved, together with more equal access to markets and to opportunities for improving the productivity of that major asset, will obviously diminish the adverse effects of unequal asset distribution on income distribution. Second, the redistributed asset is not as valuable before improvements in productivity as it is after. Redistribution with full compensation would therefore be possible, at least in principle. I have argued, therefore, for the establishment of an internationally financed land-reform fund to: 1) help countries interested in implementing land reform design the reform; and 2) provide international guarantees for the nationally issued industrial and commodity bonds used to compensate the landlords whose land is redistributed.

Chenery's recommendations are more modest. In an approach he calls "redistribution with growth," he advocates differentially allocating a larger share of the proceeds of economic growth to asset accumulation by the poor. If, for example, the growth rate is 6 per cent per year, one-third of the growth (or 2 per cent of GNP) should be devoted to investment in assets owned by the poor or in assets that are complementary to assets owned by the poor. Examples of such investments would be: nutrition, health, and education programs for the poor; investment in irrigation facilities for land owned by the poor; or investment in credit programs or input subsidies aimed at subsistence farmers.

Demand-Generating Strategies

How much of the assets owned by the poor can be monetized on the market depends largely on the development strategy chosen and on the institutions for access to factor markets by the poor. Since the assets owned by the poor consist largely of unskilled labor, development strategies that increase the absolute and relative demand for unskilled labor, coupled with institutions that enhance labor mobility and access to jobs by the poor, are the ones that benefit the poor the most.

Two strategies look promising along these lines: 1) reliance upon export-oriented growth in labor-intensive manufactures and 2) reliance upon agricultural-development-led industrialization. I shall argue that, during the coming decade, the second strategy looks more promising for most developing countries that do not yet have an established position in international markets.

Once institutional conditions that permit reallocations of the labor power of the poor to higher productivity pursuits have been established by education, by removal of barriers to migration, and by dismantling of discrimination in hiring, equitable growth requires that subsequent increases in the rate of economic growth be achieved through measures that stress rapid growth in high-productivity, labor-intensive sectors and activities. An effective anti-poverty strategy must therefore increase the rate of growth of output of high-productivity, labor-intensive sectors and assure that the poor have access to the jobs so created.

The most labor-intensive sectors in any economy are agriculture, light manufacturing, and some types of services, especially construction (many services are skill-intensive rather than labor-intensive); but these are not necessarily the high-productivity, labor-intensive sectors. Generally, labor-intensive manufacturing is a (relatively) high-productivity sector in developing countries. That is, although output per worker is lower than it would be for more capital-intensive modes of producing the same product, it is generally higher than in most of agriculture and labor-intensive services. Policies that focus on labor-intensive growth in different sectors are therefore quite different, depending upon which sectors they stress.

Strategies that emphasize employment growth in manufacturing must focus primarily on *generating* demand for the output of the labor-intensive industries. In smaller nations, this implies that development will have to be oriented toward export markets. The small countries that follow this approach must therefore adopt a strategy of export-led growth and tailor their price and non-price incentives to be compatible with such an approach. In large countries, industrialization can be oriented toward the domestic market, particularly when the distribution of income is not too skewed.[8]

By contrast, a strategy that focuses on agriculture or on services can appeal to *existing* demand but must concentrate on increasing the productivity of labor in these sectors. There are no known technologies for increasing the productivity of purely labor-intensive services. The choice, therefore, is between a labor-intensive manufacturing strategy, on the one hand, and an agricultural strategy on the other. Bhagwati as well as Solis and Montemayor in this volume espouse the first of these, while Mellor advocates the second.

The choice between the two strategies depends on two factors: 1) the size of the direct and indirect employment multipliers that result from expanding either labor-intensive manufacturing or agriculture, and 2) comparison of the cost and feasibility of entering export markets with the cost and feasibility of increasing agricultural productivity.

Simulations with the two alternative strategies in a price- and wage-endogenous multi-sectoral model of the Republic of Korea indicate that both strategies can be effective in achieving higher growth and a better distribution of income. However, they also indicate that during periods of low growth in world demand for labor-intensive manufactured exports (which is likely to characterize the rest of the 1980s), the agricultural strategy is more effective. In such conditions, this strategy results in less inequality and poverty, as well as in a higher rate of growth and a better balance of payments.

The basic reasons for the superiority of the agricultural strategy—which Mellor emphasizes in an "agriculture-and employment-led" strategy—are: 1) agriculture is much more labor-intensive than even labor-intensive manufacturing; 2) land-augmenting increases in agricultural productivity generate increases in demand for the labor of the landless—the poorest of the poor; 3) increases in agricultural incomes generate high leakages into demand for labor-intensive manufactures on the consumption side and for manufactured inputs on the production side; 4) expansion in agricultural production is less import-intensive than an equivalent increase in manufacturing production; 5) increases in agricultural output with "good-practice," developing-country technology are less capital-intensive than increases in manufacturing; and 6) the agricultural infrastructure required to increase agricultural productivity (roads, irrigation, and drainage facilities) has a high labor-output ratio.

It should be noted, however, that, to be effective, both strategies have certain institutional and asset-distribution prerequisites. The labor-intensive growth strategy in manufacturing requires a wide distribution of education and low barriers to access to jobs by the poor. The agricultural strategy requires that tenurial conditions in agriculture not be too unfavorable and that small farmers be assured access to the complementary resources (particularly credit and water) that they need to improve agricultural yields.

Both strategies also have implications for price policies. The trade-oriented strategy requires a price policy that does not discriminate against exports by means of an overvalued exchange rate and tariffs. The agricultural strategy requires a price policy that enables farmers to capture some of the benefits from improvements in agricultural productivity. The latter, therefore, implies a terms-of-trade policy that divides the income benefits of increased output more equitably between urban and rural groups.

Price-Increasing Policies

Price-increasing policies can operate through factor or commodity markets, and/or they can increase the productivity of the assets owned by the poor.

Price-increasing policies that operate through *factor markets* must raise the wages of the poor. The labor-intensive growth strategies discussed above can therefore also be wage-increasing policies, since an increase in the demand for labor can either raise the quantity of labor sold or raise the wage rate (or both); but the effects of these policies upon the wages of the poor depend critically on *how the labor market operates*. If the barriers to access to jobs by the poor are low and the amount of unemployment and underemployment is small, an increase in the demand for labor will raise the wage rate of the poor. On the other hand, if there are institutional or economic barriers (for example, obstacles to migration) to an increase in the quantity of labor that can be bought from the poor, an increase in the demand for labor can augment the wage rate of the non-poor while leaving the wage rate of the poor largely unchanged and having only a second-round effect on the employment of the poor. The effects of demand-increasing strategies on the price of labor, therefore, depend critically on the institutional organization of the labor market.

Price-increasing policies that operate through *commodity markets* must raise the prices of the goods produced with the labor of the poor. Since the poor are mostly rural, an increase in the relative price of agricultural output (i.e., an increase in the agricultural terms of trade) will tend to benefit the poor. This is true even though such an increase (if not counteracted by price subsidies for urban consumers) will tend to reduce the real wages of the urban poor—for the urban poor, poor as they are, generally are richer than the rural poor. An increase in the agricultural terms of trade will also tend to benefit landless workers, even though they are net buyers of agricultural produce, by increasing the demand for their labor. This is so because, given the usual employment elasticities in developing-country agriculture, the employment effect raises the entire income of landless labor more or less in proportion to the increase in agricultural prices, whereas the food-price effect reduces only that fraction of their income that the landless spend on purchased food.

Productivity-Increasing Policies

Another way to increase the price of the major asset owned by the poor—their labor—is to increase its productivity. This can be done through 1) upgrading the quality of labor through investment in human capital; 2) increasing the amount of complementary assets employed by the poor (e.g., land or capital); or 3) introducing productivity-enhancing technical change (e.g., land-intensive innovations in agriculture).

Human Capital Investments. Direct investments in the poor are desirable in and of themselves, as part of providing the poor with the minimal bundle of goods necessary to open up their access to opportunities for a full life. However, the discussion that follows will focus only on how such investments can affect the *productivity* of the poor, thereby enabling them to earn higher incomes, which in turn would permit them at some future date to purchase the minimal bundle of goods on the market with their own earnings.

Investments in the nutrition, education, and health of the poor not only increase their welfare directly, but also enhance their capacities for productive labor. Much of the employment of the poor is physical labor. Not infrequently, the market wage that the poor are paid is not even sufficient to allow them to purchase enough food to replace the calories used in earning that wage.[10] Such wage labor therefore results in exposing the poor to higher morbidity and mortality and to higher health hazards than if they had remained unemployed. Consequently it is not surprising that the productivity of the poor, when employed, remains low. In such circumstances, nutrition supplements or higher wages can raise the productivity of the poor.

Investments in the education of the poor—through adult literacy campaigns and increases in the availability of primary education in rural areas and in other places where the poor reside—spread the ownership of human capital. They qualify the poor for more productive jobs and narrow the distribution of wage income. They also increase the rate of rural-urban migration, thereby providing the poor with access to higher-income employment opportunities and raising the agricultural terms of trade. Primary education of females also tends to reduce population growth.

Although the availability of basic health care for the poor—through mobile clinics, "barefoot doctors," investment in environmental sanitation, potable water, and training in food preparation practices and elementary hygiene—raises the well-being of the poor, there is little evidence of significant direct links with productivity. Better health does, however, increase school attendance and learning while in school. It also raises the efficiency of transforming nutritional intake into caloric output and, therefore, substantially reduces malnutrition. Thus, from a productivity point of view, the contributions of investments in better health are mostly indirect, in that they raise the effectiveness of other productivity-enhancing investments in the poor.

Complementary Resources and Land-Augmenting Investments. The primary causes of rural poverty of the rural poor are the meager amount of land that they have to till with their own labor combined with a low demand for hired labor by large cultivators. The most effective productivity improvements for raising the incomes of the rural poor are therefore land-augmenting investments and innovations. Examples of land-augmenting innovations are: irrigation and drainage facilities, which, by allowing water control, may permit multiple cropping; improved seed, which by itself can triple the yield per acre; and fertilizer. These types of investments and innovations stretch the yields from whatever land the poor cultivate, and they significantly raise demand for hired labor by larger farmers.

To be most effective, however, these innovations and investments require making complementary resources available to the poor. For even when the more productive technologies are scale-neutral—as they are in the case of the high-yielding varieties of wheat and rice—the poor are not able to take advantage of these innovations because they do not have access to water, credit, improved seed, the wherewithal with which to buy fertilizer, or the technological know-how disseminated by extension. At least in the early stages of the diffusion of such innovations, productivity-increasing innovations tend to have two opposite effects on the rural poor: They increase the demand for wage labor, since the land-augmenting innovations are all quite labor-intensive; but they also reduce the price of the marketable surplus of small cultivators, since the increase in output from the larger farms generates an increase in overall supply in the face of inelastic demand. Large farmers benefit, since they can increase their sales—but the small ones lose, since they are not able to take advantage of the yield-increasing innovations. Therefore the net impact of agricultural innovations upon the rural poor depends, at least in the early stages, on the share of income that they derive from farming as opposed to wage labor.

The negative effects of the yield-enhancing innovations upon the nearly landless discussed above could be avoided if institutions were developed to provide them with access to the complementary resources with which they, too, could shift to more productive technologies. Small farmers need agricultural extension, improved seed and fertilizer, better irrigation and drainage facilities, and, most of all, credit.

Conclusion

Several points emerge from this review of findings derived from the experience with development, poverty, and income distribution over the past decade and a half.

1. Validated strategies, policies, and programs for poverty alleviation do exist. Indeed, there has been substantial progress toward the achievement of this goal between 1960 and 1980 in the non-communist developing countries as a group despite the fact that the distribution of income has become substantially more unequal.

2. Strategies for poverty alleviation are not compatible with just any kind of economic growth. They entail particular kinds of economic growth.

3. Approaches to poverty alleviation require the implementation of mutually consistent and reinforcing multifaceted programs. The most effective approaches entail a combination of several elements: asset-oriented policies that are supported by institutions designed to facilitate the poor's access to jobs; investments that enhance the productivity of assets that the poor possess and can sell; and development strategies that generate a rapid increase in the demand for unskilled labor.

4. More than one method exists to achieve each element of the package described above. The choice among instruments needs to be tailored to each country's particular initial conditions, resource base, size, asset distribution, institutional structure, and sociopolitical configuration—as well as to the external conditions and trends that the country faces at any point in time.

5. Choices among poverty-alleviation packages and programs are inherently *political*. A critical aspect of the political choice among competing goals and instrumentalities is the time dimension.

6. The sequence in which different policy interventions are taken up is important: The most effective approach to poverty

alleviation entails implementing asset-oriented policies and institutional changes designed to give the poor access to high-productivity jobs *before*, not after, shifting development strategies. If that is done, there is no "trade-off" between growth promotion and poverty alleviation. The same development strategy is then optimal for both goals.

7. Which strategy and which set of policies is most effective for a given country is likely to change over time—as changes take place both in the initial conditions within each country and in the economic and political environment in which the country operates.

8. With all of this in view, two strategies appear to promise the poor the most: 1) reliance upon export-oriented growth in labor-intensive manufactures and 2) reliance upon agricultural-development-led industrialization. During the coming decade— likely to be one of low growth in world demand for labor-intensive manufactured exports—the agriculture-led approach is likely to deliver more in terms of less inequality and poverty, a higher growth rate, and a better balance of payments.

Notes

[1] Irma Adelman and Sherman Robinson, *Income Distribution Policy in Developing Countries: A Case Study of Korea* (Stanford: Stanford University Press and Oxford University Press, 1978), pp. 148–151.

[2] Simon Kuznets, "Economic Growth and Income Inequality, "*American Economic Review*, Vol. 45, No. 1 (March 1955), pp. 1–28.

[3] Irma Adelman and Cynthia Taft Morris, *Economic Growth and Social Equity in Developing Countries* (Stanford: Stanford University Press, 1973); Gary S. Fields, *Poverty, Inequality, and Development* (Cambridge: Cambridge University Press, 1980).

[4] For a fuller explanation of this method, see Irma Adelman, *The World Distribution of Income*, Working Paper No. 346, Department of Agricultural and Resource Economics, University of California, Berkeley, August 1984.

[5] Adelman and Robinson, *A Case Study of Korea*, op. cit.; Frank J. Lysy and Lance Taylor, *Models of Growth and Distribution for Brazil* (Cambridge: Oxford University Press, 1980).

[6] See Irma Adelman, "Beyond Export-Led Growth," *World Development*, Vol. 12, No. 9 (September 1984), pp. 937–49.

[7] Hollis Chenery, et al., *Redistribution With Growth* (Cambridge: Oxford University Press, 1974).

[8] A. de Janvry and Elizabeth Sadoulet, "Social Articulation as a Condition for Equitable Growth," *Journal of Development Economics*, Vol. 13 No. 3 (December 1983), pp. 275–304.

[9] Irma Adelman, *Redistribution Before Growth—A Strategy for Developing Countries* (The Hague: Martinus Nijhof, 1978).

[10] Gerry B. Rodgers, "A Conceptualization of Poverty in Rural India," *World Development*, Vol. 4, No. 4 (April 1976), pp. 261–76.

Chapter 2

Agriculture on the Road to Industrialization

John W. Mellor

Economic development is a process by which an economy is transformed from one that is dominantly rural and agricultural to one that is dominantly urban, industrial, and service in composition. The objectives of the process can be usefully categorized as increased societal wealth, equity, and stability. But because these objectives require a diversification of the economy away from agriculture (no high-income, equitable, stable nations have agriculture as their dominant activity), the process is one of major structural transformation.

If economic development is a process of transforming an economy from producing mainly agricultural to producing mainly industrial and service outputs, what is the nature of a constructive role for the initially dominant agricultural sector? What is the scope for synthesizing an agricultural role into the mainstream of development thought? More specifically, what is the dynamic relation between agriculture and industry in an optimal growth strategy?

Given agriculture's initial importance, it is not surprising that it has received the explicit attention of eminent economists and has been the subject of intensive analysis by generalists and specialists alike. Yet, in view of the contemporary expansion of knowledge about how to develop agriculture, it is surprising that the principal, broad conceptualizations in development economics have not articulated a central place for agriculture. This has held true through wide-ranging shifts in development-strategy styles—from emphasis on direct allocation of resources to growth in the capital stock, to import displacement, to basic human needs, to export-led growth. In fact, each of these development fashions has had its own strong arguments for not emphasizing agriculture in either capital allocations or public policy. For countries following these mainstream strategies, occasional crises of domestic food supplies, foreign-exchange constraints in association with sudden, large food imports, or threatened cutoffs in large-scale food aid have prompted flurries of attention for agriculture. But such spurts of concern all too often have generated only such short-term palliatives as higher prices for food producers; they have not produced sustained long-run development efforts that build agriculture as part of a larger strategy.

There are, of course, numerous examples of development *practice* that have indeed given agriculture a central place. Notable are the post-Meiji restoration period in Japan as well as the developmental thrusts in Taiwan, Thailand, Ivory Coast, Malaysia, the Punjabs of India and Pakistan, and to some extent other parts of South Asia. It is ironic that, perhaps because of the critical importance of trade expansion in an agriculture-based strategy, several of these successes are perceived as examples of export-led growth rather than as a successful agriculture-based strategy.

The intellectual neglect of agriculture's role in development no doubt is rooted in an underlying view of agriculture as initially backward; development promoters have wanted to move directly to building those sectors that carry the image of modernization. An urban-based intelligentsia (including development economists), a related caste-like separation of largely micro-oriented agricultural economists and largely macro-oriented development economists, and urban-based political systems all combine to provide an intellectual basis and political pressure for directing resources to the urban sector.

In decrying this neglect, however, it is important to recognize that there is an intellectual case for downplaying agriculture in the development process. To make the contrary case, three substantial questions must be answered affirmatively:

(1) Can agricultural production be increased by means of advances in resource productivity?

(2) Can effective demand for agricultural commodities expand apace with accelerated agricultural growth?

(3) Can a dynamic agriculture provide an effective demand "pull" for growth in other sectors?

The following discussion will show why these are the vital questions, why it is not unreasonable to think that the answer to each may be "no," and what the contrary bases are for the affirmative answer that in turn defines a central role for agriculture in a dynamic process of economic transformation and growth. This exploration will make clear the essential connection between agricultural growth and employment growth—and hence the need always to speak of an agriculture- and employment-based strategy, not of one or the other independently.

The strategy described here has two key distinguishing features aside from the emphases on agriculture and employment. First, continuous, institutionalized technological change provides the basic engine of cumulative growth. Second, growth in domestic demand provides the basic markets both for the increasing agricultural output and for the activities that create rapid growth in employment. Trade is important—but mainly to serve the purpose of restraining growth in capital-intensiveness.

Before discussing the main elements of an agriculture- and employment-based strategy, common failings of alternative strategies will be briefly noted, as well as which of those failings an agriculture-based strategy might or might not meet. A sketch of the debate as to the efficacy of agricultural and non-agriculture-based strategies follows.

Development Failings and Agriculture's Potential

Robert McNamara's presidential address to the 1973 World Bank annual meeting epitomized a widespread and growing view that the ascendant development strategies of the 1950s and 1960s had an unacceptably small impact on poverty. That the expression of such concern had subsided so much by the late 1970s owed less to a diminution of the reality of the problem and more to the realization that the various direct attacks on poverty meanwhile ventured were no more successful than earlier efforts in mitigating the problem.

Failure to make a dent in the poverty problem was associated with four related phenomena:

(1) Food supplies per capita rose little or not at all, and hence the diets, nutritional status, and related well-being of the poor could not be enhanced.

(2) Employment growth rates seemed to lag even behind population growth rates, so that the poor could not obtain income to command more food or other basic wants.

(3) Growth and basic services were often available only in a small number of immense urban concentrations, with high overhead costs and little impact on the population dispersed over the rest of the country.

(4) Overall growth rates were themselves much slower and less well sustained than expected.

The first three are directly related to the lack of poverty abatement. The last, even if it was not a direct cause, certainly reinforced equity-related failings. Clearly, an agricultural emphasis strikes at one of the root causes of poverty: inadequate food supplies. Accelerated agricultural growth also provides a substantial direct increase in employment because of the large aggregate size of the sector and the nature of its technology. And agriculture, as a broadly diffused activity, spreads economic activity and employment beyond the megalopolis.

One should be clear, however, as to what accelerated agricultural growth cannot do *directly*. First, it cannot provide high overall growth rates in output or employment. For the staple foods sector, growth of 3–4 per cent is considered very rapid, and 4–5 per cent for the agricultural sector as a whole is extraordinarily rapid.[1] The constraint of limited land area, the biological nature of agricultural production, and the dispersed, variable production system explain the common experience of such low ceilings on growth rates. Similarly, it is doing well indeed to experience a 0.6-per cent growth rate in agricultural employment for each percentage point in the output growth rate.[2] Thus the agricultural sector can at best provide employment for its own population growth, and it is likely to fall far short of that. And agricultural growth alone obviously cannot supply the broadening of consumption patterns beyond food that all people desire.

These limitations explain why an agriculture-based strategy must have major *indirect* effects on growth and employment in other sectors if it is to be seen as central to development strategy. These indirect effects must come from the expenditure of increased agricultural income on non-agricultural goods and services, in turn creating not only additional output in those sectors but also additional employment. To be consistent with an agriculture- and employment-oriented strategy, one must ask of those activities that they be large in aggregate, employment-intensive, and broadly distributed geographically.

From these foundations, we can skip ahead of the story to outline what a development strategy must look like if agriculture and employment are to play a central role. *First*, the agricultural production growth rate must be accelerated; this must normally derive from technological change. *Second*, the expenditure pattern from the net additions to income arising from the accelerated growth must create demand for a wide range of goods and services with a high employment content, much of the production of which must be broadly diffused in rural areas (e.g., in major market towns). *Third*, increased food marketing will somewhat depress food prices,[3] thereby encouraging employment in other sectors by making labor somewhat cheaper relative to the goods and services it produces.

Historical Sketch of the Agriculture versus Industry Debate

Industrial Orientation

With G. S. Fel'dman's writing as the theoretical base, the Soviet Union's practice in the 1920s was to equate industrialization with modernization. The arguments constantly recurred in subsequent development literature. Capital and labor were believed to be more productive in industry. Industry was seen as having major economies of scale and external economies, while agriculture was subject to diminishing returns. Industrial "externalities," including industry's modernizing force, promoting new modes of economic behavior and new forms of social organization, were all seen as supportive of growth. Given the diminishing returns in agriculture, if underemployed labor could be mobilized out of agriculture with no loss of production, the argument for industry was compelling. In this context, it is fitting that Paul Rosenstein-Rodan's piece on economic development, published in 1943, was entitled "Problems of Industrialization of Eastern and South-Eastern Europe."[4]

A major force in the development literature of the 1950s and 1960s and in the practice of both India and China[5] grew out of the conceptualization by Fel'dman, as further developed by P. C. Mahalanobis, and related to the concepts of Roy Harrod and Evsey Domar.[6] Increase in the capital stock was the source of growth. It followed in the view of Fel'dman and Mahalanobis that this resource should be directly allocated to capital-goods production, and not to consumer-goods, including agricultural production. In practice, industrialization became highly capital-intensive, with little employment growth and consequently little growth in demand for food; hence there was little upward pressure on food prices, even though agriculture was doing poorly. The strategy, since it was inward-looking, spawned a whole generation of closed-economy growth models showing how capital should be deployed among subsectors. The push was always on industry.

A substantial ancillary literature dealt with the balance of growth and the issue of whether or not capital intensity could be reduced by choice of technology. The answer, in the confines of an inward-looking strategy, was that it could not. A. K. Sen provided the definitive rationalization of that conclusion, basing it on the inevitable need for more food to underpin the increased wages from employment growth and diminishing returns (increasing capital intensity) in agriculture.[7] The proponents of this capital-intensive strategy realized that equity and poverty abatement would be postponed by the strategy, although they hoped that relatively inexpensive efforts in agriculture and cottage industries (e.g., community development in India) would mitigate the problem.

The import-substitution strategy popularized for Latin America by Raul Prebisch[8] was driven by the view that primary-commodity prices, particularly including those of agricultural commodities, would inevitably trend downward relative to the prices of manufactured goods. It followed that a developing country should shift out of agriculture and into industry as quickly as possible. The market would come from displacement of previously imported goods. In practice, however, as implementation of the strategy progressed, more and more capital-intensive imports were displaced by domestic production. Thus as expansion proceeded, capital intensity increased, employment growth slowed, income distribution became more skewed, and the growth rate decelerated.

By the mid-1960s, concern was growing that development was moving too slowly, and the poor were not participating significantly in such growth as was occurring. At the same time, agricultural research was demonstrating the capacity to provide major new technology to increase agricultural productivity—the green revolution. Why did the concurrence of these breakthroughs and the concern for poverty reduction of that time not bring a sharp swing in development strategy toward an agriculture- and employment-based strategy of growth?

The green revolution is based on new technology and rapid growth in fertilizer use, increased commercialization of agriculture, and a complex set of national-level institutions run by a large and rapidly growing number of highly trained people. The sharp rise in energy prices led to a wish to de-emphasize the use of fertilizer and even of irrigation based on energy-using pumps. Western environmental concerns also were on the ascent and did not favor fertilizer. Mounting attention to equity problems strengthened interest in dependency theorists, who in turn also had a negative view of fertilizer as an instrument of Western multinationals. Concurrently, anti-elitism favored primary over higher education, turning foreign aid away from advanced training of the scientists and technicians essential to the success of the green revolution. Concern with poverty reduction, energy depletion, environment, dependency, and elitism all seemed associated with each other. All this was reinforced by a literature decrying the then reputed negative effect of the green revolution in further skewing the rural income distribution; it was said (incorrectly, it is now clear) that only the larger farmers benefited from the new technology[9] and that they would use their new wealth to buy out small farmers and tenants.

The combined impact of these forces retarded response to the essential requirements of the green revolution and spawned a "basic human needs" approach that emphasized social welfare functions and agricultural production only in highly complex regional projects. The integrated rural development projects that resulted not only were not integrated into national support structures for agricultural growth; they tended to raid the latter for personnel. Almost universally, the integrated rural development projects failed due to excessive complexity and a lack of central support services.[10] (Local institutions are, of course, central to the green revolution, but they are effective only when serviced by national-level support structures, including research.) The basic-needs approach had a major influence on foreign assistance in the 1970s, particularly in the least developed countries that include the bulk of Africa but also a few other countries, such as Nepal, in Asia.

Asian countries that had benefited from earlier foreign assistance emphasizing large-scale, high-level technical training and well-developed agricultural research systems were able to pursue the green revolution effectively and even to restrain foreign aid from single-minded pursuit of the new directions of the 1970s. In that context, the basic-needs strategy could be used to deal with "second-generation" problems in the context of the other requisites of a successful green revolution. It is notable, however, that where—as in India and the Philippines—the green revolution was not associated with an employment orientation, it served substantially to displace food imports and build food stocks rather than as the base for a new development strategy. The basic-needs strategists, while often vigorously and specifically attacking the green revolution, were generally silent about strategies giving priority to capital-intensive industry and import-substitution. There was urgent need to change those strategies to provide the essential employment complement to the green revolution.

The failings of the capital-intensive strategies, dependent as they were on market interference, also prompted a trend quite separate from the equity-oriented basic-needs strategy: a renewed interest in a market-oriented strategy commonly emphasizing export promotion. With the gradual demise of the basic-needs orientation in the early 1980s, the strategy of export-led growth or export promotion became the new fashion. Of all the post-World War II strategies, this was the one least deleterious to agriculture. It argued against overvalued currencies, which discriminate so strongly against agriculture. It argued generally for prices favorable to agriculture, supported commercialization of agriculture (including import of key inputs), and fostered better domestic markets for agricultural output by favoring employment-intensive industries—with beneficial effects on employment for the poor and hence greater expenditure on food. In practice, however, the export-promotion strategy looks explicitly to markets abroad—rather than to the broad-based domestic markets that accelerated agricultural growth can provide. This, combined with an anti-governmental bias, works against support for large public investments in the key areas of research, education, rural roads, and rural electrification that are so critical to an agriculture- and employment-based growth strategy. In practice, the export-promotion strategy also emphasizes trade to allow economies of scale, thereby favoring more capital-intensive industries relative to relying more on vigorous domestic markets.[11]

Agricultural Orientation

Although a clear agriculture- and employment-based strategy has not been ascendant, agriculture has never lacked for a good word from an eminent economist. During the postwar renaissance of concern for the macro-economics of growth, Nicholas Kaldor stated:

> Economic development will, of course, invariably involve industrialization . . . this can be expected to follow, almost automatically, upon the growth of the food surpluses of the agricultural sector. . . . Once this is recognized, the efforts of under-developed countries could be concentrated—far more than they are at present—in tackling the problem of how to raise productivity on the land, as a prior condition of economic development.[12]

It is, however, clear from succeeding lines in Kaldor's piece that he had little grasp of what was involved in the modernization of agriculture and least of all as to what was required to provide a stream of land-augmenting technological changes—although his intuition as to the importance of agriculture and the importance of education to agricultural growth, were both correct. Perhaps Kaldor was also facile in his perception of the near-automaticity of agriculture's growth converting into industrial growth. Our knowledge of these processes has improved immensely since 1954, although its scant diffusion to macro-economists still prejudices thought about development.

Paralleling the broad orientation of development economics away from agriculture was an evolution of knowledge about how to develop agriculture. Farmers were presented as economically rational responders to prices and technology;[13] understanding of the need for radically improved technology was articulated in economic terms,[14] and the nature of a range of complementary agricultural growth requirements was set forth.[15] Myriad empirically based analyses have filled in the picture. More important, the scientific groundwork for the green revolution was laid by the activities of the Rockefeller Foundation in Mexico and India, and by the Ford and Rockefeller Foundations in establishing the International Rice Research Institute, the precursor of and role model for the Consultative Group on International Agricultural Research. The result was the bursting of the green revolution in Asia in the late 1960s and a clear appreciation of the requisites of accelerated agricultural growth.

Compared with the imme: ¨¨ ains in our understanding of the agricultural development process *per se*, the relationships between agriculture and the rest of a developing economy remain less fully explored. While there have been many contributions on the subject, the empirical data underlying the relationships asserted are much less complete than is the case with the micro-economics of agriculture—and hence the policies implied remain more speculative.

Nevertheless, four major threads of the analysis can be defined. First, the critical role of food as a wage good (the object of consumption from the increased income of employment) was elegantly defined in W. Arthur Lewis's classic paper.[16] Second, the need for productivity increase in agriculture and the role of technology was laid out by Johnston and Mellor.[17] Third, the resource transfers from agriculture that so facilitate growth of the non-agricultural sector were delineated from the Japanese experience by Kazushi Ohkawa, Bruce Johnston, and I. Ishikawa,[18] and meticulously documented for Taiwan by T. H. Lee.[19] Fourth, the critical role of agriculture in stimulating growth in the non-agricultural sector has been explored with respect to both consumption goods[20] and producer goods.[21]

An Agriculture- and Employment-Based Strategy of Economic Growth

An agriculture- and employment-based strategy of economic growth has three basic elements. *First*, the pace of agricultural growth must be accelerated despite the limitations of fixed land area. Technological change solves a major, special problem of agricultural growth and allows low-income countries to use the most powerful element of growth. *Second*, domestic demand for agricultural output must grow rapidly despite inelastic demand. This can occur only through accelerated growth in employment (more precisely, increased demand for labor), which is facilitated by the indirect effects of agricultural growth itself. *Third*, the demand for goods and services produced by low capital-intensity processes must increase. This, too, is facilitated by the technology-based increase in agricultural income. As we proceed, we will see that these three elements continually interact in the strategy.

Technological Change in Agriculture

One of the most important theoretical and empirical findings in analysis of Western economic growth is the identification of technological change as a major source of growth. Hence it is initially surprising that in the various ascendant macro-economic theories of economic growth for developing countries, technological change has not been assigned a central role.

On second thought, however, the neglect is understandable: These ascendant theories have been preoccupied with growth in the initially minuscule industrial sector, where the first concern necessarily has been to expand the capital stock as the basis of growth. Only if the dominant agricultural sector is to be central to growth can technological change play an immediate, major role. It happens that, because of Ricardian diminishing returns, technological change is in any case essential to agricultural growth. The land area for agriculture being generally limited, increased output is traditionally obtained via declining increments in output per unit of input as input intensity increases. The result is rising costs, which must be offset by rising prices if incentives are to prevail. It is apparent that cumulatively increasing relative food prices are not socially acceptable. Thus it is essential that the incentive to produce more in the face of constantly rising costs be met by technological change rather than by price increases. Continuous, cumulative technological change is the proven effect of institutionalized agricultural research systems.

The rudiments of getting agriculture moving through technological change have been fully understood for a long time.[22] Development of a technology system (including research) and technically competent extension are primary. The nature of agricultural technology is such that rapid growth of sophisticated input delivery systems is essential. For this latter, and for effective multipliers of other sectors, a highly developed infrastructure of roads is required. Underlying the total process is rapid growth in the number of highly trained people and of the institutional structure within which they can work effectively.

In all of these elements, the public sector must play a key role in physical investment and institution building. The essential financial and organizational requirements of governments are so immense that every effort must be made to maximize activities in the private sector and to concentrate public-sector attention on only those essential agricultural support activities not taken up by the private sector. Agriculture, with its small-scale orientation, is more in need of public-sector support than industry. The sharp turnaround in Asian agriculture—resulting in a 30-per cent increase in growth rates in basic food-staple production from the 1960s to the 1970s—impressively demonstrates the results of turning the public sector's attention to the requisites of technological change in agriculture.

The urgency of moving the agricultural sector is underlined by its role as a supplier of food as essential backing to employment growth. It is generally understood that developing countries have a large pool of extremely low-productivity if not idle labor. In effect, this provides a highly elastic labor supply. If jobs become available, labor is ready to march into them. What has not been fully recognized is that the supply of labor is a function of two independent markets: a labor market and a food market.[23] Increased employment provides the labor class with added income, 60 to 80 per cent of which is spent on food. If the food supply is not expanded, increased employment will cause the price of food to rise, squeezing the real incomes of laborers back nearly to the previous level, reducing the incentive to work, placing upward pressures on wages, and reducing employment. Thus, accelerated growth in employment must be accompanied by accelerated growth in food supplies.[24] Three arguments have been used against the need to emphasize domestic food production in this context.

First, the labor-surplus arguments take the position that labor is already maintained and idle in the rural sector; hence, until there is a "turning point" at which labor is fully absorbed, food supply is available for labor transferred to other occupations.[25] This argument neglects the theoretically and empirically verifiable fact that increased employment, even in the face of surplus agricultural labor, results in increased wage payments in the hands of people with high marginal propensity to spend on food. A related argument is that employment can only grow very slowly due to the capital constraint. The striking contrary evidence is that developing countries that have done well in agriculture expand employment rapidly enough to have to increase food imports.[26] We will, however, return to this argument later.

Second, there is a widespread belief that the aggregate supply of food is elastic with respect to price. If such is the case, higher food prices induced by increased purchasing power in the hands of the poor will readily bring forth the needed increased supply of food. The theoretical and empirical evidence is clear on this point: Under essentially all conditions, the aggregate supply of food is only slightly responsive to price.[27] Most simply, this is due to Ricardian diminishing returns. It is possible to accelerate the growth rate of food production sharply, but only through the processes of technological change. With existing technology, the aggregate supply response to higher prices is comparatively limited.

Third, it is believed that the supply of food from imports is highly elastic. Up to a point, this assumption is probably correct. Certainly Singapore and Hong Kong have been able to expand employment rapidly and to meet the consequent increased demand for food with imports. It is less certain that supplies would be adequate if the bulk of the developing countries succeeded in a rapid employment growth strategy without increasing domestic food production. But the possibility of importing food to meet the demands of increased employment strengthens the argument that generating demand and resources for growth of other sectors must be an important part of the argument for an emphasis on agriculture.

Adequate Effective Demand for Food

There is an important theoretical problem in realizing the full potential of accelerated technological change in agriculture. The demand for food tends to be inelastic. If food production increases rapidly without increased employment, prices will tend to fall sharply and eventually cause reduced production. The way to deal with the problem is through accelerated growth in employment, which under the low-income conditions of developing countries is efficiently translated into increased demand for food. The correct response to increased food production is no more through constantly decreasing prices than the way to meet the need for increased production is through constantly increasing prices. The correct response to the former is employment; to the latter, it is technological change.

Prices, it must be emphasized, are not so much problems as indicators of problems. If food prices are rising, this indicates that the supply is not being increased rapidly enough through technological change. One should in such circumstances redouble efforts in the technological change arena. While waiting for those redoubled efforts to succeed, food would have to be imported, so as to prevent employment being held back by rapidly rising food prices.

Conversely, declining food prices mean that the success in technological change is moving ahead of the employment strategy. Governments may come under substantial pressure from organized farm interests to maintain agricultural prices as technology moves ahead even though demand is not keeping pace. The result will be either subsidized exports or, more likely, rapid growth in domestic stocks. India's record in the early and mid-1980s has been a prime example: Stocks were built up to four times the level that would be justified by optimal stocking policies. This is an example of a country achieving modest success in technological change and doing badly on employment growth. One should in those circumstances examine the allocation of capital and of demand structures to see what can be done on the employment side.

Just as the preceding discussion emphasized the need to meet food requirements by domestic production, so this discussion stresses growth in domestic income, not exports, for generating effective demand for growing supplies of food. If one is exporting staple foods, this means that one has a more-than-adequate supply of food to provide for the growth in demand from the existing rate of growth of employment. In a low-income, low-employment economy, one should obviously be striving for policies that increase domestic employment as a way of fully taking up food supplies.

Demand Stimulus to Non-Agricultural Employment

The role of agriculture in providing effective demand for production from the non-agricultural sector has received little emphasis in the literature and has been poorly understood. In the most extreme phase of its evolution, this view was: "Agriculture stands convicted on the count of its lack of direct stimulus to the setting up of new activities through linkage effects—the superiority of manufacturing in this respect is crushing."[28] This position overlooked that technological change in agriculture can increase net national income and thereby generate added demand for consumer goods. The neglect of this aspect was reinforced by capital-centered growth theory, which tended to view consumption and the production of consumption goods as antithetical to growth. This bias was aggravated by excessive emphasis on "modern" consumer and capital goods to the neglect of services and more traditionally produced consumer goods. A more careful review of early Western development history, despite the weak technological base of its agricultural growth, would have helped avoid this misreading.[29]

A central problem of contemporary development practice is illuminated by a quote from Sir John Hicks that has roots in a long history of his own work: "That it is possible for a 'developing country,' by choice of techniques that are too capital-intensive, to expand employment in its modern sector less rapidly than it might have done is nowadays familiar."[30]

The failures in economic development to which Hicks refers have been associated with a poor record in agricultural growth and failure to connect success in agriculture to driving the rest of the economy. These failures have been associated with a marked dualism in capital investment—a small portion of the labor force operating with high capital intensity and a large portion with low capital intensity. The result, as Hicks would lead one to expect, is generally low productivity of both capital and labor. That dualism exhibits itself partly in low allocations of capital to agriculture, occasional instances of investment in state farms and other capital-intensive elements within agriculture, and a widespread tendency to place the bulk of additional capital in large-scale, capital-intensive industries with few additional employees, leaving little capital for the dominant remainder of the labor force.[31]

Agricultural development offers a potential for rapid growth in domestic demand for labor-intensive goods and services. Incremental consumption patterns of peasant farmers have a large rural-services component, and a large share of other goods consumed is also produced relatively labor-intensively.

It is essential to note two needs if the favorable demand effects of agricultural growth are to be achieved. *First*, the increments to demand must come from volume-increasing and unit-cost-decreasing technological change. Raising prices is not likely to help. Although the income transfer from urban to rural people arising from higher agricultural prices may provide some modest, net restructuring of demand favorable to employment, only a major, continuous increase in net national income from new technology can be expected to provide a continuous aggregate effect. *Second,* the infrastructure of communications essential to growth of rural industry and services must be in place. Highly developed infrastructure is essential to agricultural production growth, favorable consumption incentives, and to the complex, interactive system of region-based urban centers that are so essential to a high-employment content in an agriculture-based growth strategy.

Capital stock must grow rapidly if employment is to do the same. In an agriculture-led strategy, however, market mechanisms should work well to raise the savings rate. Much of the capital needed for agricultural growth can be generated in agriculture itself in response to technology-induced high rates of return. The non-agricultural supply response to increased demand may well be highly elastic. If capital proves to be a constraint, higher prices will result, transferring resources from newly prospering agriculture to those activities. The critical investment bottlenecks are more likely to be in the public sector, with government at the local or national level not gathering or allocating adequate resources for the massive rural infrastructure that is essential to agricultural and employment growth. The 20- to 30-per cent savings rates that characterize so many contemporary developing countries are inadequate to the task only because the capital intensity of many productive processes is excessive and because too small a share of the savings is invested in infrastructure. Agricultural linkages can contribute to reducing that intensity and to spreading capital more thinly.

Policy Issues

Pursuit of an agriculture- and employment-based strategy of growth requires quite different public-sector policies than those comprising alternative strategies. Discussion of key policy requirements serves to bring out distinguishing characteristics of the strategy as well as to indicate what policy shifts are needed if it is to succeed.

Trade

An agriculture- and employment-based development strategy requires an open trading regime. That point must be made explicitly because of the emphasis on meeting the demand for wage goods arising from employment growth from domestic food production and on providing domestic demand for the increased food production. Those inward-looking emphases are a product of comparative advantage, reinforced by high transfer costs typical of developing countries, and do not require protection. (Thus this strategy is highly complementary to and supportive of the points made elsewhere in this volume by Jagdish Bhagwati.)

The high employment-growth leg of the strategy requires that capital be spread thinly over a rapidly growing labor force. There is little scope to restrain rising capital-labor ratios in a closed economy. Although particular goods and services may have low capital-labor ratios, they always seem to have component parts that have very high capital-labor ratios (e.g., fertilizer for agriculture, and steel, aluminum, and petrochemicals for otherwise labor-intensive manufactured goods). Thus while agricultural growth generates direct demand for a final product that is efficiently produced by labor-intensive processes, there must be rapid growth in imports of capital-intensive intermediate goods and services. Clearly, accelerated growth of such imports must be matched by accelerated growth of exports. The latter should be goods and services with relatively high employment content. This fits obviously with standard trade theory. The need to foster such exports will further restrain increases in aggregate capital-labor ratios. The rapid growth in domestic markets for labor-intensive manufactures would itself be favorable to low-cost production and therefore to their external competitiveness. Taiwan's rapid success in exports in the late 1950s was based on prior development of domestic demand.[32] A somewhat undervalued exchange rate facilitates full pricing of agricultural commodities; encourages restraint in using inputs that are capital-intensively produced because they will be imported and thus more highly priced; and provides some additional incentive to export the more labor-intensive commodities, helping to overcome the various institutional hurdles to exports that inevitably exist in developing countries. This is, of course, the opposite of the exchange-rate policy that is consistent with the capital-intensive approaches.

If employment does move ahead of the capacity to produce domestic food staples, one should obviously take advantage of that opportunity and import food to support the more rapid growth rate of employment. If, on the other hand, food is being exported, one should examine carefully whether trade policies are restraining the imports of capital-intensive goods and services and the export of labor-intensive goods and services, or whether infrastructure investment is inadequate for rapid growth in domestic employment.

Poverty Reduction

The agriculture-employment strategy is innately favorable to reducing poverty. Thus it is important to mobilize resources for its
vigorous pursuit. The strategy increases the supply of less expensive food and increases the demand for labor. These are the two
essentials for removing poverty through growth. Wherever poverty
is massive, a shift to such a strategy of growth should be the first
priority of poverty alleviation. In the context of such a strategy,
special attention is properly given to removing frictions that are
especially deleterious to the poor. Thus attention may be needed for
infrastructure to bring more remote areas into the process; credit
for small, labor-intensive processes; and technical assistance in
production and marketing of vegetables and other less capital-
intensive, small-scale activities.

In the longer run, the new agriculture- and employment-based
strategy does bring a problem of regional disparities. Agriculture
will move more rapidly in some regions than others simply because
of the accident of technological breakthrough. Even over the long
term, there may be some regions with physical resources for which
it will be impossible to come up with improved technologies. The
first-round effect of widening regional disparities through differential progress in agriculture will be strongly reinforced by the favorable local multiplier effects of accelerated agricultural growth. Historically, migration has proved the most common means of dealing
with this problem. With potential for migration, it makes little
sense to invest in technology at low rates of return in areas that
have very little capacity for its development while at the same time
starving areas that could provide faster growth of such an equity-
oriented type. On the other hand, the social problems of migration
need to be recognized and alternative measures sought.

There is also, of course, a residual problem of equity for persons
who are handicapped by their circumstances. Income transfers are
necessary for meeting such a problem. Far more pervasive is the
problem of poverty during the transition while an agriculture-
employment growth strategy is getting under way. Since shifting to
such a strategy is so very favorable to poverty reduction, dealing
with the interim and transition problems by redistribution of resources is apt to be costly to later reductions in poverty. Large-scale
rural public works may be redistributive and assist the growth
strategy itself. Urban food subsidies may serve to stabilize the
urban labor force. If non-fungible foreign food aid is used to support
such efforts, the cost in terms of less growth and reduction of
poverty in the future may be close to nil.

The Role of Government

The role of government is critical to an agriculture- and employment-oriented strategy. Because agriculture is a small-scale sector, there has to be substantial public-sector investment in the support for that sector in the form of, for example, transportation, power, communication, research, education, and input supplies systems. Because these burdens are so heavy, government needs constantly to seek ways of transferring these activities to the private sector. Thus activities such as marketing, which the private sector performs fairly well, should remain as much as possible in that sector. Input distribution should be moved into the private sector as quickly as the latter can take it up.

Since agricultural development is diffused over a wide geographic area, the infrastructure requirements are massive. And since the process is one of rural modernization, development of small- and medium-scale industry, and upgrading of consumption patterns, the needs for rural electrification and communications are critical. Thus, while a heavy-industry-oriented strategy requires large-scale, public-sector investment in major urban areas, a more rural-oriented strategy still requires considerable investment of this type to service market towns. This will sorely strain the capacity of government to raise capital resources; there will be a tension between the need for private incentives and the need for public revenues. Governments will need to make tough budgetary choices that allow scope for little beyond the investments in infrastructure, education, and technological change in agriculture that are the centerpieces of the strategy. The agriculture-employment strategy founders because governments do not recognize its large resource requirements and, therefore, the need to drop activities that may be appropriate only for alternative strategies. This explains why, for example, India and the Philippines have combined success in agriculture so inefficiently with employment growth, as compared with, for example, Taiwan or Thailand.

Price Policy and Technological Change

As pointed out earlier, prices are indicators of, not solutions for, the problems of agricultural production and employment. The answer to the problem of agricultural production is technological change. When the latter has been inadequate, rising prices will indicate a problem and, one hopes, induce corrections. However, because the processes of technological change entail substantial lags between investment and results, prices are an extremely inefficient way to send signals. It is much better to analyze the need, as has been done here, and to act before the price changes indicate a problem. Of course, grossly overvalued exchange rates or other interventions may provide price relations unfavorable even to a technologically dynamic agriculture. However, such policies are probably an essential element of an alternative strategy and will only change as that whole strategy, particularly its capital allocations, changes.

A more serious price problem may arise from a highly dynamic agriculture. Technology may increase agricultural production in specific sub-regions much more rapidly than effective demand can be created in those regions, which in turn may be isolated by poor infrastructure. In such circumstances, it may be desirable for government to serve as buyer of last resort, build stocks, and transport basic agricultural staples to other regions. Governments must be very careful, however, not to spend massively on building stocks of food, as has been happening in India in recent years, instead of spending to accelerate technological change in agriculture and to provide the infrastructure that is so essential to increasing employment.

The role of agriculture as a stimulator of non-agricultural growth probably means that some of the benefits of lower costs of production in agriculture will be used to stimulate production in other sectors by a swing in the terms of trade in favor of the non-agricultural sector. Indeed, some market-induced depression of agricultural prices in response to lower costs seems an inevitable part of the process.[33]

Foreign Assistance

The critical role of foreign trade in supporting an agriculture-employment-based strategy of development requires that the industrial countries keep their markets open for relatively labor-intensive goods and services from developing countries—so that those countries will have the foreign exchange for purchasing the capital-intensive goods and services they need for a high-employment strategy.

In initiating the strategy, foreign aid has a tremendously important role to play in accelerating the growth of education—particularly higher education, which is so essential to the agriculture- and employment-based growth strategy. Vast numbers of trained people are critical to developing and running agricultural research systems, extension systems, and input supply systems.

The details of public policy for an agriculture-employment strategy require constant development and analysis of data, and fine adjustments, which in turn require trained people. Decades of effort can be saved by major commitments of developed countries to expand education through foreign training and technical assistance.

It should also be noted that, although Japan and Taiwan moved into technological change in agriculture after they had already built a very substantial infrastructure in irrigation and transport systems, present-day developing countries may have to make these investments concurrently. Foreign assistance can help with these heavy investments.

Foreign assistance also can contribute to financing imports of capital-intensive goods and services during the early stages of the strategy, when exports may still lag; and food aid can help provide infrastructure, facilitating a stable political environment through food for work and food subsidies.

Foreign assistance may have a powerful role to play in aiding the transition from an inappropriate capital-oriented strategy or an import-displacement one into the more appropriate agriculture- and employment-based strategy. There will be substantial equity problems in the transition. Because the alternative strategies are so inequitable in the short run, they are usually accompanied by food subsidies and other elements to redress the inequities. Foreign assistance can help with the sorting out of these matters, but it must take care to do so in a way that facilitates a genuine transition to the new strategy instead of delaying it.

Today, Africa faces special problems substantially because of unusually inappropriate national and foreign assistance strategies applied in the 1970s. African countries are particularly short of the trained personnel for an agriculture- and employment-oriented strategy of development. They have traditionally had some of the worst infrastructure situations of any of the developing countries, and they suffer from a high degree of instability in principal export commodities. Comparatively massive foreign assistance is needed in the realms of training, investment in infrastructure, and stabilization of export earnings.

Looking Ahead

In most Asian countries, the green revolution has demonstrated both the potential and the basic requisites of accelerated growth in agriculture. Unfortunately, the role of investment in rural infrastructure has been inadequately understood, slowing the selective spread of technology to new areas to maintain high growth rates. Similarly, the dynamics of agricultural growth, calling for gradual diversification beyond initially dominant cereals, has not been sufficiently understood to favor continued expansion of research capacities and the dynamic development of complex marketing systems for perishables. Far more important, however, has been the very laggard response of employment growth in countries such as India and the Philippines compared with that in Taiwan and Thailand. The employment record in India and the Philippines, both of which have done moderately well in agriculture, is puzzling. The answer probably lies with a strong import displacement and a capital-intensive development strategy that has left both economies poorly structured to benefit from accelerated growth in agriculture. That problem requires considerable attention. Major past, inappropriate investments may have to be written off and a new start made.

In Africa, the situation is at once conceptually simpler and in practice more difficult. The basic act of moving the agricultural sector has not yet been put together. Training, national institution-building, and giving development priority to the needs of the most responsive regions and commodities must be pursued vigorously. A complete reorientation of foreign assistance as well as of national policies is needed.[34] Given the gross inadequacies of trained personnel, institutions, and rural infrastructure, the task will be difficult and lengthy. Obviously, complex political compromises will be needed, but an urgent effort must be mobilized if measurable progress is to be made.

Once an economy gets moving, the non-agricultural sectors will rapidly increase in relative importance and take on a life of their own. Institutions must be developed to foster technological improvement in those activities. As the economy diversifies, so must the capacity to support and foster that diversification. The demands for trained personnel and institutional capacity will burgeon. But these longer-term needs must not be allowed to diminish the here-and-now priorities for agriculture and employment growth upon which the economy's post-agricultural prospects so largely depend. Africa, in particular, has suffered from such a lack of priority on the part of national policies and donor-country assistance alike.

Notes

[1] For calculations of a high potential, see John W. Mellor, *The New Economic of Growth: A Strategy for India and the Developing World* (Ithaca, N.Y.: Cornell University Press, 1976).

[2] See, for example, C.H. Hanumantha Rao, *Technological Change and Distribution of Gains in Indian Agriculture* (Delhi: Macmillan Company of India, 1975).

[3] Uma Lele and John W. Mellor, "Technological Change, Distributive Bias and Labor Transfer in a Two Sector Economy," *Oxford Economic Papers*, Vol. 33, No. 3 (November 1981), pp. 426–41.

[4] Paul N. Rosenstein-Rodan, "Problems of Industrialization of Eastern and South-Eastern Europe," *Economic Journal*, Vol. 53 (June–September, 1943).

[5] P.C. Mahalanobis, "Some Observations on the Process of Growth of National Income," *Sankhya* (Calcutta, September 1953), pp. 307–12; and Anthony M. Tang and Bruce Stone, *Food Production in the Peoples Republic of China* (Washington, D.C.: International Food Policy Research Institute, Research Report No. 15, 1980).

[6] A review of these concepts in the context of agricultural growth is found in John W. Mellor, "Models of Economic Growth and Land-Augmenting Technological Change in Foodgrain Production," in Nural Islam, ed., *Agricultural Policy in Developing Countries* (London: Macmillan, 1974), pp. 3-30.

[7] Amartya K. Sen, *Choices of Technique: An Aspect of the Theory of Planned Development* (New York: Augustus M. Kelly, 1968).

[8] Raul Prebisch, *The Economic Development of Latin America and its Principal Problems* (United Nations: Economic Commission for Latin America, 1950).

[9] For this view, see Keith Griffith, *The Political Economy of Agrarian Change* (London: Macmillan Press Ltd., 1979); and for the contrary evidence, see John W. Mellor and Gunvant M. Desai, eds., *Agricultural Change and Rural Poverty: Variations on a Theme by Dharm Narain* (Baltimore, Md.: The Johns Hopkins University Press, 1985).

[10] Uma Lele, *The Design of Rural Development: Lessons from Africa* (Baltimore, Md. and London, U.K.: The Johns Hopkins University Press, 1975 and 1979).

[11] Bela Balassa, "The Policy Experience of Twelve Less Developed Countries, 1973–1979," in Gustav Ranis et al., *Comparative Development Perspectives* (Boulder, Colo.: Westview Press, 1984).

[12] Nicholas Kaldor, *Essays on Economic Growth and Stability* (London: Duckworth, 1960), p. 242.

[13] T.W. Schultz, *Transforming Traditional Agriculture* (New Haven, Conn.: Yale University Press, 1964).

[14] John W. Mellor and Robert W. Herdt, "The Contrasting Response of Rice to Nitrogen: India and the United States," *Journal of Farm Economics*, Vol. XLVI, No. 1 (February 1964), pp. 150–60.

[15] Bruce F. Johnston and John W. Mellor, "The Role of Agriculture in Economic Development," *American Economic Review*, Vol. 51, No. 4 (September 1961), pp. 566–93.

[16] W. Arthur Lewis, "Economic Development with Unlimited Supplies," *The Manchester School*, Vol. 2 (May 1954).

[17] Johnston and Mellor, "The Role of Agriculture in Economic Development," op. cit.; and John W. Mellor, *The Economics of Agricultural Development* (Ithaca, N.Y.: Cornell University Press, 1966).

[18] Kazushi Ohkawa, *Differential Structure and Agriculture: Essays on Dualistic Growth* (Tokyo: Institute of Economic Research, Hitotsubashi University, 1972); Bruce F. Johnston, "Agricultural Productivity and Economic Development in Japan," *Journal of Political Economy*, Vol. 59 (December 1951), pp. 498–513; Shigeru Ishikawa, *Conditions for Agricultural Development in Developing Asian Countries*, (Tokyo: Committee for the Translation of Economic Studies, 1964.)

[19] T. H. Lee, *Intersectoral Capital Flows in the Economic Development of Taiwan, 1895–1960* (Ithaca, N.Y.: Cornell University Press, 1971).

[20] John W. Mellor and Uma Lele, "Growth Linkages of the New Foodgrain Technologies," *Indian Journal of Agricultural Economics*, Vol. 28, No. 1 (January–March 1973), pp. 35–55.

[21] Bruce F. Johnston and Peter Kilby, *Agriculture and Structural Transformation: Economic Strategies in Late-Developing Countries* (New York: Oxford University Press, 1975).

[22] John W. Mellor, *The Economics of Agricultural Development* (Ithaca, N.Y.: Cornell University Press, 1966).

[23] Lele and Mellor, "Technological Change," op. cit., pp. 426–41.

[24] Ibid.

[25] Gustav Ranis and John C. H. Fei, "A Theory of Economic Development," *American Economic Review*, Vol. 51, No. 4 (September 1961), pp. 533–46.

[26] Kenneth L. Bachman and Leonardo Paulino, *Rapid Food Production Growth in Selected Developing Countries: A Comparative Analysis of Underlying Trends, 1961–76*, IFPRI Research Report No. 11 (Washington, D.C.: International Food Policy Research Institute, 11, 1979).

[27] For a careful example of a difficult *genre*, see Robert Herdt, "A Disaggregate Approach to Aggregate Supply," *American Journal of Agricultural Economics*, Vol. 52, No. 4 (November 1970), pp. 512–20.

[28] Albert O. Hirschman, *The Strategy of Economic Development* (New Haven, Conn.: Yale University Press, 1958).

[29] Mancur Olson, *The Rise and Decline of Nations: Economic Growth, Stagflation and Social Rigidities* (New Haven, Conn.: Yale University Press, 1984).

[30] John Hicks, *Economic Perspectives: Further Essays on Money and Growth* (Oxford: Clarendon Press, 1977).

[31] See Mellor, "New Economics of Growth," op. cit., for data on potential job losses in India due to increasing capital intensity.

[32] Kou-shu Liang and T.H. Lee, "Process and Pattern of Economic Development." Mimeographed. (Taipei, Taiwan: Joint Committee on Rural Reconstruction, 1972).

[33] Lele and Mellor, "Technological Change," op. cit., pp. 426–41.

[34] John W. Mellor, Christopher Delgado, and Malcolm J. Blackie, eds., *Accelerating Food Production Growth in Sub-Saharan Africa* (Baltimore, Md.: The Johns Hopkins University Press, 1985).

Chapter 3

Rethinking Trade Strategy

Jagdish N. Bhagwati

The task assigned to me is to rethink the orthodoxy of the export-promoting (EP) strategy for advancing development and to analyze whether a return to the import-substitution (IS) approach may now be called for.

I must begin by distinguishing between orthodoxy among economists and orthodoxy among policy makers in the developing countries, where the clients of our advice are located. It is indeed true to assert that the conventional wisdom among economists (insofar as any kind of consensus can ever be found in our tribe) has swung from the IS strategy to the EP strategy. This shift began in the mid-1960s, I would say, when the success stories of the Far Eastern "gang of four" (Taiwan, Singapore, the Republic of Korea, and Hong Kong) began to attract interest and then were widely disseminated—to the chagrin of many who had put their bets on IS-strategy countries such as India and China. By the late 1960s, and particularly the late 1970s, professional opinion had indeed moved away completely from the IS and in favor of the EP strategy as a desirable option. I shall have more to say about this shift. For the moment, however, let me add that for several reasons of circumstance, the EP orthodoxy also has found its way into policy-influencing institutions such as the World Bank. In view of the considerable exposure of many developing countries to an unappetizing external environment in the last few years, and their sense of vulnerability to the conditionalities imposed by these institutions when they offer aid or liquidity, the sense that the EP orthodoxy is very strong, and possibly suffocating, has certainly increased among the policy makers in the developing countries.

Many of these same developing-country policy makers seem, for reasons that are specific to the countries in question, not only not to share the new EP enthusiasm but to remain unabashed in their adherence to the old IS orthodoxy. In India, for instance, the shift from the IS to the EP strategy has been impossible to achieve for many reasons: partly because the intellectuals and economists have been enamored of impractical investment allocation and control schemes that they misidentify as being optimal simply because they maximize an objective function in a bureaucratic exercise; partly because proponents of such controls identify them as being tantamount to true socialism; partly because once controls and protection regimes have been adopted, their managers of course become partial to the patronage they afford (a point that I elaborate below). The "Reaganomics"-led worldwide recession, and subsequent capital-inflow-led "overvaluation" of the dollar, and the growing threat (and indeed some actuality) of protection that these phenomena have spawned in the West have only reinforced thinking along these lines—especially among the intellectuals who influence policy in several developing countries.

The clash of orthodoxies among these two groups is therefore evident. It provides, in fact, the rationale for looking at this question again. I must confess that, having been for many years engaged in the analysis of foreign trade strategies of the developing countries, I have developed rather pronounced views on the subject. Therefore, although I shall try to be as objective as possible in taking yet another look at the problem, and even shall try to poke the EP strategy in the eye, the IS-proponents may well think that my hand trembles a trifle too much as I do this.

Some Important Clarifications

Let me first clarify that, by EP strategy, the literature now simply means a policy such that, on balance, the effective exchange rate for exports (EER_x) is not significantly different from that for imports (EER_m), so that the EER_x is roughly equal to the EER_m. In short, the effective exchange rate does not show a "bias against exports." Since the IS strategy is defined as one characterized by EER_m greater than EER_x, the definition of EP as one in which EER_x is roughly equal to EER_m may appear asymmetrical. But the motivation is simply that the EP strategy *eliminate the bias against exports*, thereby restoring the incentive to export as much as to produce for the home market. Moreover, this as it were minimalist definition of EP conforms closely to the actual experience of the successful East Asian export promoters mentioned earlier. In their cases, their EER_x exceeded their EER_m only relatively insignificantly—in contrast to the great excess of EER_m over EER_x in the IS countries most widely studied.[1] Perhaps we need to distinguish between EP regimes where EER_x roughly equals EER_m and the "ultra"-EP regimes where, instead, EER_x is substantially greater than EER_m.[2]

We also need to remember always that the average EER_x and EER_m can and do conceal very substantial variations among different exports and among different imports. In view of this fact, I have long emphasized the need to distinguish between the questions of the *degree* of import substitution and the *pattern* of import substitution. Thus, within the broad aggregates of an EP country case, there may well be activities that are being import-substituted (i.e., their EER_m exceeds the average EER_x). Indeed there often are. But one should not jump to the erroneous conclusion that there is therefore no way to think of EP versus IS and that the distinction is an artificial one—any more than one would refuse to acknowledge that the Sahara is a desert, whereas Sri Lanka is not, simply because there are some oases.[3]

Clarity requires us also to distinguish among different types of IS strategies. On the one hand, there have been those (as during the 1950s and 1960s in many Latin American countries, I believe) that have simply reflected the side outcomes of overvalued exchange rates. Regimes of so-called reluctant exchange-rate adjustment (that preceded the later onset of gliding, sliding, and otherwise lissome-sounding exchange-rate policies) implied protectionist regimes and hence the de facto adoption of an IS strategy. On the other hand, there have been such country cases as India, Egypt, and Ghana, in which IS policies have been explicitly and consciously driven by theories of investment allocation and where protection for import substitution has been designed to accommodate the derived targets. These important differences, often ignored by those who rush in with preconceived assessments of the IS and EP strategies, need to be remembered in analyzing the costs of the IS strategy.

One other question needs to be answered and then put aside: Is the EP strategy to be identified with laissez faire? Many in the IS camp are of that view, and I cannot say that no EP proponent would answer in the affirmative. But I certainly do not. The reason is simple enough: Since governments exist, and certainly cannot be prevented from providing occasional intervention of one kind or another, I think that the close association of the governments of the East Asian economies, and indeed of Japan, with the EP strategy (and the involvement of different institutions in supporting export-oriented enterprises as is widely known to be the case with banks in South Korea) provides the *key assurance that governments will not behave erratically*, changing their minds and their rules. This assurance supplies the lubrication that is essential for the "strategic" pursuit of the development strategy in question. I recognize, especially from the insightful writings of Gary Saxonhouse, that the Japanese MITI is not the omnipotent and omniscient agency that industrial-policy proponents in the United States would like to believe. I believe instead that the correct way to analyze its role is precisely to see it as an agency that plays this assurance-providing role. While Mitsubishi, Sanyo, et al. really take the decisions, MITI is giving them the assurance that stems from a symbiotic relationship between the capitalists and the government. In short, there is indeed an important role for government even in an EP strategy.[4]

EP versus IS Strategy: Old Arguments and Findings

This is not the place to restate the old arguments and findings of numerous studies that established the orthodoxy among economists in favor of the EP strategy. But a brief backward glance may be useful.

The birth of development economics at the end of the Second World War was attended by the commonly shared assumption among development pioneers that the external environment was no longer one that would promote growth and that an inward-looking strategy, rather than an outward-oriented trade strategy, was called for. I have argued elsewhere that the writings of Rosenstein-Rodan, Prebisch, Hirschman, and Nurkse, in alternative but reinforcing ways, were founded on this export pessimism.[5] The most explicit writer in this vein, of course, was Ragnar Nurkse, whose writings are very reminiscent of Arthur Lewis today, in that he advocated an IS (so-called "balanced growth") strategy because of a diminished external opportunity. Nurkse called for "balanced growth," but *not* in Rosenstein-Rodan's sense, which implied the need to coordinate a big plan. Nurkse's case in essence corresponded to the optimal-tariff argument in the presence of less than perfectly elastic foreign markets. Arthur Lewis and other current proponents of South-South trade will have noted that this avenue was also explicitly explored by Nurkse in his Wicksell Lectures,[6] but was considered not to be significant enough to alter the need for what we would today call the IS strategy.

This export, or elasticity, pessimism was not shared by Alex Cairncross or by Anne Krueger among the early skeptical writers in the 1950s. And, as we now know, it was also not allowed to become the basis of the trade-cum-development strategy that the smaller East Asian economies adopted as they quickly shifted from an early, and (in my view) inevitable IS phase into the EP stage, thereby laying the world's markets at the feet of their new industries.

A number of international research projects have now thoroughly examined these questions, and the evidence is overwhelming that the countries that adhered to IS too long, instead of shifting to EP, lost out on the opportunity for an impressive economic performance that the growing postwar economy liberally provided. These projects were organized at the World Bank by Balassa; at the OECD by Little, Scitovsky, and Scott;[7] at the National Bureau for Economic Research (NBER) by Krueger and myself; and at the Kiel Institute by Donges. Analyzing the trade and payments policies of several developing countries, these projects demonstrated the costs of an IS strategy that creates a bias against export performance.

Paradoxically, in some developing countries, the IS strategy was promoted on the ground that it would imply greater industrialization. However, exactly the opposite happened in the semi-industrialized countries such as India, where the discrimination against export markets *reduced* the size of the market, imposed protectionist costs, and indeed impaired the growth rate of the economy in aggregate and in the industrial sector in particular. That IS would promote industrialization rather than impede it might have been relevant to more primitive economies that had little industrial base and exports that were almost exclusively non-manufactures; the opposite applied to semi-industrialized countries, where exports already included a growing quantity of manufactures.

Skeptics have argued that the EP strategy may produce greater allocative efficiency in the short run, but that growth rates many not be superior. Such a divergence may arise due to several causes. Thus the IS strategy may lead to a higher savings rate, reflecting an altered income distribution; and this may lead to a conflict between current efficiency and increased growth rate. In the Harrod-Domar model of the growth process, the growth rate is S/V, where S is the average savings ratio and V is the marginal capital-output ratio. It is argued that, although the IS strategy may increase V, it may raise S more, thereby accelerating growth. Or again, it is suggested that the IS strategy may lead to increased entrepreneurship or to enhanced research and development (R&D). The NBER project (headed by Krueger and myself), in particular, examined several such claims for specific countries.[8] Yet these studies failed to turn up any compelling evidence to rank-order EP and IS strategies on these dimensions. Hence, in the NBER synthesis volume, I reached a firm conclusion: The statistical evidence was overwhelming that better export as well as economic performance (measured by GNP growth), was associated with the EP strategy, so that, indeed, a policy maker had little choice but to concede this.[9] More work needed to be done, however, to establish the relative roles of different factors contributing to this outcome.[10]

In a subsequent NBER study,[11] Anne Krueger has followed up yet another objection that was leveled at the findings of the NBER and, indeed, of other projects that I listed earlier—namely, that the IS strategy would do better by employment even though it was outdone on growth by the EP strategy. I find it difficult to imagine how anyone could have thought this an objection likely to be sustained by empirical analysis. And, in fact, it is not. The finding of Anne Krueger and her research collaborators is generally the opposite of what the IS proponents hoped for. For various reasons, including the fact that the manufactured exports of many developing countries tend to be labor-intensive, the EP strategy, compared with the IS alternative, appears to generate more demand for labor per dollar of investment, other things being equal.

Finally, one may raise the important issue of comparative impacts on poverty and ask whether an IS strategy, even if inefficient in raising growth, would not do a better job of curbing poverty. My own view, expressed at length elsewhere, is that growth indeed has had an anti-poverty effect wherever the growth has been sustained and substantial.[12] Furthermore, I find the view that the objective of poverty elimination has been invented only recently, whereas GNP growth was the basic development objective during the 1950s and 1960s, simply ludicrous. Except perhaps in Neanderthal circles, which can always be discovered, GNP growth always was regarded as an *instrumental* variable for reducing poverty. In any event, it is a non sequitur to argue that if growth does not reduce poverty, lack of it does.

Someone may still wind up arguing that growth under EP affects poverty adversely, whereas growth under IS (even though less) has a stronger anti-poverty effect. I would rule out nothing in economics a priori; but I have not encountered a single argument or piece of evidence in the literature that supports such a proposition.[13]

EP versus IS Strategy: Old War, New Battles

As I have said, IS proponents have remained comfortable in their convictions despite the mounting evidence. Recently, however, they have drawn inspiration from a new set of arguments that would seem to militate against EP proponents. Thus, for instance, John Ruggie's recent foray into the subject,[14] which I discuss below, received the stamp of editorial approval in *The Third World Quarterly* simply because of its skeptical, if not critical, stance toward the EP strategy. Since we are collectively rethinking strategies, evidently a focus on these new arguments is in order.

I have been able to distinguish and will here address, four different types of arguments in the recent literature:

1. *Recession and Debt Crisis Costs?* Proponents of IS tend to congratulate themselves by noting that the EP countries must have suffered a greater adverse impact than the IS countries in view of their greater exposure to the external environment when the last great recession struck.

Moreover, those who borrowed much to indulge in what Albert Fishlow has christened "debt-led" growth would be in double jeopardy because of the attendant collapse of world credit markets and the resulting imposition of severe adjustment costs by the international institutions to which they had to turn. Ex post, therefore, an IS strategy would have been advisable.

The following are reasons why I do not feel that EP proponents need to shed tears over this counterattack. The fact is that the prototype EP countries, the East Asian four, remained among the best growth performers during the recession as they slowed down along with the rest of the world. Indeed, Bela Balassa's 1983 cross-sectional analysis of the comparative performance of a broader array of EP and IS countries during this lean period suggests little to confirm that an EP stance has made countries fare worse.[15]

More important, even had these countries been disrupted more, they did so much better during the long, preceding period of prosperity that any cost-benefit calculus addressed at appraising the wisdom of their strategy choice surely must weigh these gains against the later losses (which, if Balassa is correct, do not exist in any event and may even be gains).

I believe that the same argumentation must be applied to the second contention about the costs of debt-led growth. The debt-burdened countries of Latin America, in particular, enjoyed years of high growth as they sucked in the OPEC surpluses. Now that they must reckon with lower expectations and performance, the gains of the 1970s must be looked at in relation to the current losses. My own impression is that in the end most of these debts will prove to be simply not repayable. If so, the long-run evaluation of these countries' "excessive borrowing" may turn out to be entirely favorable.

2. *Protection in the World Economy?* The really interesting and important new issue concerning EP, it seems to me, centers on the question of whether the world trade environment is now being overwhelmed by protection, and whether, therefore, the elasticity pessimism (which so badly served the interests of the developing countries in the nearly three decades of postwar expansion) has now finally come into its own, endowing the IS stance with a legitimacy after all.

I think that it is profitable to address this question at several levels. First, we have to determine whether the protectionist threat of the last few years has actually managed to deter trade expansion by leading to protectionist actions. Of course, as I myself have often argued, the mere *threat* of protection could inhibit investment in exportation by the developing countries, so that the actuality of the protection is not necessarily an accurate guide to what a climate of protection can do to inhibit trade. It is therefore worth looking at actual trade flows. Adjusting for the income effects of the last recession, it is not clear that the *actual* protectionist effect on trade has been sufficiently severe to make us fear that the world trade order has begun to collapse. There are good reasons to infer rather that world trade has shown remarkable resilience in the face of these fears and threats, that the bark has been more evident than the bite, and that the revival of export pessimism may be premature.[16]

Second, even if world markets do not expand rapidly, this does not mean that developing countries, one by one, will necessarily face less than perfectly elastic demand curves for their exports. The demand curve for the product of a country contributing a small fraction of the global supply may be perceived by the country as being perfectly elastic, while at the same time the individual demand curve shifts along a less elastic global demand schedule. In such a case, support for an IS strategy cannot be derived legitimately from the traditional argument defining and justifying optimal tariffs for large countries.

Third, I should like to emphasize that I do not find persuasive the frequent contention that the East Asian economies' EP model cannot be exported because, if every developing country exports like them, the world cannot possibly absorb the resulting exports. Those making this argument often hypothesize that all developing countries would try to raise their exports to the same share of GNP as in Korea or Taiwan. But the EP strategy simply implies *eliminating the bias against exports*. There is absolutely no reason to conclude that this would yield, for every country, the same share of trade to GNP as for the small group of current EP countries. Moreover, such extrapolations ignore the fact that trade can occur in all kinds of differentiated products and in unpredictable ways. Export pessimism in the 1950s was in no small part a result of the inability of planners in developing countries to think up, in their armchairs, the possible sources and composition of trade expansion. For example, before the trade in similar products seized our empirical and theoretical attention, who could have not thought that "similar economies" would have less, rather than more, trade with one another? Again, devaluations are often successful in promoting exports of "miscellaneous" items that no bureaucrat or economist can predict but that the opportunity for gainful trade often seems to galvanize. Finally, it cannot be denied that rapid trade expansion, if many more countries chose the EP strategy, could put pressure on specific sectors in specific countries. But, interestingly, the reaction need not be simply protectionist; it may also be to pressure your rivals into freer trade—as, in fact, is happening in the case of Japan at the insistence of Europe and the United States. Expanding trade needs, therefore, may drive Western leadership into redoubling efforts to keep its doors open *and* to open other people's doors.

3. *Wages and Labor Markets?* A recent argument against the adoption of the EP strategy has been advanced by Gary Fields.[17] Contrasting the prototype EP economies in East Asia principally with the countries of the Caribbean, Jamaica included, Fields has argued in effect that the latter countries have suffered from excessively high wages that make protection desirable and that their reliance on the EP strategy therefore has been harmful rather than helpful.

However, I am afraid that Fields does not establish the basic contention that these countries have an EP strategy in the first place. As I have spelled out above, the EP strategy consists of eliminating the bias against exports (the overvalued exchange rates and the resulting protection, etc.) that the IS strategy implies. As far as one can tell, Fields has not produced the evidence on the relative effective exchange rates on exports (EER_x) and on imports

(EER$_m$) that would support his contention that the Caribbean countries are EP economies, i.e., that they are characterized by an EER$_x$ roughly equal to EER$_m$, rather than by an EER$_m$ greater than EER$_x$, as with the IS countries. In fact, for Jamaica at least, I am assured that my presumption that it is really a classic case of an *IS strategy* is corroborated by such evidence. Fields seems to have mistaken the island nature and smallness (with associated high ratios of trade to GNP)[18] of these countries for the altogether different concept of what is an EP strategy.[19]

Besides, note that the *theoretical* contention that labor-market imperfections *may* require a departure from the EP strategy is well known from the work of trade theorists, including Richard Brecher, V.K. Ramaswami, T. N. Srinivasan, Harry Johnson, and myself, during the 1960s. Our demonstration that the optimal policy intervention in these cases is to intervene in the factor markets *directly*[20] of course may not be feasible where political or institutional factors inhibit the implementation of such policies. If this case is persuasively established, then a protectionist departure from the EP strategy may well make sense. But I see no such case persuasively established by Fields for the Caribbean countries either.

Fields's reliance instead on the argument that wages are kept under control in the East Asian "gang of four" countries seems to me to point to a very different line of reasoning. The "gang of four" countries appear to have used authoritarian methods to keep trade-union wage demands under control and to build on this basis a successful macro policy of low inflation. Thus, the good micro-economics of EP strategy has been built on the necessary macro foundations without which one would likely lapse into repeated overvaluations, occasional exchange controls, and the attendant inefficiencies of implied import substitution. I had already hinted at this explanation in my NBER synthesis volume,[21] but it is a thesis that requires further intensive empirical examination.

4. *Political Requirements?* Many critics of EP strategy have been worried about the association of this strategy with the authoritarian regimes of the prototype EP countries: Does this association not imply that the iron fist is essential for the adoption and successful implementation of this strategy?

Of course, since many developing countries are unfortunately authoritarian, this argument would not constitute a widespread barrier to the adoption of the EP strategy. More seriously, however, the argument simply ignores the fact that many authoritarian countries (e.g., the U.S.S.R.) have followed the IS strategy, whereas the degree of authoritarianism varies within the Far Eastern economies—and not necessarily in proportion to economic performance. Quite plainly, authoritarianism is neither a necessary nor a sufficient condition for EP.

Nevertheless, I would venture the modest hypothesis that it has been hard for democratic countries such as India to graduate from their early IS strategy and easy for the less democratic, more authoritarian countries of the Far East to embrace the EP strategy—after a brief and necessary IS phase—simply because pluralistic democracies may find it much harder to dismantle the controls, protection, etc., that inevitably accompany the IS strategy. These policy instruments carry patronage and confer on the politicians the power to collect funds for their re-election, so that the economic regime under the IS strategy tends to become a critical source of political power. By contrast, in authoritarian political regimes, power is seized directly, freeing the rulers to shift to the EP strategy with its diminished patronage potential.[22]

A "satisficing" political theory has recently been advanced by John Ruggie and his associates, all distinguished political scientists, suggesting that the advantages of an EP strategy cannot be exploited by political regimes that cannot successfully address the distributional conflicts and tensions that would follow from this strategy.[23] Fundamentally, this appears to me to be a persuasive argument as far as the political feasibility of *any* developmental strategy is concerned. Where I part company from Ruggie and his associates is in the implied contention that the EP strategy leads to *more* such demands on the political system. An IS strategy, while relatively insulating the system from external disturbances, may create yet more tensions if the resulting loss of income expansion accentuates the zero-sum nature of the other policy options in the system. Therefore, I would rather convert the Ruggie thesis from its current version into the necessary and valid caveat that, in the pursuit of any development strategy, the compatibility of it with the political structure and resilience of the country needs to be considered. And this particular caveat is, I would stress, not one that I would address only to EP-strategy proponents.

The caveat does imply, in my view, that those who seek to include the EP strategy as a necessary ingredient of conditionality imposed by the World Bank or the IMF (as is the case with many structural adjustment loans from the Bank, for example) should be urged to exercise some caution lest their prescriptions are counterproductive because of ignored political prerequisites. It was once said—too harshly—of the eminent Nicholas Kaldor that political upheavals tended to follow his advisory missions. Such is the risk run by all outside intervenors who fail to place their economic prescriptions into political context.

In conclusion, I fail to find compelling reasons for thinking that orthodoxy among economists should revert to the IS strategy. Not that this will make much difference to what most policy makers will do in any event in the developing countries. My guess is that those who have remained wedded to the IS strategy through the last two decades will embrace the arguments dissected above and proceed, if their countries listen to their advice, to retreat inside their IS shell. These countries will then experience, as before, the self-fulfilling prophecy of diminished export and economic performance—these being the demonstrated disadvantages of shunning the EP strategy and failing to exploit the advantages offered by the external trade opportunities. The traditional EP countries will redouble their efforts to keep their foreign markets open and will successfully get through the door. If so, the leadership in the EP countries will again have demonstrated the capacity to recognize and seize economic opportunity. Again, time will tell.

Notes

This paper has benefited considerably from comments received from Irma Adelman, Colin Bradford, Gerald Helleiner, and John Mellor at the Wingspread Conference on Rethinking Development Strategies sponsored by the Overseas Development Council and the Johnson Foundation. Special thanks are due to John Lewis, who has gone beyond normal editorial duties to offer valuable suggestions.

[1] All this and more has, of course, been amply discussed in the literature. See, for instance, Jagdish N. Bhagwati, *The Anatomy and Consequences of Exchange Control Regimes*, NBER (Cambridge, Mass.: Ballinger and Co., 1978).

[2] Paul Streeten has reminded me that at least one distinguished proponent of export promotion, Anne Krueger, has happened recently to discuss this strategy as being characterized by an effective exchange rate for exports that is higher than that for imports. (Anne O. Kreuger, "Trade Policy as an Input to Development," *American Economic Review: Papers and Proceedings of the Ninety-second Annual Meeting*, Vol. 70, No. 2 [May 1980], p. 288.) In my judgment, however, the standard usage of the export-promotion terminology is where the rates are equal. Plainly, the reader is well-advised to make sure in each instance which usage the author has in mind, in view of this possible ambiguity.

[3] I should also note that the phrases "export promotion" and "import substitution" are used in some development literature in quite different senses. Thus, economists who follow in Hollis Chenery's footsteps will typically decompose overall growth into components described as being due, respectively, to import substitution and export promotion. Useful as such decompositions and corresponding descriptions are, they have no relationship at all to the incentives-related concepts of EP and IS in the theoretical and policy literature on developmental strategy that I use in this paper.

The theoretical appropriateness of these and other measures of import substitution, has been dealt with by Padma Desai ("Alternative Measures of Import Substitution," *Oxford Economic Papers* [November 1969]). Note also that Bela Balassa has recently used the incentives-related definitions (using EER_x and EER_m) to classify countries into

EP and IS categories, while simultaneously undertaking a Chenery-type decomposition analysis of export-promotion and import-substitution components of growth. (Bela Balassa, *Development Strategies in Semi-Industrial Economies* [Baltimore: Johns Hopkins University Press, 1982]). While Balassa's own usages are careful, the coexistence of two wholly unrelated ways of using these phrases in one paper may have caused the reader some confusion (as was manifest in some of the discussion, drawing on Balassa's work, at the conference on the papers for this volume).

[4] Thus the observations at the Conference that the South Korean government played an active export-promoting role are quite consistent with the case for export promotion. I should also add that the comments that detailed interventions implied *necessarily* non-neutrality of incentives must be treated with care. What appears to the naked eye as great noise may amount to nothing when quantified. In the NBER project (discussed later in this chapter), we started out with exactly the view that the Republic of Korea represented a case of a chaotic, physical-planning-oriented system that would result in great variances in EERs. Only with reluctance did we then yield to the detailed estimates, carried out carefully by Larry Westphal, Charles Frank, and others, that suggested that it all boiled down to relative non-neutrality and moreover to an EER_x only slightly higher than EER_m. I might add that a case for having an EER_x that is only slightly higher can ideed be made: The implied export substitution may be justified on several grounds, which have been advanced and formalized in the trade-theoretic literature by Wolfgang Mayer, Robert Feenstra, and others.

[5] Bhagwati, in Gene Grossman ed., *Essays in Development Economics: Wealth and Poverty, Vol. 1* (Cambridge, Mass.: MIT Press, 1985).

[6] For Nurkse's Wicksell Lectures, see Ragnar Nurkse, *Equilibrium and Growth in the World Economy*, Chapter 11, "Patterns of Trade and Development," (Cambridge, Mass.: Harvard University Press, 1962), pp. 282–336.

[7] Ian Little, Tibor Scitovsky, and Maurice Scott, *Industry and Trade in Some Developing Countries*, OECD (London: Oxford University Press, 1970).

[8] In fact, the India volume (Jagdish N. Bhagwati and T.N. Srinivasan, *India*, NBER [New York: Columbia University Press, 1978]) is explicitly addressed to an in-depth analysis of precisely these types of issues, aside from a detailed examination of the 1966 devaluation-cum-liberalization episode, and in that sense is a complement, and not just a sequel, to the OECD project volume on India that Padma Desai and I wrote earlier (*India: Planning for Industrialization* [London: Oxford University Press, 1970]).

[9] Bhagwati, *Exchange Control Regimes*, op. cit. Some discussants have raised the objection that EP can at best yield low-order gains relative to IS since removal of distortions is seen in computable models to result in minor income gains. Even if this were true, it would be a non sequitur to argue that export promotion therefore should not be preferred: Any gain in income should be welcome unless some important offsetting objective is compromised and a tradeoff has to be considered. The writings of Krueger, Balassa, and others have considered this question at greater length.

[10] See, in particular, the concluding Chapter 8 in Bhagwati, *Exchange Control Regimes*, op. cit., where I advanced several alternative hypotheses for further investigation. This chapter has been reproduced in Bhagwati, *Essays in Development Economics, Vol. 2* (Cambridge, Mass.: MIT Press, 1985).

[11] Anne O. Krueger, *Trade and Employment in Developing Countries: Synthesis and Conclusions* (Chicago: University of Chicago Press, 1982).

[12] Bhagwati, *Essays in Development Economics, Vol. 1*, op. cit.

[13] I can, of course, readily construct a model where this will happen. I am simply saying that I would like to see a "plausible" model where it will happen.

[14] John Gerard Ruggie, *The Antinomies of Interdependence: National Welfare and the International Division of Labor* (New York: Columbia University Press, 1983).

[15] Bela Balassa, "External Shocks and Adjustment Policies in Twelve Less Developed Countries: 1974–76 and 1979–81," Paper presented to the Annual Meeting of the American Economic Association, San Francisco, December 1983.

[16] On this point, see the interesting paper in *The World Economy* that takes, consistent with work by Anne Krueger and Helen Hughes at the World Bank, an optimistic view of world trade trends in the teeth of protectionist voices and actions. Bela Balassa and Carol Balassa, "Industrial Protection in the Developed Countries," *The World Economy*, Vol. 7, No. 2 (May 1984), pp. 179–96.

[17] Gary Fields, "Employment, Income Distribution and Economic Growth in Seven Small Open Economies," *Economic Journal*, Vol. 94 (March 1984), pp. 74–83.

[18] On four alternative ways of defining these ratios, and their conceptual underpinnings, see Padma Desai, *How Should the Role of Foreign Trade in the Soviet Economy be*

Measured, Working Paper No. 42 (New York: International Economics Research Center, Columbia University, 1984).

[19] Thus, an EP strategy is wholly consistent with a "low" ratio of trade to GNP, however defined.

[20] For a synthesis of these findings, Jagdish N. Bhagwati, "The Generalized Theory of Distortions and Welfare," in J. Bhagwati et al., eds., *Trade Balance of Payments and Growth: Essays in Honour of Kindleberger* (Amsterdam: North Holland Co., 1971).

[21] Bhagwati, *Exchange Control Regimes,* op. cit.

[22] I have advanced this hypothesis in Bhagwati, *Exchange Control Regimes,* op. cit., drawing on elements of the argument in Jagdish N. Bhagwati and Anne O. Krueger, "Exchange Controls, Liberalization and Economic Development," *American Economic Review,* Vol. 63, No. 2 (May 1973), pp. 419–27.

[23] Ruggie, *Antinomies of Interdependence,* op. cit.

Chapter 4

A Mexican View of the Choice Between Outward and Inward Orientation

Leopoldo Solis and Aurelio Montemayor

The first half of the 1980s has been a period of wrenching adjustment for many developing countries, not the least for Mexico. The interaction of accumulating problems produced a crisis. Not only was there a decline in the output and incomes of industrialized countries; many other countries were faced with extremely serious problems in their commitments abroad—Poland, for one, and, among developing countries, Mexico, Brazil, and Argentina.

The capacity of the world economy to adjust to random shocks has been severely tested in recent years. Growth has been slow to resume in many countries, and there are weak spots in the commercial and financial sectors. Yet in the midst of this scene of predominant difficulty and hardship, the performance of some developing-country economies has been very satisfactory.

The various middle-income developing countries of Latin America and Asia adjusted their economies in different ways to the circumstances of the 1970s, which included violent price increases in the real costs of energy and the slowdown of industrial-country growth to stagflation rates. Some middle-income countries resorted to sharp expansion of their foreign debt to delay or stretch out the adjustments necessitated by these circumstances. Others, particularly several Asian countries, borrowed less and adjusted faster. Thus they started the period of renewed and aggravated shocks that hit all the middle-income countries from 1979 onward with a smaller overhang of debt. But they also have managed their subsequent economic affairs more effectively. Like all developing countries, they have felt the effects that policies adopted in the industrialized countries and the oil-exporting countries have had on the international economic environment. But the successful adjusters have looked out for themselves in two ways: First, they have pursued domestic economic policies that have mobilized internal resources and promoted their efficient allocation and use. Second, and perhaps decisive, their adjustment performance has rested heavily on their choice of external trade regimes. Their trade strategy has been outward-oriented, i.e., export-oriented. Although some implemented import-substitution policies in the initial stages of their industrialization, more recently they have shifted toward export promotion and have avoided burdening their exports with the high-cost inputs that would have been needed to press import substitution into the range of intermediate goods.

We define outward orientation as Jagdish Bhagwati does in his chapter: It entails, simply, a set of government policies that do not tilt incentives against exports relative to indigenous substitutes for imports. Policies in the successfully adjusting countries have promoted *both* industrialization and trade. Typically, such evenhandedness means ending subsidies to the capital-intensive sector and offering smaller, labor-intensive enterprises equal access to credit, technical expertise, and marketing support.

The differences between the fortunes of the outward-oriented and the still substantially inward-oriented middle-income countries in the 1970s—and, more particularly, since 1979—have been so striking that we make them the theme of this chapter. As observers who look at the recent record from the viewpoint of Mexico—one of the larger countries still having an inward orientation in the first half of the 1980s—we have been anxious to explore the comparative growth and equity experiences, as well as the comparative adjustment difficulties, of the two middle-income country groups.

The Experience of Outward-Oriented Countries

Among the most successful outward-oriented countries have been the Republic of Korea, Singapore, Taiwan, Hong Kong, and Spain. In all of these countries, manufactures are important in both domestic output and exports. In terms of income, all are among the more prosperous developing countries.

Real growth in the manufactures exported by semi-industrialized countries averaged 27 per cent annually from 1960 to

1973, compared to a global growth of only 9 per cent. Some of these economies showed spectacular growth rates in their exports of manufactures: for example, Korea, 51 per cent; and Taiwan, 29 per cent. The share of the semi-industrial countries in total world exports climbed from 3 per cent in 1960 to 8 per cent in 1974. For this group of countries, expansion of manufactured exports was an important source of swift economic growth.

Moreover, countries that adopted outward-oriented policies have been the most successful in adjusting to shocks originating abroad. They have done less foreign borrowing than their import-substituting counterparts; they have been quite successful in adjusting the mix as well as the destinations of their exports; and they have succeeded in mending their growth rates quickly. The flexibility gained by outward orientation has been more than adequate to offset the vulnerability that this might imply.

Let us examine the case of Korea. In terms of scale, the Republic of Korea is the largest of the East Asian economic "success stories," and it provides a good illustration of the potential of externally oriented strategies.[1] From being one of the poorest developing countries at the start of the 1960s—predominantly agricultural and with a very weak balance of payments—it has become a semi-industrialized country of medium income and one in which industry plays an important role, providing the major impetus to what has been a rapid growth rate. The sharp transformation of its economy resulted from a deliberate modification of government policy in 1964 toward a strategy of development based on boosting exports. This strategy, combined with the abilities of Korea's work force and the pragmatism of its leaders, paved the way for accelerated economic growth. The effectiveness of the strategy's implementation became even more significant after 1973, since the country lacked internal energy resources.

Although the success with which export markets were cultivated became the "pull" factor on economic expansion, it was rapid growth in domestic investment that permitted Korea to exploit the opportunities that were developed in the international market. Domestic investment as a proportion of gross domestic product (GDP) more than doubled. The combination of rapid growth in the demand for exports with a major influx of foreign technology and capital and a high level of investment served to maintain an average annual economic growth rate of 10 per cent between 1963 and 1978.

The reduction of Korea's deficit on current account through rapidly growing exports and a greater flow of foreign capital made it possible to augment international reserves. When the oil crisis of

1973–74 occurred, the Korean economy was able to absorb the shock without major problems. The value of imports jumped, and the growth of exports slowed, yielding a considerable deficit on current account. But the authorities chose 1) to reduce the economic growth rate in order to keep the rise in imports within a range that could be financed by moderate foreign borrowing, and, simultaneously, 2) to boost exports through more incentives. By maintaining a constant supply of equipment, parts, and raw materials for Korean producers, the Korean government was able to ensure that the supply of exportable goods was not interrupted, thereby generating foreign exchange to pay for the oil and also renewing confidence in the ability of the country to service its obligations.

The government took three steps to prevent export incentives from being cancelled out by subsequent increases in costs: 1) It devalued the country's currency; 2) it gave a higher priority to fiscal incentives for exporters; and 3) it stepped up efforts to diversify export markets and to change the mix of goods exported. These measures improved the competitive position of Korean exports, allowing them to rise again to high levels despite Korea's lower growth rate and the overall dampening of demand experienced by the country's principal customers.

The Record of Inward-Oriented Countries

Economies inclined to look inward—with the idea of diminishing their vulnerability to shocks from abroad—have tried to establish greater self-sufficiency in an increasingly wide range of products, as well as to reduce relations with the rest of the world in commercial matters somewhat beyond what comparative advantage recommends. Included in this group are most of the countries of Latin America. Some of these countries have experimented briefly with commercial policies directed toward boosting exports. In the twenty-five-year period since 1960, however, the orientation of Latin American countries as a group generally has tended to be inward—not just inward toward the region as a whole but inward toward their own domestic markets. This may also be said of most African countries and certain Asian countries, especially the Philippines, Indonesia, and India.

In the cases of Brazil, Mexico, and Argentina, the import-substitution strategy of industrialization implied favoring manufacturing over farming, as well as domestic over foreign sales. Up to the end of the 1970s, this meant obtaining a significant growth rate in GDP despite the high levels of inefficiency and foreign financing involved. In many of the inward-oriented countries, price policies discriminated against domestic agricultural producers. Mexico, for example, became dependent on importing basic products from 1973 onward.

Although the share of investment in GDP in these countries has tended to rise, it has been financed largely through involuntary savings or sharp increases in foreign debt. Foreign commercial banks in the 1970s offered abundant credit; in Mexico's case, credit availability kept rising in parallel with the country's oil exports. Given the fiscal link between the oil and the government sector, public investment expanded as oil revenue grew. Although public-sector savings initially increased, they later fell as a proportion of GDP, partly because non-oil fiscal income grew at a slow rate. At the same time, public-sector spending remained at high levels, following plans drawn up immediately after the oil-price rise, and large sums were allocated to expanding infrastructure and providing other public services. Compared with the growth of the public sector, private investment stagnated. When oil prices fell, however, spending needed to be cut and reductions achieved in the fiscal and commercial deficits. Mexico was able to postpone this adjustment for one year—but only one year—by obtaining an extra round of foreign credit.

In the inward-oriented countries, public-sector investment in industry tended to favor capital-intensive projects. As an anti-inflationary measure, oil-exporting countries subsidized domestic prices of petroleum products. These subsidies not only diminished government revenue but also reduced incentives to conserve energy. Furthermore, the appreciation that occurred in the real exchange rate of oil-exporting countries not only reduced incentives for industry but also led to the substitution of labor by capital goods that could be imported more cheaply.[2]

In the case of Mexico—where a major effort was launched to exploit growing oil reserves beginning in 1977—not only was the currency kept overvalued for several years, but important amounts of debt were also contracted abroad. These resources, in turn, were quickly traded for unessential imports, or for artificially cheap trips to foreign countries, or were taken out of the country as capital seeking safe haven abroad.

Although there were differences among the oil exporters and importers, a common pattern emerged among several of the larger Latin American countries, including Mexico, Argentina, Brazil, and Venezuela. They all made the same mistakes. This, in turn, had something to do with the propagation by international agencies over the years of theories in support of the import-substitution strategy of industrialization, wherein planning and protectionism were advocated and inflation was seen as essentially a problem of bottlenecks, not lack of monetary discipline.

Such doctrines have powerful interest-group allies—for example, among protected industries and city workers who have benefited from the situation as it is. These groups resist fiscal reform and elimination of the host of distortions that encrust the economic system. But the inward-oriented countries have paid a heavy price for these favors to special interests. Both their budgetary and current-account deficits have been high; in contrast, calculations carried out for a sample of developing countries show that, on average, the economies with a higher growth rate were those in which both deficits represented smaller fractions of GDP. The faster growing systems also had fewer distortions in their basic prices—for example, exchange rates, interest rates, and wages.

Moreover, although the import-substitution approach to industrialization has worked in the sense of having sustained a high rate of growth in some of the large countries, it has not been able to reduce inequalities. These remain especially alarming in view of the conditions that persist in rural areas and in the poorer sections of cities, and the continuing imbalance between urban and rural areas. Income inequalities are mainly rooted in unequal distributions of land and human capital. Some African and Latin American countries have tried to supply more public services than they can afford—thereby shifting real income from the poorest rural segments to relatively better off urban segments and, in general, inflicting strong disincentives on agricultural production.

The Vista for the 1980s

If economic growth slows down in the industrialized countries in the coming years, the adverse effects on developing countries are likely to be aggravated by greater protectionism—especially with regard to manufactures. Moreover, such protectionism will not only directly retard developing-country exports, but also reduce incentives to institute technological change and increase productivity. Thus it will further diminish growth.

External shocks impose greater immediate losses in GDP on countries whose economies are more outward-oriented. But in the past, such economies also have proved to be more resilient; they recover faster, and they become less dependent on external financing. They can accept a temporary loss in the growth rate while they adjust by increasing exports, limiting imports, and endeavoring to control imported inflation; at the same time, they retain room for growth, since this form of adjustment does not usually imply restrictions of a deflationary type for any significant length of time. This is perhaps the most valuable lesson to be learned from the recent experience of semi-industrialized and oil-exporting countries.

It is important that countries facing shocks coming from outside their borders not only balance the incentives to export with those for import substitution, but also furnish incentives for savings. Funds obtained from abroad should be allocated to productive investments that augment the country's capacity to both produce exports and substitute for imports. Such a reform in domestic policy is not easy. Developing a symmetrical, balanced incentive system takes time; and greater savings are simply not going to materialize by themselves unless there is general confidence in the authorities' management of the economy.

Economic policy reform usually has to be supported by substantial external transfers during the implementation period. In the case of a trade liberalization program, for example, external funding can provide the inputs needed for exporting industries as well as finance a flow of imports to ease inflationary pressures. Without such financing, governments will attempt to avoid economic policy reform, claiming—often justifiably—that they are blocked by a combination of political obstacles and scarce foreign exchange. But the reverse is also true: If financing from abroad is available but is not supported by internal policy reform, a crisis is merely postponed.

The theme of our argument also can be turned on its head: We have been urging that, as a strategy, export promotion generally is preferable to import substitution. But expanding exports is not equally easy for all countries. Those with only one or two exportable products and a modest capacity for manufacturing have less room for maneuver. In such cases, being able and ready to undertake efficient import substitution in direct response to international shortages and comparative advantages may be an important part of having an outward orientation.

Policies favoring development and growth—such as those promoting domestic savings and improving the efficiency of markets—also help adjustment toward financial balance. Although there is no one path for development, the countries that have been relatively more effective in adjusting their policies to changing international conditions had better growth records over the past twenty-five years; moreover, they were able to improve their average standards of living without damage to the equity with which living standards are shared. One must admit that in countries whose economies have stressed inward orientation—especially in those with extensive domestic markets such as Mexico and Brazil—average growth over the long period has been acceptable. But in some years, it was necessary to sacrifice income and pay high costs in the form of aggravated inequity due to the strategy and/or the policies chosen for its implementation.

Each country requires policies that are suited to its particular conditions. We are not proposing that all countries implement the same strategy as Korea, Taiwan, Singapore, or Hong Kong. What *is* important, however, is that sectors as critical as farming not be denied incentives and that economies not be subjected to either over-protection or over-regulation. In practice, it has proved very difficult for a strategy of inward orientation to provide adequate yields of both growth and equity. Typically, such countries must not only reduce the deficits of the public sector but also redirect public spending—current as well as investment—to improving health, housing, nutrition, and education. Research indicates that the required effort need not be so large;[3] what is necessary is a genuine political commitment to reduce poverty. Finally, currently or recently inward-oriented countries require realistic price policies in the public sector, as well as interest rates and an exchange rate that promote savings and do not discourage exports. Recently, the experiences of Brazil and Mexico have been positive in these latter respects. However, the accumulated scale of the adjustments required has been so great that the costs in terms of living standards have been high indeed.

Conclusions

Not everyone agrees that a growth strategy oriented toward boosting exports is right for a country that wants to maintain an acceptable rate of growth—together with an equitable distribution of income, and without serious problems of adjustment to external shocks. But the cumulative experience gained between 1960 and 1984 seems to show that countries that shifted their development strategy toward external markets fared better in their quest for the several objectives mentioned above. The superior performance of this type of economy is not surprising. The challenge is to assure competitive exchange rates, an adequate and well-known system of incentives, and, for export-producing enterprises, access to imported inputs on which the duties have been waived.

In contrast, countries that continued along the import-substitution path to industrialization, concentrating on the domestic market, encountered serious problems of adjustment—especially during the last recession. Since they had relied heavily on foreign debt in the first years of this decade, they now had to modify their growth patterns. Such countries had to apply policies of contraction that worsened their income distributions.

It is clear that semi-industrialized countries attempting to make their economic strategies more outward-oriented cannot rely on any single-track export promotion. They need an accompanying set of consistent economic policies. While avoiding overvaluation of their currencies and an import-substitution bias in their industrialization efforts, they must also see to it that their farming sector does not suffer worsened terms of trade relative to the urban economy. They need to generate domestic savings and to assure its allocation to socially profitable sectors. More generally, they need to maintain a commercial environment in which potential investors— whether interested in production for export or for the domestic market—will encounter defined rules of the game that invite their confidence in planning and risking their enterprise and capital.

Although it promises no miracles, the outward-oriented approach *can* yield generous equity as well as growth dividends, and it is available to more countries than have yet adopted it.

Notes

[1] Part of what is mentioned about this country is based on F. Jaspersen, *Adjustment Experience and Growth Prospects of the Semi-Industrial Countries*, World Bank Staff Working Paper No. 477 (Washington, D.C.: The World Bank, 1981).

[2] The foregoing is another case of the so-called "Dutch disease." The phenomenon was actually noted earlier—by W. Arthur Lewis in 1963 in the case of bauxite in Jamaica, and by Dudley Seers with respect to oil in Trinidad-Tobago. But the label derives from the effects of the rapid exploitation of natural gas by the Dutch.

[3] Marcelo Selowsky, "Nutrition, Health, and Education: The Economic Significance of Complementarities at Early Age," World Bank Series No. 218 (Washington, D.C.: The World Bank, 1981).

Chapter 5

East Asian "Models": Myths and Lessons

Colin I. Bradford, Jr.

Not long ago, surveys by the "pioneers" of development theory were gloomy about the prospects of this subdiscipline of economics. W. Arthur Lewis, for example, noted in 1984 that "development economics is said to be now in the doldrums."[1] Some critics even have gone so far as to hail the demise of development economics.[2]

It is odd that development economics should be perceived by some to be in such difficulty in the wake of a period in which there has been remarkable development success. New concepts and terminology for categorizing the developing world are required today precisely because of the increased differentiation among countries over the last two decades. The term "Third World" no longer seems appropriate. Arthur Lewis has called the rapid growth rate of the "success stories" of the developing world an "outcome without precedent."[3] Yet, as Albert Hirschman has observed, development economics seems to have suffered more than profited from development success: "The concept of a unified body of analysis and policy recommendations for all underdeveloped countries, which contributed a great deal to the rise of the subdiscipline, became in a sense a victim of the very success of development and its unevenness."[4]

The Debate: Theory, Politics, and Policy

There has traditionally been a healthy tension between economics as a discipline and development economics as a subdiscipline. With economics becoming increasingly formal, and with development economics confronting diversity in economic performance and understandably falling short of a single theory to account for differentiation, the tensions have grown. The debate has heated up in recent years as more theoretically inclined economists have celebrated the triumph of neoclassical assumptions in the development success stories in East Asia. This celebration is the latest manifestation of what Hirschman calls "monoeconomics"—the view that there is only one economics just as there is only one physics.[5] The rapture with which the East Asian cases are celebrated derives from the view that they constitute proofs of the results achieved when neoclassical theory, relying on markets and getting prices to reflect real scarcities, is put into practice. It is a way for economics to take over development economics by destroying the subdiscipline's basic underlying premise: that developing countries are different from advanced market economies and require different theories and policies to promote development. Not surprisingly, this attempted takeover has spurred a lively response.

The highlighting of the East Asian cases goes beyond the boundaries of economics. It is rooted in the larger realm of public opinion, where confidence in the market system was shaken in the last two decades by stagflation, oil shocks, productivity declines, and perceptions of loss of power in the United States and Western Europe. In the wake of the crisis of the welfare state in the West and the rise of fiscal deficits as a generalized problem, there has been a reaction that argues in favor of a reduced role for the state in the economy and an enhanced role for market forces. This reaction in the West has been given further encouragement by interpretations of the success stories of Hong Kong, Singapore, Taiwan, and Korea as having been market-driven. Commenting on such explanations, Staffan Linder has argued that: "This will yield what may be called an ideological effect. Political thought and economic thinking will be influenced in the old industrial countries, where faith in the system which once brought these countries their wealth is again rising after a long period of erosion."[6]

In addition, of course, this trend in public opinion has been reinforced and reflected in the political thrust of the Reagan, Thatcher, and Kohl governments, which have extolled the virtues of the marketplace and built their political support on opposing the governmental structures that they themselves command. The result is that the political mood of our time is to trust most governments that govern least. This political outlook has carried over into North-South relations. Jagdish Bhagwati has commented in a recent lecture that:

> The Reagan administration's revisionist approach to North-South relations was twofold. It not merely sought to reverse what it perceived as an ideological surrender to statism and intervention in the different multilateral agencies via their very existence or through their methods of functioning. It also proceeded, in consequence, to become intolerant of the pluralistic political and economic approaches to development.
>
> The conviction with which the advantages of the invisible hand, and the disadvantages of the visible hand, were propagated and sought to be imposed on the faithless infidels whenever possible tempts one to describe this period as *The Age of Certainty*.[7]

A second extension of the debate beyond the confines of economic theory is the convergence of views between the short-run stabilization requirements of the International Monetary Fund (IMF) and the longer-run development policy perspective now predominant in the World Bank. During the 1970s success stories occurred not only in East Asia but in many regions: in Latin America (Mexico and Brazil), in Southern Europe (Portugal, Spain, Turkey), and in Eastern Europe (Yugoslavia, Poland, Hungary). However, the greater exposure of Latin America to financial shocks—due to its large variable-interest-rate debt—led to a stylized contrast between the development trajectories of East Asia and Latin America. The stylized version highlights Latin America's policies as inward-oriented, interventionist, import-substituting while the East Asian model is seen as outward-oriented, market-driven export promotion based on internal liberalization.

The stylized version of the East Asian success stories meshes with the conclusions of the price distortion research presented in recent annual volumes of the World Bank, *World Development Report*.[8] The research concluded that high price distortion was associated with low growth; and, conversely, low price distortion was associated with high economic growth.[9] Further World Bank research showed "that big distortions also lead to slower growth of exports and a greater likelihood of debt-servicing difficulties."[10]

If the commitment to an outward-oriented growth strategy is construed to mean internal liberalization, then adopting the stylized version of the East Asian model will achieve high economic growth through both efficiency gains and increased exports.[11] In explaining why the economic growth of the Asian-Pacific countries has outpaced that of other countries, Helen Hughes has observed that: "The only hypothesis that explains why some developing countries have grown rapidly, while others have not, links the adoption of a positive development philosophy with a policy framework that leads through market mechanisms to efficient resource allocation and utilization."[12]

This stereotyped contrast fits well with the IMF's short-run demand management stabilization policy outlook. In the late 1970s, there had been greater flexibility in the policy approach of the Fund, most notably in the March 1979 Executive Director's conditionality guidelines, which embodied not only the possibility of medium-run stand-by arrangements, but also more sensitivity to social and political constraints and more openness toward supply-side dimensions of policy emphasizing additional investment and economic growth. The recent predominance of the more orthodox concerns for price stability and balance-of-payments equilibrium has overshadowed the structural elements in the 1980s.

The idealization of the East Asian model as having succeeded in development through getting prices right for resource allocation reasons and the shift toward demand-management stabilization policies that emphasize getting prices right to achieve balance-of-payments equilibrium constitute a consistent policy package. Both emphasize the need to give priority to removing import controls and adjusting the exchange rate to bring internal prices into alignment with world market prices. Both emphasize price stability and open markets prior to economic growth and export promotion. Both argue that the costs of the new orthodoxy of liberalization and conventional stabilization will be compensated for by balance-of-payments equilibrium and efficiency gains in the short run and by export-led growth in the longer run.

The short-run requirements of conventional stabilization are consistent with the policy reforms—based on the East Asian model—necessary for success in the long run. It could be argued that this signals a new conventional wisdom about stabilization and development—a new consensus that gives the Fund and the Bank a single, uniform policy approach—one that spells the triumph of neoclassical economics over development economics. If one believes the orthodoxy, "monoeconomics" prevails in both theory and practice.

The East Asian Experience: Another Look

Closer study of the East Asian economies reveals a different explanation of their success. The story is more complex, and not so easily told or summarized, as is necessary here; but it is precisely this complexity that creates some doubt about the advisability of construing the East Asian cases as a singular model for economic policy. First, there are differences among the four principal success stories—Hong Kong, Singapore, Taiwan, and Korea. Of the four, Hong Kong is the closest to the stylized version; Korea is probably the furthest removed.

Second, there are different phases in the development experience of these four countries in which the mix of factors has shifted over time; what is true in one period gives way to a different configuration in the next. This problem is exacerbated today by the lags necessarily involved in publishing results of major research projects. Three major studies of development policy became available in the late 1970s, when attention was being focused on success of the East Asian success stories and other newly industrializing countries (NICs).[13] These research endeavors mainly focused on experience through the mid-1970s. This appeared largely to fit the stylized version: a shift from import-substitution industrialization to export-led growth seemingly coinciding with a shift from government intervention to internal liberalization. Studies published in the 1980s, focusing on the experience of the 1970s, generally reveal a more complex story, involving a mix of private market forces and public sector actions that overall yields a more *dirigiste* cast to the success story. This general conclusion, too, is out of phase, because in the mid-1980s—as the more balanced story of the 1970s is only now being highlighted—a shift toward more reliance on markets is in fact occurring in several countries.

Let me illustrate briefly. Wontack Hong estimates that "the annual provision of credit subsidies in the Republic of Korea amounted to at least 10 per cent of GNP each year on average in the 1970s."[14] He concludes that "the increasing exports of highly capital-intensive goods may only be explained by the extensive subsidies on capital use in Korea in the 1970s."[15] Credit rationing to preferred sectors accompanied this subsidization. Targeting sectors and establishing export targets for specific industries played a significant role.[16] Hong finds that the nine largest general trading groups increased their share of total commodity exports from 15 per cent to nearly 50 per cent from the beginning of the 1970s to the early 1980s and that this increased concentration was "at the expense of the share of small- and medium-size exporting firms."[17] This is not exactly an Adam Smith world of an invisible hand operating in an atomistic marketplace of small firms. Although these policies had a major effect on Korean economic performance in the 1970s, they also had some negative effects that are being corrected in the 1980s.[18]

The Brazilian development story, which is not dissimilar from that of Korea, also relied heavily on the involvement of the government in achieving an export boom that began in 1967 and entailed a major expansion in the export of manufactured goods in the 1970s. There is now movement in Brazil toward a more realistic exchange rate, a higher real rate of interest, cutting subsidies, reducing the public-sector deficit, mobilizing internal savings, and providing incentives for private-sector innovation and investment. Brazil is trying to continue export promotion and at the same time is seeking new opportunities for import substitution.[19] The Korean case was also characterized by import-substitution industrialization along with export promotion. A French study comparing Mexico and Korea shows that in both countries import substitution took place in sectors that were initially protected and then in later phases moved toward production for the export market; thus initial-stage industries spurred upstream industries such as steel that eventually produced for export.[20] The dichotomy between export promotion and import substitution is overdrawn in descriptions of the experiences of both Brazil and Korea in both the 1970s and in the 1980s.

Taiwan is also interesting from the perspective of the mythology of East Asian development success. Its trade regime has involved very selective management of both the volume and the composition of imports to boost the technological capability of the economy. Fiscal incentives were highly selective by product, reflecting the government's clear sectoral strategy to change the structure of the economy. Even though the country's banking system was government-owned, credit allocations were less prevalent in Taiwan than in Korea. On the other hand, public-sector enterprises constituted almost a third of fixed-capital formation in Taiwan in contrast to slightly more than a fifth in Korea. In comparison to Japan, government expenditures in Taiwan accounted for 30 per cent of GNP in contrast to Japan's 19 per cent in the mid-1970s. Taiwan also made a strong effort to keep macro policies in balance, keeping the exchange and interest rates realistic and inflation low. Along with other measures, this helped to keep the prices of labor, capital, and other factors of production close to their scarcity value.[21]

In the Taiwan case, import substitution was also found to accompany, rather than simply precede, export promotion. As Chi Schive puts it: "During the last two decades, the great success of export-led economies in East Asia, in particular Taiwan and South Korea, has led critics to label import substitution as inefficient, unnecessary, and even a sin." The results of Schive's analysis of Taiwan from 1966 to 1976 show that "secondary import substitution is clearly present at the industrial level during the period when Taiwan's exports increased rapidly." Schive goes on to say that "secondary import substitution industries in Taiwan seem to have been developed with little policy intervention"—he suggests a full investigation of this question—and that "the sequence of import substitution in Taiwan is directly in line with the backward linkage hypothesis," whereby downstream industries are spurred by dynamic final-goods sectors.[22]

The Taiwan development experience, then, is very difficult to stereotype *either* as a market-oriented success story *or* as an illustration of the triumph of dirigisme and policy intervention. Instead, its success is due to a mixture of both elements in effective and powerful interaction—and to a mixture, rather than sequencing, of import substitution and export promotion.

Singapore seems to be another case of development mix rather than dichotomous choice. Chung M. Wong points out that although Singapore has relied mainly on private enterprise, its government has tried to influence resource allocation in various ways, including incentives to industries regarded as desirable for the country. He cites the findings of Pang and Tan as having singled out the government as the most important factor behind Singapore's economic success. Wong goes on to argue that:

> At present the "pioneer status" (with relief of five to ten years from the 40 per cent tax on profits arising from an approved pioneer activity) and the investment allowance incentive (with tax deduction equal to up to 50 per cent of new fixed investment in plant, machinery, and factory buildings) are the main incentives used in investment promotion. Pioneer certificates are now mainly awarded to projects manufacturing new and high-technology products, while the investment allowance incentive is increasingly being used to promote the upgrading and mechanization of existing operations. Tax incentives are also given to encourage manufacturers to undertake research and devel-

opment activities. Projects believed to be of strategic importance to Singapore's industrial development can obtain long-term fixed-rate loans at favorable interest rates under the Capital Assistance Scheme (CAS) administered by the Economic Development Board.[23]

Ralph C. Bryant describes a similar set of circumstances—"the gradual extension of incentives and dismantling of constraints"—as part of Singapore's "aggressive," "conscious and active" policy to "create an environment for financial activity to flourish."[24] This priority to the development of the financial sector included favored regulatory and tax conditions. Here also, Singapore's emergence both as a major exporter of manufactures and as an international financial center relied heavily on supportive policies, some of which may have temporarily "distorted" prices in favor of priority sectors. Markets and private enterprises were also important. Pragmatism, rather than ideology or a single-formula model, seems to have been crucial to Singapore's success.

Against this background, it seems a bit overdrawn to conclude that "in South Korea and Taiwan, growth did not really start until around 1960 when, in both countries, there was a far-reaching redirection of economic policies away from regulation and interventionism over to a reliance on market mechanisms"[25]—or that "the East and Southeast Asian experience suggests that if the basic policy framework is appropriate, only limited sectoral policies are required to stimulate areas of actual and potential comparative advantage."[26]

Conclusions and Implications

Instead of providing a sound basis for the new conventional wisdom on development policy, the experience of the East Asian newly industrializing countries is at odds with this view. The real story of what constitutes successful development is more subtle and indeed quite different from what the stereotypes suggest. In the end, effective development relies on both market forces and public policies, and even on government intervention; it rests on *both* import substitution and export promotion. Credit and interest-rate subsidies, tax preferences, differential exchange rates, preferential treatment of capital goods imports, and other deviations from unfettered market signals have been integral parts of development policy. As Albert Fishlow has pointed out, "the more fundamental proposition is that the correctness of the prices must be decided by reference to a comprehensive development strategy, not independently of it."[27]

Sectoral priorities and industrial policies have been essential ingredients in the East Asian success stories. In Korea, Taiwan, and Singapore, the evolution of the production structure and the composition of exports was not left to the market but was the result of deliberate government design. On balance, the exchange rate, the interest rate, the tax system, and public-sector investment were not neutral factors subordinate to market forces in these cases; rather, they were leading indicators and important instruments of development strategy. What seems to distinguish the East Asian development experiences is not the dominance of market forces, free enterprise, and internal liberalization, but effective, highly interactive relationships between the public and private sectors characterized by shared goals and commitments embodied in the development strategy and economic policy of the government. The dichotomy between market forces and government intervention is not only overdrawn; it misconceives the fundamental dynamic at work. It is the *degree of consistency* between the two sectors—rather than the extent of implicit or explicit conflict—that has been important in the successful development cases. A coherent development strategy was not only formulated but followed by both the government and the private sector in providing an unusual degree of common direction to national energies in these cases.

The implications of this reality for development theory and policy thinking are far-reaching. As uncomfortable as it is for the social sciences in U.S. academic institutions to recognize the limitations of increased insights through specialization, understanding the fundamental courses of development success requires an interdisciplinary approach. The East Asian cases reviewed here clearly suggest this. Arthur Lewis asserts that "the wide range of performance of underdeveloped countries today, of whom one-third have been growing continually at more than 5 per cent a year . . . [is the] kind of question [that] belongs as much to history as it does to economic analysis."[28] It is interesting to realize that Albert Hirschman, whose intellectual role in political economy is seminal, views himself as a "dissenter" and that his intellectual framework was set inductively through his early experience (1952–56) in Colombia. Of that period, he writes that "my instinct was to try and understand better *their* patterns of action, rather than assume from the outset that they could be 'developed' by importing a set of techniques they knew nothing about."[29] Lloyd Reynolds, in his survey of the spread of economic growth to the Third World, comments that the explanation of differences in economic growth "does not seem to be mainly in the realm of factor endowments. . . . At this point, as a properly modest economist, I disclaim further responsibility and pass the problem to my political science colleagues."[30]

Far from a triumph of "monoeconomics," differential growth in the Third World highlights the limitation of explanations derived from economic theory alone. The success stories of East Asia point to a messier realm of interdisciplinary, political-economy research with strong historical and inductive methodologies.

The implications for policy practices in the World Bank and the IMF are also important. The eclectic reality of the East Asian cases contradicts the conventional wisdom. The consensus in which stabilization and development policy paradigms have become fused is brought into question. In the name of evenhandedness, it is not a helpful circumstance to have our premier international financial institutions wedded to a single model of a successful development policy or to a narrow definition of an effective stabilization program. The present convergence of paradigms seriously undermines the role of the Fund and the Bank in the world economy by restricting their scope and their effectiveness. It politicizes them by having them represent what Staffan Linder has rightly pointed out is an ideology, when their role is to be responsive to a variety of types of governments and economic systems.

The most serious result of the formation of the new conventional wisdom and the degree to which it has either been imposed on or embraced by the Fund and the Bank is the degree to which this set of ideas, and the molding of Fund-Bank instrumentalities in accordance with them, restricts the freedom of national governments around the world to determine their own policies and shape their societies in keeping with their distinct values and traditions. Lost in the trumpeting of the East Asian success stories are the views of others who recognize the excesses of intervention, who are concerned by overburdening the role of the state, who believe that getting prices right is an important part of development, but who nevertheless see national economic policy and the state as crucial instruments for shaping the destiny of their countries according to national norms.[31]

Given entrenched interests, structural problems, and a highly fluid international environment, the state and its economic policies can be vehicles for enhancing freedom, self-determination, and democratic values. Single-formula solutions are confining at best and undermining at worst to policy makers who are seeking to balance short-run and long-term requirements, stability and growth, real and financial dimensions in defining their nations' futures and their roles in the world economy.

The World Bank and the IMF need to exercise more flexibility and diversity—both in their instrumentalities and in their policy outlooks—in dealing with the world economy of the mid-1980s and with the variety of policy mixes that can, in complex and varied circumstances, be effective in coping with the economic challenges currently facing national leaders.

The East Asian success stories do indeed provide a model for development strategies, but one that is different from the stylized version. More than this, they illustrate the joining of short- and long-run policy problems, macro-economic and structural forces, in what could be characterized as the new policy nexus.

Economic stabilization has been a global problem for nearly two decades.[32] Between the 1970s and 1980s, however, there was a shift in emphasis. Whereas in the stabilization policies and programs of the 1970s were driven more by inflation, the principal driving forces in the 1980s are balance-of-payments disequilibria and debt. The inflation-driven stabilization problems of the 1970s raised an issue of the degree of internal determination versus the extent of external transmission.[33] In contrast, economic stabilization issues in the mid-1980s, seem clearly linked with the degree of openness of national economies; the degree of interaction between trade, macro policy, and financial patterns; and the degree of interdependence among major nations in the world economy, now including new powers from the developing and socialist worlds.[34] This open-economy dimension is a major distinguishing characteristic of the stabilization problems in the mid-1980s.

A second major characteristic is the degree to which stabilization problems and policies are now embedded with structural issues related to growth, industrial policy, and the international division of labor and are not limited, as in the past, to short-run demand management policies. The short-run tensions and tradeoffs between growth and stabilization are well known in policy experience and in the literature. In the 1980s, the new element of restructuring has become a matter of equal policy priority. The pressure on industrial structures due to rapid technological change and diffusion and to the transnationalization of both production and financing is now global. France and the United States, Poland and Brazil, Korea and Japan are struggling in different ways and in distinct circumstances to find their niches in the international division of labor.

The embedding of the restructuring issue within the more conventional macro-economic framework gives economic policy a decidedly medium-run horizon. For many developing countries, this is largely attributable to the pressures of the debt burden that force a longer-term framework for scheduling debt payments and projecting export earnings. The need to export in order to finance debt adds to the structural pressures to find a niche in the world economy. The design of sectoral development strategies that are consistent not only with internal endowments and capabilities but also with the rapidly changing structure of trade relations has become a more pressing policy imperative.

Therefore, longer-term financial planning, sectoral development strategies, and export requirements play a more decisive role in shaping short-run macro-economic policies. In turn, macro policies have a crucial bearing on the realization of the longer-term goals. The sustainability of short-run macro policies is critical to the viability of the longer-run trajectory, just as the long-run trade and financial requirements shape short-run policies. Hence, achieving a sustainable balance between growth and stabilization in the short run becomes *inseparable* from the longer-term structural dimensions. The policy nexus of growth, stabilization, and restructuring now poses the central challenge for economic policy makers.

If there is a "new synthesis" of development strategies, it is that the confluence of these formerly separate forces and perspectives defining the policy nexus of the 1980s requires a new fusion of structurally oriented development and macro-economic policies. The East Asian success stories provide models of this new synthesis, integrating the multifaceted elements of policy into an effective strategy, eschewing one-dimensional solutions rather than enshrining them.

Notes

[1] W. Arthur Lewis, "The State of Development Theory," *The American Economic Review*, Vol. 74, No. 1 (March 1984), pp. 1 and 10.

[2] Thus Deepak Lal recently wrote: "In seeking to improve upon the outcomes of an imperfect market economy, the *dirigisme* to which numerous development economists have lent intellectual support has led to policy-induced distortions that are more serious than, and indeed compound, the supposed distortions of the market economy they were designed to cure. It is these lessons from accumulated experience over the last three decades that have undermined development economics, so that its demise may now be conducive to the health of both economics and the economies of developing countries." "The Misconceptions of 'Development Economics,'" *Finance and Development*, Vol. 22, No. 2 (June 1985), p. 13.

[3] Lewis," State of Development Theory," op. cit., p. 9.

[4] Albert O. Hirschman, "The Rise and Decline of Development Economics," in *Essays in Trespassing: Economics to Politics and Beyond* (Cambridge: Cambridge University Press, 1981), p. 20.

⁵ Ibid., p. 4.
⁶ Staffan Burenstam Linder, "Pacific Protagonist—Implications of the Rising Role of the Pacific," *American Economic Review, Papers and Proceedings of the Ninety-seventh Annual Meeting*, Vol. 75, No. 2 (May 1985), p. 280.
⁷ Jagdish Bhagwati, "Ideology and North-South Relations," Bernard Fain Lecture, Brown University, Providence, R.I., April 18, 1985.
⁸ "Pricing for Efficiency," in World Bank, *World Development Report, 1983* (New York: Oxford University Press, 1983), pp. 57–63, and World Bank, *World Development Report, 1985* (New York: Oxford University Press, 1985), pp. 54–55.
⁹ Ramgopal Agarwala, *Price Distortions and Growth in Developing Countries*, World Bank Staff Working Paper No. 575 (Washington, D.C.: World Bank, 1983). See critiques by Colin I. Bradford, Jr., in "The NICs: Confronting U.S. 'Autonomy,'" in Richard E. Feinberg and Valeriana Kallab, eds., *Adjustment Crisis in the Third World* (New Brunswick, N.J.: Transaction Books, for the Overseas Development Council), especially pp. 121–26; and by Albert Fishlow, *The Economic and Social Progress in Latin America, External Debt: Crisis and Adjustment* (Washington, D.C.: Inter-American Development Bank 1985), pp. 123–148.
¹⁰ World Bank, *World Development Report, 1985*, ibid.
¹¹ Anne O. Krueger, "Import Substitution versus Export Promotion," *Finance and Development* Vol. 22, No. 2 (June 1985), pp. 20–23.
¹² Helen Hughes, *Policy Lessons of the Development Experience*, Occasional Paper No. 16 (New York: Group of Thirty, 1985), p. 16.
¹³ I.M.D. Little, T. Scitovsky, and M. Scott, *Industry and Trade in Some Developing Countries: A Comparative Study* (Oxford: Oxford University Press, 1970); Bela Balassa, "Export Incentives and Export Performance in Developing Countries: A Comparative Analysis," *Weltwirtschaftliches Archiv*, Vol. 114, 1978; Anne O. Krueger, *Foreign Trade Regimes and Economic Development: Liberalization Attempts and Consequences* Vol. 10 (Cambridge, Mass.: Ballinger, 1978).
¹⁴ Wontack Hong, "Export Oriented Growth and Trade Patterns of Korea," in Colin I. Bradford, Jr., and William H. Branson eds., *Trade and Structural Change in Pacific Asia* (Chicago: University of Chicago Press, NBER, forthcoming).
¹⁵ Ibid.
¹⁶ Yung Whee Rhee, Bruce Ross-Larson, and Larry Pursell, *Korea's Competitive Edge* (Baltimore: The Johns Hopkins University Press, 1984), Chapter 3.
¹⁷ Hong, "Export Oriented Growth," op. cit., p. 40.
¹⁸ "South Korea: A Special Economic Report," *International Herald Tribune* (Paris), October 6–7, 1984.
¹⁹ Peter T. Knight, *Economic Stabilization and Medium Term Development Strategy in Brazil*, (Washington, D.C.: World Bank, 1985); Persio Arida, *Economic Stabilization in Brazil*, Working Paper No. 149, Latin American Program, (Washington, D.C.: The Wilson Center, 1984).
²⁰ Centre d'Etudes Prospectives et d'Informations Internationales, *Coree Mexique: Deux Experiences de Development Face a la Crise* (Paris: La Documentation Francaise, 1982).
²¹ Robert Wade, "Dirigisme Taiwan-Style," in Robert Wade and Gordon White, eds., *Developmental State in East Asia: Capitalist and Socialist, IDS Bulletin*, Vol. 5, No. 2, (Sussex, U.K.: Institute of Development Studies, 1984).
²² Chi Schive, *A Measure of Secondary Import Substitution in Taiwan*, (Cambridge, Mass.: Harvard-Yenching Institute, 1985).
²³ Chung M. Wong, "Trends and Patterns of Singapore's Trade in Manufactures," in Bradford and Branson, *Trade and Structural Change*, op. cit., citing Pang and Tan, "Employment and Export-led Industrialization: The Experience of Singapore," in Rashid Amjad, ed., *The Development of Labor Intensive Industry in ASEAN Countries* (Geneva: International Labour Office, 1981).
²⁴ Ralph C. Bryant, "Financial Structure and International Banking in Singapore," *Brookings Discussion Papers in International Economics*, Washington, D.C., May 1985.
²⁵ Linder, "Pacific Protagonist," op. cit., p. 280.
²⁶ Hughes, *Policy Lessons*, op. cit., p. 17.
²⁷ Fishlow, "State of Latin American Economics," op. cit., p. 141.
²⁸ Lewis, "State of Development Theory," op. cit., p. 9.
²⁹ Albert O. Hirschman, "A Dissenter's Confession: 'The Strategy of Economic Development' Revisited," in Gerald M. Meier and Dudley Sears, *Pioneers in Development* (New York: Oxford University Press, 1984), p. 91.

[30] Lloyd D. Reynolds, "The Spread of Economic Growth to the Third World," *The Economic Literature*, Vol. 21, No. 3 (September 1983), pp. 975–76.

[31] See Enrique V. Iglesias, "Latin America: Crisis and Development Options," and Aldo Ferrer, "Debt, Sovereignty and Democracy in Latin America: The Need for a New Orthodoxy," in Colin I. Bradford, Jr., ed., *Europe and Latin America in the World Economy* (New Haven, Conn.: Yale Center for International and Area Studies, 1985), pp. 44ff.

[32] William R. Cline and Sidney Weintraub, eds., *Economic Stabilization in Developing Countries* (Washington, D.C.: The Brookings Institution, 1981); and William R. Cline and Associates, *World Inflation and the Developing Countries* (Washington, D.C.: The Brookings Institution, 1981).

[33] Surjit S. Bhalla, "The Transmission of Inflation into Developing Economies," in Cline and Associates, *World Inflation*, op. cit., pp. 52–101.

[34] Colin I. Bradford, Jr., "New World Economy," in Bradford, Jr., *Europe and Latin America*, op. cit., pp. 7–14.

Chapter 6

Aid Effectiveness in Raising Adaptive Capacity in the Low-Income Countries

Alex Duncan

In setting out to consider development strategies for low-income countries, this chapter takes as its starting point the fact that development is a process of constant change in which new opportunities and new constraints emerge continually. In T. W. Schultz's phrase, it is a process beset by various disequilibria.[1] Sustained development demands increasing not just productive capacity but also adaptive capacity—the ability constantly to pursue allocative efficiency in the context of change. The capacities with which we are concerned are those which enable decision makers—whether in the private or public sector—to analyze and understand current circumstances, to identify the costs and benefits of feasible options, to decide the best course of action, and to mobilize or reallocate resources successfully.

What any one country needs in terms of the resources to sustain development will vary in significant respects from other countries and will itself vary over time. Thus this chapter does not set out to prescribe what specific resources or skills an economy may need at any given level of development; instead, it asks what can be done to ensure that each country has the ability to adapt as appropriate to its circumstances.

Although much of what will be said will apply in some degree to all developing countries and to some developed countries as well, my primary emphasis is on low-income countries (other than the two giants, India and China).[2] The reason for this emphasis is that, without minimizing differences among the low-income countries I have in view, most of these countries share characteristics that differ in two important respects from those of most other countries: 1) their institutions tend to be weak; and 2) foreign aid plays a large and in many cases growing role in their economies (in contrast with the middle-income countries, where aid is marginal and decreasing). There is a danger that in trying to generalize across even this limited group of low-income countries, I will not do justice to the diversity of the subject. There are real exceptions to virtually every statement. Some low-income countries have maintained growth better than others, some have stronger institutions, and so on. Common distinguishing features of low-income countries do exist, however, and the broad-brush approach, for all its dangers, is the only means of elucidating them.

In parallel with my focus on low-income countries, I will pay considerable attention to the role of aid, given its importance to these countries. My conclusion will be that aid can be of great value in increasing local capacities. But in practice it often falls short of doing all it could, and in some cases it can even exacerbate the institutional difficulties of the recipient.

Recent Trends and the Growth of Aid

During the decade of the 1970s, the economic performance of many low-income countries worsened, especially in Sub-Saharan Africa (Table 1); and from our admittedly close perspective, the early 1980s may mark a watershed for some of them. Previously, large investments, with considerable assistance from aid, were made in human capital, physical infrastructure, and direct production to provide the resources and skills for sustained growth. Economies grew quite rapidly, if variably, although in some cases no faster than population. Poverty showed no sign of disappearing. From the late 1970s to the present, however, even these modest achievements have not looked sustainable in many countries. The ability of economies to hold their own has been challenged by a constellation of events and circumstances that included civil unrest, climatic variability, weak policy formulation and administration, structural budgetary problems, unfavorable international terms of trade, accumulated indebtedness, and rising debt-service ratios.

One feature of the economies of low-income countries since 1970 has been the high level of official development assistance (ODA). In all cases but two (Ghana and Pakistan), total ODA increased in real terms over the period; and per capita ODA in-

Table 1. Annual GDP Growth Rate

	1960–1970[b]	1970–1979[c]	1979–1982[d]
Low-Income Countries[a]			
Chad	0.5	−0.2	−9.8
Bangladesh	3.7	3.3	6.5
Ethiopia	[4.4]	1.9	3.1
Nepal	2.5	2.7	2.7
Mali	3.3	5.0	2.2
Burma	2.6	4.3	7.1
Zaire	3.4	−0.7	1.3
Malawi	4.9	6.3	−3.6
Upper Volta	3.0	−0.1	13.9
Uganda	5.6	−0.4	−4.8
Rwanda	2.7	4.1	8.9
Burundi	4.4	3.0	5.0
Tanzania	6.0	4.9	1.3
Somalia	1.0	[3.1]	5.9
Haiti	0.2	4.0	1.6
Benin	2.6	3.3	3.3
Central African Republic	1.9	3.3	−4.3
Guinea	3.5	3.6	4.4
Niger	2.9	3.7	2.5
Madagascar	2.9	0.3	−0.1
Sri Lanka	4.6	3.8	6.6
Togo	8.8	3.6	1.2
Ghana	2.2	−0.1	−1.7
Pakistan	6.7	4.5	6.5
Kenya	5.9	6.5	9.5
Sierra Leone	4.3	1.6	3.2
Selected Middle-Income Countries[e]			
Indonesia	3.9	7.6	8.0
Ivory Coast	8.0	6.7	2.7
Malaysia	6.5	7.9	7.1
Korea, Republic	8.6	10.3	3.5
Brazil	5.4	8.7	4.3

[a] Countries with 1982 gross national product per capita of less than $410, listed in ascending order of GNP per capita.
[b] World Bank, *World Development Report 1984* (New York: Oxford University Press, 1984), Table 2. Figure in brackets is for 1961–1970.
[c] *World Development Report 1981* (New York: Oxford University Press, 1981), Table 2. Figure in brackets is for 1970–1978.
[d] Calculated from 1970–1979 and 1970–1982 average growth rates.
[e] Countries with 1982 GNP per capita of $410 or more.

creased in real terms in all but five countries (Table 2). As a proportion of GNP, ODA rose in all but three of the twenty-six countries listed. As a proportion of total investment, ODA increased in almost all of the countries listed; in 1982, it represented more than one-third of gross domestic investment in all but eight of them.[3]

This picture contrasts with that of most middle-income countries, a small number of which are included in the tables for comparison. The recent growth record in middle-income countries is by and large better than in the low-income countries, and in financial terms, aid is marginal to total resource availability and, moreover, is commonly declining in relative and often absolute terms.

Building Capacities

It is arguable that one reason for the more successful performance of the middle-income countries is that, compared to the low-income countries, they so far have proved more able to adjust as new difficulties and new opportunities have presented themselves. This has been especially true of the newly industrializing countries (NICs). Their economies have become more diversified in the production of other-than-traditional goods and services, and their people and institutions have proved adaptable.

The capacity to adapt has two aspects. The first is analytical capacity—the ability to understand issues and to identify and choose between alternative possible solutions. With respect to human resources, for instance, this entails designing, among other things, the right curricula, the right balance between different levels and types of educational institutions, and effective mechanisms for disseminating skills through employment. The second factor required for adaptive capacity is that which allows the lessons of analysis to be put into effect by mobilizing the appropriate combination of human, organizational, and financial resources.

These analytical and implementation components of countries' capacities to adapt also can be sliced along input lines: The low-income countries need management and institutional capacity, human resources development, and improved technology. These input needs are examined in succession.

Management and Institutional Capacity

At every level, from small farms and private businesses to government ministries, organizations that work effectively and can change when change is called for are a defining characteristic of a successful economy. They require entrepreneurship and organizational, technical, and intellectual skills and discipline, as well as financial resources.

Policy Formulation and Management. The policy framework in many low-income countries, especially many of the African ones, has been subjected to a good deal of criticism and is held to be at least partly responsible for their disappointing economic performance.[4] Evaluations of many donor-supported projects suggest that failures are often attributable to policy.[5] There are two interrelated aspects of poor policy formulation: the technical and the political. The capacity of the civil service to analyze policy and to evaluate alternatives is often rather weak, and the political process is frequently unable to arrive at decisions that are other than short-term or narrowly sectional.[6] It is premature to expect consistent and farsighted political decision making in the absence of an indigenous analytical capability that can define alternatives in a clear and convincing manner; equally, technical analysis can weaken if policy analysts become discouraged by an environment in which political decisions regularly override their recommendations. Increasing the capacity for sound policy analysis is of course no guarantee that the policies actually adopted and implemented will be an improvement on what has gone before, as policies are primarily an outcome of a political process. But, although sound analysis is not a sufficient condition for improvement, it is a necessary one.

The weaknesses of policy formulation and management manifest themselves at three levels. (They are by no means unique to low-income countries, or even to developing countries as a whole, but they are clearly evident at present in a number of the countries with which we are concerned.) First, strategic priorities are not articulated and acted upon consistently. Thus the priority accorded to agriculture in rhetoric may not be reflected in policies and expenditure patterns. Second, capacity is often inadequate for a competent and timely technical analysis of alternative policy instruments. For instance, information and statistical systems may not provide sufficient data for pricing or marketing policies to be soundly formulated. Third, administrative and budgetary processes are often not adequate for ensuring that policy will be implemented effectively on a sustained basis. A special case of this—one that is significant for the role of aid—is that many countries have not established a framework whereby the activities of numerous aid donors can be matched to local needs.

Table 2. Official Development Assistance: Net Disbursements in Real Terms, Total and Per Capita

Low-Income Countries[a]	Total ODA[b] (U.S.$ millions 1980)			Per Capita ODA[b] (U.S.$ 1980)		
	1970[c]	1980	1983[c]	1970	1980	1983
Chad	58.2	35.3	85.3	16.0	7.9	18.0
Bangladesh	—	1,262.4	1,061.3	—	14.3	11.2
Ethiopia	104.0	216.0	255.1	4.1	7.0	7.5
Nepal	61.4	163.1	197.9	5.4	11.1	12.5
Mali	55.4	252.1	212.0	10.8	37.6	29.1
Burma	60.1	308.7	298.2	2.2	9.3	8.4
Zaire	232.4	427.5	315.1	10.9	14.8	10.0
Malawi	96.2	143.3	115.6	21.3	23.7	17.3
Upper Volta	57.2	212.3	188.0	11.7	34.5	28.2
Uganda	86.1	113.6	133.4	8.8	9.0	9.6
Rwanda	56.7	155.3	147.5	15.9	30.1	25.8
Burundi	46.3	117.2	139.6	12.8	28.5	31.3
Tanzania	133.4	666.2	598.4	10.0	35.9	29.3
Somalia	72.3	446.5	332.5	23.2	104.5	71.6
Haiti	20.5	72.8	72.9	4.8	14.5	13.8
Benin	39.0	90.4	86.3	14.7	26.1	22.7
Central African Republic	37.4	111.0	92.3	23.4	48.6	37.4

Guinea	26.8	89.5	67.8	6.6	18.5	—
Niger	82.2	170.2	165.8	20.6	30.8	27.4
Madagascar	125.3	200.2	239.2	18.4	23.0	25.4
Sri Lanka	127.9	392.5	465.0	10.2	4.8	5.2
Togo	44.2	91.0	110.2	22.6	35.3	38.7
Ghana	154.2	191.6	106.2	17.9	16.7	8.5
Pakistan	1,095.1	1,040.2	713.1	18.1	12.7	7.9
Kenya	150.0	396.5	394.5	13.3	23.8	20.9
Sierra Leone	17.9	92.9	64.4	6.6	30.4	19.7
Selected Middle-Income Countries[c]						
Indonesia	1,209.8	949.5	736.5	10.3	6.5	4.7
Ivory Coast	137.0	210.3	154.9	27.4	25.4	16.7
Malaysia	68.9	135.0	175.7	6.4	9.7	11.8
Korea (Republic)	714.5	139.0	8.3	22.8	3.6	0.2
Brazil	490.4	85.4	100.4	5.2	0.7	0.8

[a] Countries with 1982 GNP per capita of less than $410, listed in ascending order of GNP per capita.
[b] OECD, *Geographical Distribution of Financial Flows to Developing Countries, 1969–1975 and 1980–1983.*
[c] Deflator from World Bank, *World Development Report 1984* (New York: Oxford University Press, 1984), p. 252, table 18; see also note, p. 280.

Making good these deficiencies calls for efforts on several fronts: investments in education to ensure that individuals are available with the specialized qualifications needed for policy analysis; a working environment that is conducive to retaining talent within the public service; decision makers who take policy advice seriously, even if they do not always accept it; and technical assistance that is explicitly designed to strengthen the institutional capacity for policy analysis.

Providing for Recurrent Costs. Development institutions need adequate financing—and financing of the right type. It may not be feasible in the near term to increase the total funds supplied to many of the countries we are considering. Hence it is important to make more effective use of what funds are available by reallocating existing resources. Specifically, there is evidence that failure to provide adequately for recurrent expenditures is a major cause of the disappointing performance of many development investments.[7] In a survey of developing countries,[8] twenty-eight were classified as "having a recurrent cost problem," while fifteen did not. A recurrent cost problem arises when the overall productivity of a given level of budget funds would be increased by a transfer of funds from capital expenditure to recurrent expenditure, but, for institutional or other reasons, such a transfer cannot be made. Thus the problem is one of the relative availability of the different types of funds, not of the total size of the budget.

The problem arises primarily because of differences in the ease with which a government is able to acquire funds for capital and recurrent expenditures. Governments of low-income countries with a weak tax base find it hard to obtain additional recurrent revenues from domestic sources in a non-inflationary manner; and the political costs of doing so are high. By contrast, the existence of aid programs with a preference for project aid reduces the cost and difficulty of obtaining capital funds for the recipient government.[9] The problem is not that donors refuse to finance recurrent expenditures during project implementation. In recent years, they have increasingly done so; for example, the United Kingdom will now finance 100 per cent of local project costs in some countries. Moreover, the growth of balance-of-payments support through lines of credit from donors has generated local funds that are used to relieve the shortage of recurrent revenues either through contributions to general government revenues (e.g., U.K. aid) or through project-specific application (e.g., U.S. aid). But the real problem emerges in its most acute form *after* the end of donor involvement in a project;

this is one reason why projects that look promising at the end of the implementation phase often cannot be sustained.

The scarcity of funds to meet recurrent costs has pervasive effects on the recipient system. At the most prosaic level, vehicles and roads are not maintained, and industry and services operate well below capacity. It is also difficult to maintain the right balance between personnel and other components of the recurrent budget as reductions in personnel are politically costly. Thus, at a time of budget stringency, a numerically large civil service finds itself without basic supplies and services, and efficiency suffers in consequence.

With a scarcity of recurrent resources, pressure naturally builds up to blur the distinction between capital and recurrent items in government's accounts. Development projects extend from phase to phase; they are kept separate from a government's routine activities; and the rehabilitation of stalled projects becomes a "normal" method of management. Donors increasingly fund non-incremental items within projects, and faster depreciation substitutes for recurrent spending. The idea of "handing over" projects to a government after the establishment phase becomes more and more unrealistic, except in those comparatively few cases where the project is financially self-sufficient.

A study of government finances in southern Sudan, one of the poorest areas in Africa, found the problem in an acute, but not atypical, form.

> There is no possible way for the Southern Region Government to assume the recurring costs of agricultural development projects or other development projects now being conducted in the Southern Region with donor aid. Either donors must plan to continue carrying these recurrent costs, or the gains from implementation of most of the projects will have contributed little. This fact may necessitate a reduction in the number of projects undertaken and/or a reconsideration of the strategy of development in the Southern Region.[10]

The Budgetary Process. Effective budgeting is basic to both the allocation and control of productive resources. Unfortunately, deficiencies in budgetary management are characteristic of many low-income countries. They include the failure to articulate priorities, to project revenues and expenditures with accuracy, to ensure the timely availability of funds, to supervise and audit expenditures, and to monitor implementation. Of particular significance is the failure of budgets to relate capital expenditures to their subsequent recurrent requirements. Governments thereby lose the mechanism available to them for controlling the aggregate financial effects of numerous projects and for minimizing the recurrent cost problem. The need for closer integration of development and recurrent budgets is indicated by studies of several countries, including Gambia and Kenya.[11]

These budgetary weaknesses contribute to several features of poor development performance, including the recurrent cost problem, the absence of a rational basis for implementing financial cuts when necessary, the poor performance of many public sector institutions, and the weakness of fiscal policy as an instrument of economic management.

In the low-income countries, aid programs bear on the budgetary question in several ways. In many of the country cases, aid has made a significant contribution to strengthening the budget process through financial support, training, and technical assistance. But the record is not wholly satisfactory. In the first place, the inflow of aid funds, unless integrated with a disciplined system of budgetary ceilings, may contribute to a weakening of the integrity of the budgetary process. Thus a Kenya budget study, for example, found this to have occurred during the 1970s:

> Why did Ministry of Agriculture and Ministry of Livestock officials play the Kenya budgetary game in such a cavalier way? The refusal to establish priorities among programs and projects was due to the tremendous expansion in resources in the mid-1970s. Coffee revenues were high and donors were anxious to put more money into smallholder agricultural development. The correct presumption was that any development project that was well conceived or had donor support would be funded. . . . Far from being disciplined for being financially uncontrolled, officers were, in effect, rewarded with more funds.[12]

Second, aid programs have increased the complexity of the budget task by introducing multiple sources of funds and different procedures and conditions for disbursement. Many national budgetary processes are not structured appropriately or operated effectively to bring order into the fragmented approaches of donors. Budgets may not succeed in incorporating aid-supported revenues and expenditures. Some projects are entered in the budget as a notional figure only, while their actual financial dimensions, if funded directly from the donor, may be independent of the national budget and perhaps not even recorded. It may therefore be difficult to establish budget ceilings as a basis for financial discipline. An example of this is provided by the administration of counterpart funds generated by U.S. commodity-import programs in Somalia. Up to 1983, these funds were disbursed in parallel to, but separately from, the Somali national budget and were made available for approved purposes (e.g., U.S.-assisted projects). However, eligible projects also had funds approved under the national recurrent budget. The two sources were not always fully articulated, and project managers were on occasion able to sidestep budget restrictions by drawing on both sources. The system has since been changed to permit only one budget submission.

Public Administration. Conventional wisdom regarding low-income countries seems to have gone through a cycle from the colonial period, when priority was given to efficient administration, through stages of localization, infrastructure, capital requirements, human capital, and back to efficient administration. Particularly in Africa, there is certainly now a widespread perception that poor institutional performance is a key to the failure to achieve development aspirations.[13] The need for improvement is now all the greater if ambitious aims of effective donor coordination and better policy formulation are to be achieved.

Aid programs can contribute positively to bringing about this improvement if the recipient governments demonstrate the will to achieve such gains. In the past, however, aid has not made the most of its potential in this respect. On the contrary, the aggregate effect of the aid agencies, programs, and procedures with which the recipient has to deal has been to overload an already weak system. Anyone who has worked in a ministry in a low-income country will be aware, for instance, of the number of visiting missions that must be prepared for and received by a small number of senior officials. In some cases, special departments have been set up to handle donor affairs; and these departments can themselves develop parochial interests—e.g., to maximize the number of projects initiated—that may not reflect those of the government as a whole.[14]

Aid projects introduce another important bias into the process of the recipient's institutional development: Recipients need to achieve results quickly. This has been particularly evident at times of expanding aid funds, when donor organizations are anxious to disburse their appropriations. For donors, the old dilemma of whether to work through existing institutions or to establish special-purpose, often semi-autonomous, units for implementation persists.[15] Where an administration is very weak, speedy implementation may appear to demand such units. But they contribute far less to strengthening local institutions than the latter need. In some cases, the ad hoc units actually weaken the established structures, and certainly they militate against continued good performance by the project after the withdrawal of donor support. It can be argued, for instance, that one reason for the poor results of national agricultural research in Africa has been that, during the critical post-independence phase, much financial and technical assistance was provided in a series of discontinuous projects rather than in the form of a more coherently structured program that would have strengthened the indigenous capacity to conduct research.

Human Resources

Human skills and abilities—technical, intellectual, organizational, entrepreneurial, and physical—are central to the productive and adaptive capacities required by an effective development process. As an economy changes, so does the relative importance of specific skills and abilities; what does not change, however, is the demand for the right mix of skills to match evolving and growing needs.

The qualities that allow people to play their full roles in a process of economic development are generated by a satisfactory physical quality of life in terms of health, nutrition, and living conditions, and by a process of education that develops the necessary skills and abilities. The issue of whether some philosophies or forms of political organization are more conducive than others to making full use of these qualities in economic development is addressed elsewhere in this volume by Atul Kohli. Here, however, the focus is on education, using the term in a broad sense to cover all learning activities, including, but not limited to, formal schooling.

The World Bank's *World Development Report, 1980* made a strong case for investment in education in developing countries as both a means and an end.[16] In the first place, education directly enriches the lives of those affected. But education also helps to improve nutritional levels and child health, and lowers fertility; and education leads to improved incomes and *sometimes* to greater equality.

The central importance of education is clear. But much less so are the questions of what fraction of resources it should claim, compared with competing uses, and what should be the balance between different types of educational expenditures. The answers will be country- and time-specific, underlining how important it is that each country build up its own capacity to analyze educational policies. Overwhelmingly rural societies with little medium-term scope for industrialization should probably adopt a different educational strategy from those in which a rapidly growing proportion of the population will make a living from non-traditional skills. Different political values will call for different educational systems.

Even though education may be an end in itself, its case for bidding financial and human resources away from other uses must insofar as possible be based on an assessment of the associated benefits to which education leads. The difficulties of measuring the benefits are, however, very considerable, as has been demonstrated by the numerous studies that have attempted to identify the relative role played by the human factor in economic growth.[17] Many such studies have treated the human factor as a residual; others have attempted to identify it as a distinct explanatory variable. In studies of twenty-two countries between 1950 and 1962, education was reckoned to have contributed more than 10 per cent of economic growth in only four countries—and those were the slowest growers.[18] However, such calculations are fundamentally unconvincing. Spending on education, perhaps more than any other investment, has very powerful external effects on virtually every field of human endeavor, and attempts to distinguish its influence from other factors probably understate its full role. This is especially true if the definition of education includes all forms of learning. There is likely to be a high level of correlation with other variables that explain growth. For instance, some studies indicate that "learning by doing" may be as important as formal schooling to human capital formation. This implies that investment in physical capital, which itself generates economic growth, is also an effective means of building up human resources.

Even if the precise effect of education, broadly defined, on economic growth is elusive, it seems clear that formal education has a particular importance in increasing the adaptive capacity of an economy. Moreover, the greater the rate of modernization, the more central will be the role of education in permitting efficient and timely responses to change. Schultz, in his analysis of the process of adapting to disequilibria, suggests that in a traditional economy, people are nearer to an economic optimum, given available resources, than they are in an economy in which new possibilities are crowding in.[19] Where the productive arts are fairly constant, people learn what they need to know from their parents; the process of modernization and change, however, involves to a considerable degree influences originating outside the experience of the productive unit. The need for, and value of, formal education is correspondingly increased.

During a time of economic difficulty, aid has a particularly significant role in education in low-income countries. The benefits from spending on the sector may take some years to become apparent. Thus at a time when public finances are under stress, investments that provide quick pay-offs may be correspondingly more attractive. Without contesting the public investment priorities of the recipient government, aid funds may usefully provide the means by which expenditures on the development of human skills can be insulated from the worst effects of economic stringency.

Technology

In the process of economic development, technology always has been important. But it may well be becoming more so. If it remains a servant and not master, technology has great scope for contributing to development. Technology can be defined as "the skills, knowledge and procedures for providing useful goods and services"[20]; these skills, knowledge, and procedures permeate every economic activity and are constantly being added to and changed by a process of generation, diffusion, and adaptation that is intrinsic to investment and growth. All decisions on the allocation of physical resources for directly productive investments, on increasing human skills, and on strengthening institutions are a part of the process of technological change. Making good a technological deficiency thus is not a question of identifying a missing resource and setting out to provide it, but rather of influencing the direction of future decisions in such a way that their technological implications are better suited to local conditions.

Unfortunately, there is plenty of evidence that, in low-income countries at least, much of the technological change that occurs is not optimal—it may lead to unbalanced internal development; it may not suit local factor availability and thus may cause an inefficient use of limited resources; it may do little to ease unemployment problems; or it may lead to an undesirable degree of economic dependence.[21] The source of concern is that the great majority of research and development—over 90 per cent by most estimates— takes place in industrialized countries. This research inevitably addresses the issues of concern to the firms, inhabitants, and governments—of the developed countries—issues that reflect the nature of these economies as more and more capital-abundant, with high-cost and highly skilled labor forces. The nature of the technology that results from these imperatives is at variance with the needs of low-income countries, where enterprises are typically capital-scarce, labor is abundant, and needs are for employment as well as broad-based income generation and economic growth.

Although technological change has received a great deal of attention from economists, deep disagreements persist on such issues as how far the choice of technique is determined by relative prices and whether a dualistic pattern of development is wholly undesirable. But a framework of analysis has been provided that is useful in explaining patterns of technological change.[22] It classifies influences on an economy's technological mix as being demand or supply-related.

Demand factors influencing the direction of technological change are:

- The state of factor prices and other incentives facing decision makers;
- Income distribution, which determines the effective market demand for various products and sectors;
- The nature and situation of those who make decisions about the technology to be used in concrete projects.

Some of these factors are fundamental to the social and political structure of the society and cannot readily be changed by policy. Thus in the Asian subcontinent, an extensive literature confirms that the impact and pace of agricultural mechanization and the scale of the equipment demanded was greatly affected by land ownership patterns.[23] Income distribution is also crucial; as Stewart and James point out, the nature of the final product that is demanded is a key determinant of what technology is feasible. If income distribution is such that purchasing power is substantially in the hands of those who wish to buy advanced modern products, a basic, labor-intensive technology simply may not exist to produce them.[24]

Other demand-related influences on technological change may, however, be more immediately susceptible to policy action—take, for instance, the relative prices of capital and labor. The extent to which these prices, rather than such other factors as management convenience, determine the technique chosen is a matter of continuing debate, and it is probably in part country-specific.[25] Nevertheless, there can be little doubt that the relative costs of capital and labor are one influence on the direction of change. In developing countries, these prices are quite commonly distorted and incline investments toward greater capital intensity than is warranted by the factor endowment of the economy. The more common causes of these distortions (currency overvaluation or subsidized interest rates from formal lending institutions, for instance) are susceptible to correction—and there are plenty of cases of this being done.

Aid has less to contribute directly in the evolution of demand-related influences on technology than it has with respect to supply issues. Indirectly, however, by strengthening the analytical capacity of the recipient's private and public sectors, aid resources can enable the relevant issues to be better understood. This of course does not necessarily mean that the political process, which so strongly influences the demand-related issues, will be transformed by this improved understanding.

Supply factors affecting the direction of technological change are:

- Existing technologies—the "technological shelf" from which technologies are selected, transferred, and disseminated;
- A country's ability to adapt existing technology to its own special and changing conditions; and
- A country's ability to create a national or indigenous technology suitable for and specifically geared to its objectives and circumstances.

These three factors correspond to three levels of technological capacity. At the lowest level, technology developed elsewhere is put into service without adaptation; what is important in this case is that adequate knowledge about existing alternatives be available so that the options chosen are the best in the available range. At the second level, there is an ability not just to select among alternatives, but also to take the most promising and adapt it to local circumstances. At the highest level, a country will itself have the capacity to undertake more basic research and development; naturally, the institutional and human requirements at this level are substantialy greater than at the other levels.

These three levels of capacity do not represent a scale up which all countries in all areas of technology should aspire to move. It will make sense for very few developing countries—or indeed developed countries—to attempt to reach a competence in basic research

across a wide band of technologies. If the research is being conducted elsewhere and the results are accessible, there is little point
to reinventing the wheel; the financial and human costs will be too
high and the benefits doubtful. However, to the extent that there
are barriers to the transfer of the findings of basic research—posed
by patents, for instance—the case becomes stronger for at least the
larger and more sophisticated developing countries to undertake
some basic research.

By contrast, a strong case can be made that, in the immediate-
and medium-term, many of even the lowest-income countries
should strengthen their capacity for adaptive research in the sectors most important to their economies. The case is strong because
adapative research cannot be done elsewhere, and because the
skills involved in many instances will be less specialized than those
needed for basic research. Agricultural research is perhaps the
single most important example. Returns on agricultural research
have been some two to three times higher than on any other major
type of investment in developing countries;[26] the international research structure—comprising specialist centers undertaking fundamental research, linked to national capabilities for selection and
adaptation—provides a mechanism that has led to some highly
beneficial results. The results, however, are patchy. For many countries and farming systems, the counterpart of the seed-fertilizer-
water package that has been so successful in parts of Asia has not
yet been developed. Progress in doing this depends to a considerable
extent on the strength of the national, and even local, research
capability; thus in India, one of the main reasons for the effective
diffusion of high-yielding varieties of wheat and rice has been the
high quality of national and regional research capacity.[27] Unfortunately, in many countries this capacity is low, greatly weakening
the potential benefits to farmers of the international research
effort. The World Bank found that "perhaps 10 per cent of developing countries already have adequate research skills, good national
research programs, and effective linkages with international research institutions."[28]

Aid programs have a continuing role in supporting the supply
factors that influence technological availability. In the first place,
aid can support technological policy-making capacity—that is, the
analysis of needs and the identification of the most appropriate
means for fulfilling them. In the second place, aid can do much to
strengthen the actual capacity to undertake research within the
country. Moreover, "the development of local technological capacity
reduces dependence on advanced countries, permitting countries to

strike a better bargain for imported technology, as well as contributing to objectives of independence and self-reliance." It also "can lead to comparative advantage in this area and significant export earnings."[29]

Aid can provide crucial finance, manpower, and institutional support to enable public and private research groups to play these roles with respect to technology. Reinforcing research capacity is of the highest importance, but it is more difficult to achieve than providing a solution for a particular research problem. In the context of most low-income countries, donors who would help build research capacity must persevere in the effort for extended periods.

Tailoring Aid for Specific Needs

The quantitative importance of aid finance to the countries we are considering was shown earlier in this chapter. But aid does more than just provide funds—especially in countries in which indigenous institutions are still comparatively weak. Aid agencies assist in policy analysis, provide technical assistance to institutions, plan projects and evaluate the outcomes, and assist in assembling cofinancing arrangements for the more complex investment schemes. By and large, they are successful in the range of things they try to do.[30]

However, in a number of respects, the form and substance of aid programs do not match the needs of recipients. To the greatest extent possible, what aid programs do and how they do it should be determined on the basis of the recipient country's needs rather than the donors' priorities and procedures. In many recipient countries, the latter hold sway over project identification, design, management, and other matters that are generally recognized to be the responsibilities of host governments in countries with more effective institutions.

The donor bias that can enter into program design—especially in the case of bilateral programs—may reflect a relationship between donor and recipient that extends well beyond the purpose of development promotion. In the first place, donors pursue *commercial interests* in competition with others; examples of this consideration affecting aid are legion, from aid-tying to the use of aid to soften the terms of commercial contracts. Commercial interest, however, probably influences the aid program within the recipient country more than it influences the overall direction of aid flow.[31] Second, the direction and volume of aid are influenced by *donors' domestic political considerations*, arising, for instance, out of their histories as colonial powers. Other political considerations, such as the bureaucratic imperative to disburse the budget, lend urgency to spending even when this may not be indicated by the status of the aid program. Third, there are *procedural considerations* that may run counter to the most desirable form for aid programs. Perhaps the most important of these is donor unwillingness to undertake lingering financial commitments. Aid tends to be provided in the form of clearly defined and circumscribed four-to-five-year projects even where the needs of the recipient (for instance, in the case of research efforts) clearly are longer-term.

The *ideological* inclinations of donors also influence the nature of their aid. Consequently, changes have occurred as the political complexion of donor governments has varied. Currently, Scandinavian aid gives more emphasis to basic needs and services than that of many others, while U.S. and British aid is more concerned to expand the role of the private sector. There is clearly a danger that prescriptions for the recipient economy that are based on a priori inclinations of the donor may not be the most appropriate for the recipient's current state of development; there is no substitute for careful country-by-country analysis to determine this. Finally, the *geopolitical interests* of some donors, especially the United States, United Kingdom, and France, influence the direction and volume of their aid flows, as well as the weight they are prepared to accord issues of aid effectiveness in determining the future of aid to any one recipient.

These donor concerns may be perfectly legitimate ones for sovereign governments. Nevertheless, they influence the form and content of aid programs in ways that are not necessarily fully in accord with the needs of the local situation. The resulting costs and distortions detract from the effectiveness of aid programs in achieving the aims of sustained economic growth and institutional development.

These distortions and costs are of three main types. First, inherent in the project approach that still characterizes much aid is a tendency toward heavy expenditures on capital and underfunding of operating costs, especially after the initial establishment phase. As we have seen, the difficulty of providing for recurrent expenditures undermines the effectiveness of development institutions in low-income countries. Second, the aggregate effect of so many donors, unless they are effectively coordinated by the recipient, complicates policy formulation and planning and overburdens the local civil service and budget. Third, some characteristics of aid—such as the preference of donors for short-term commitments—detract from the contribution of aid to strengthening indigenous institutions. Inevitably, the greater the proportion of domestic investment that comes as aid, the weaker the recipient's institutions and the greater the impact of these influences.

To argue for a closer matching of aid forms to aid needs is not to suggest that donors are completely insensitive to local needs, or that they are wholly inflexible when change is indicated. Indeed, the changes to aid programs over the past five years—for instance, in response to the gathering crisis in Africa—demonstrate the opposite. Nevertheless, the persistence over many years of some of the causes of the mismatch we have identified indicates that they are deeply rooted in the institutions and interests of donors and recipients. It would be naive, therefore, to expect a marked all-around improvement simply as a result of the disadvantages being clearly recognized. Rather, it will take dynamic interaction between such technical perceptions and political determination.

Clearly, it is neither true that donor or recipient actions are uninfluenced by technical analysis nor that technical prescriptions always predominate. There is an untidy dialectical relationship between the technical and the political, and it shifts in response to changes in the participants' priorities and in perceptions of the effectiveness of the aid. The time for most radical and effective change under such a relationship is when existing practices and received wisdom are most clearly seen to be failing to meet the exigencies of the situation—that is to say, in a time of crisis. It is an open question whether the present dire economic circumstances of many of the low-income countries constitute a sufficient catalyst to bring about the changes needed.

Building Capacities: What Is To Be Done?

I conclude on a prescriptive note even more explicitly focused on lessons that can be drawn for the aid enterprise. What are some ways in which donors and recipients can improve the match between aid and the recipient's need for better adaptive capacities?

Donor Coordination

A high priority must be to establish within the recipient country a mechanism for matching the form and scale of aid with the needs. There are two levels at which the necessary coordination should take place. The first is where national priorities and the budget are discussed, total aid flows agreed, and the appropriate balance decided between different sectors as well as between project and program aid. For many recipient countries, such a forum already exists at least nominally in consultative groups or roundtables. The second level is where routine in-country coordination of aid donors takes place; here the recipient government takes the leading role, with the active collaboration of donors. In many countries, this will probably best take place at the sectoral level, in part because the number of interested major donors in any one sector is unlikely to exceed a manageable half-dozen, and in part because at this level the benefits of increased program coherence are likely to be felt most immediately.

Sectoral coordination requires supporting sectoral analysis— again ideally carried out by the recipient government, with or without donor assistance. However, in many countries, much of the analysis at present is carried out by the World Bank. This organization will inevitably play a leading role in coordination mechanisms—because of the large scale of its lending, because its professional capacity is greater than that of any other agency, and because it is seen by many recipients to be free of commercial bias and therefore in a better position than bilateral agencies to act as the honest broker.

Aid Management

A coordination mechanism will only be effective as an instrument of aid management (rather than as a simple information exchange) if government is able to integrate aid effectively within its budget. As noted previously, this will require that the budget incorporate the recurrent cost implications of all development projects and aid revenues and expenditures. Furthermore, government requires a method for monitoring the progress of all projects. These changes are essentially technical, involving little political disadvantage although some administrative cost, particularly at the time of initial establishment. Donors are able to assist in this effectively, however, provided that government demonstrates the necessary intent. A good current example of this that deserves wider emulation is provided by Kenya, which—in response to its financial crisis of the early 1980s—has brought about a significant improvement in its budgetary procedures and aid management with multi-donor assistance.[32]

More Effective Recipient-Country Institutions

If the negative aspects of encroachment of donor institutions and procedures are to be avoided, and if aid is to be more effectively managed, there is no alternative to continued efforts to strengthen the local implementing institutions. Donors can assist through resources and advice, but the remedy is ultimately in the hands of the recipient.

Growing awareness of the need for more effective support to recipient-country institutions has implications for the way in which donors provide this support. One of the main instruments that has been employed has been technical assistance. Experience with this form of aid has been mixed, and in many countries reliance on it continues at a higher level than was generally expected ten to twenty years ago. Despite widespread acknowledgment that a longer time-scale is needed if support to many institutions is to be effective, donors and recipients find it necessary to continue with technical assistance on an almost exclusively short-term basis. In consequence, advisors are normally appointed in a sequence of short contracts and without a career structure. This has a predictably adverse effect on the average quality of the appointees and leads to disruption as inevitable discontinuities occur. The effectiveness of technical assistance is further reduced by the weakness of outside professional and logistical support—also the result of unwillingness to treat this form of aid as needed for the medium term at least. A related point is that donor agencies need to increase their own expertise in carrying out detailed analyses of the reasons for institutional weaknesses and in drawing up detailed agendas for remedial actions.

Policy Analysis

Policy analysis is a special case of the need for improved institutional performance. The need to strengthen this capacity in low-income countries has been emphasized throughout this chapter. An essential step in the long-term improvement of the policy framework is to increase indigenous analytical capacity to the point where decision makers are advised at a high level of competence by their compatriots. Experience has shown that development of this capacity requires not just post-graduate training (which donors can and do provide), but also the right incentives and institutional framework. Some countries (Bangladesh and the Republic of Korea, for example) have set up policy analysis institutes for this purpose. Donors and recipients both have a great deal to gain by creating such a capacity and should collaborate in working toward achieving this objective.

The Long View

The recent acute difficulties of low-income countries have prompted most major donors to change their operations significantly. Balance-of-payments support has expanded at the expense of project aid in some countries; donors are more prepared to fund recurrent expenditures; and closer attention is perhaps being paid to strengthening institutions than in the past. Many of these changes have, however, taken place in an atmosphere of crisis management, with participants reacting to events beyond their control and partly unforeseen.

For donors and recipients alike, the priority now is to work out the set of principles that should underlie aid for the next ten to fifteen years. One of these principles must be to take the long view and to design aid accordingly. Another must be to tailor aid on the basis of a country-by-country analysis of needs, prospects, and constraints. A third must be sustained attention to strengthening productive and adaptive capacities in the private and public sectors of the recipient countries.

Notes

[1] T. W. Schultz, "The Value of the Ability to Deal with Disequilibria," *Journal of Economic Literature*, Vol. 13, No. 3 (1975), pp. 827–46.

[2] In this essay, "low-income" is used in the sense of the World Bank's *World Development Report 1984*: countries with 1982 gross national product per person of less than $410.

[3] OECD, *Geographical Distribution Financial Flows to Developing Countries, 1969–75*, and *1980–83*.

[4] See, for example, The World Bank, *Toward Sustained Development: A Joint Program of Action for Sub-Saharan Africa* (Washington, D.C.: The World Bank, 1984).

[5] See R. H. Cassen and associates, *Does Aid Work?*, The Independent Consultants' Study of Aid-Effectiveness, report to the Task Force on Concessional Flows, established by the Joint Ministerial Committee of the Boards of Governors of the Bank and Fund on the Transfer of Real Resources to Developing Countries (forthcoming).

[6] The interaction of politics and policies is addressed in Robert H. Bates, *Markets and States in Tropical Africa: The Political Basis of Agricultural Policies* (Berkeley: University of California Press, 1981).

[7] See, for example, Organisation for Economic Co-operation and Development, Development Assistance Committee, "Guidelines on Local and Recurrent Cost Financing," (Paris: OECD, 1979); M.F. McPherson, 1979, "Study on the Financing of Recurrent Costs," CILSS/Club du Sahel, Harvard Institute for International Development Working Paper; CILSS/Club du Sahel, "The Recurrent Costs in the Countries of the Sahel: How to Evaluate, Finance and Control Them," (Paris, 1982); John Howell, ed., *Recurrent Costs and Agricultural Development* (London: Overseas Development Institute, 1985).

[8] Peter S. Heller and Joan C. Aghevli, "The Recurrent Cost Problem: An International Overview," in Howell, *Recurrent Costs and Agricultural Development*, pp. 44–8.

[9] Ibid. An attempt has been made on the basis of a sample of forty-four countries, to identify the factors most likely to lead to a recurrent cost problem. Heller and Aghevli concluded that the only indicator that appeared to distinguish countries with a recurrent cost problem from those without one was having a relatively large share of capital expenditure financed from abroad.

[10] Jean M. Due and John F. Due, "Financing of Agricultural Development Projects in the Southern Region of the Sudan and Long-Run Prospects for Financing and Operation of the Projects by the Government of the Southern Region," Report prepared for the Sudanese government (Juda, 1980).

[11] McPherson, "Study on the Financing of Recurrent Costs," p. 14; David K. Leonard, John M. Cohen, and Thomas C. Pinckney, "Budgeting and Financial Management in Kenya's Agricultural Ministries," *Agricultural Administration*, Vol. 14 (1983), pp. 105–20.

[12] Leonard, Cohen, and Pinckney, "Budgeting and Financial Management in Kenya's Agricultural Ministries," p. 112.

[13] This is the conclusion of numerous analyses conducted by donors and is also indicated by some recipients. See, for example, Government of Kenya, *Report and Recommendations of the Working Party on Government Expenditures* (Government of Kenya Printer, Nairobi, 1982).

[14] See, for example, Malawi component of the aid-effectiveness study, by R.H. Cassen and Associates.

[15] Uma J. Lele, *The Design of Rural Development* (Washington, D.C.: The World Bank, 1975), Chapter 8.

[16] The World Bank, *World Development Report, 1980* (Washington, D.C.: 1980).

[17] An excellent survey of such studies is provided by M. J. Bowman, "Education and Economic Growth: An Overview," in Timothy King, ed., *Education and Income*, World Bank Staff Working Paper 402 (Washington, D.C.: 1980).

[18] Ibid., p. 55.

[19] Schultz, "The Value of the Ability to Deal with Disequilibria."

[20] H. W. Singer *Technologies for Basic Needs*, Second edition (Geneva: International Labour Office [ILO], 1982).

[21] J. Stewart and J. James, *The Economics of New Technology in Developing Countries* (Boulder, Colo.: Westview Press, 1982).

[22] P. Kilby, "Appropriate Technology at the National Level: A Survey," International Labour Office Working Paper (Geneva: 1976), discussed in Singer, *Technologies for Basic Needs*.

[23] See, for example, C. Gotsch, "Technical Change and the Distribution of Income in Rural Areas," *American Journal of Agricultural Economics*, Vol. 54, No. 2 (1972); C. E. Finney, *Farm Power in Pakistan*, Development Study 11 (Reading, U.K.: University of Reading, 1972).

[24] Stewart and James, *New Technology in Developing Countries*.

[25] There is a good presentation of the arguments in Singer, *Technologies for Basic Needs*.

[26] E. Evenson and Y. Kislev, *Agricultural Research and Productivity* (New Haven, Conn.: Yale University Press, 1975).

[27] M. Lipton and J. Toye, *Aid Effectiveness: India* (Brighton and Swansea, U.K.: Institute of Development Studies and Centre for Development Studies, 1984).

[28] The World Bank, Agricultural Research Sector Policy Paper (Washington, D.C.: 1981).

[29] Stewart and James, *The New Economics of New Technology in Developing Countries*, p. 11.

[30] This was the conclusion of both the recent report (October 1985) of the Task Force on Concessional Flows of the World Bank/IMF "Development Committee" (Joint Ministerial Committee of the Boards of Governors of the Bank and Fund on the Transfer of Real Resources to Developing Countries) and of the study of aid effectiveness under the of the Task Force by R. H. Cassen and associates, op. cit.

[31] Evidence for this is the increase in the proportion of aid that goes to Africa, a continent whose prospects as a commercial purchaser of the exports of industrial countries appear less promising that those of, for instance, Southeast Asia, whose aid receipts have declined in relative terms.

[32] Kenya operates a "forward budget" that spells out the recurrent-cost implications of the development budget three to five years ahead.

Chapter 7

Democracy and Development

Atul Kohli

Democracy's failure to take root in many developing countries often has led scholars and policy makers to conclude that a democratic government may not be able to cope with the pressing problems of development. A frequent corollary of this conclusion has been that authoritarian regimes may well be inevitable in the Third World.

In challenging this rather popular line of thinking, this essay argues that the developmental record of Third World democracies is relatively impressive. It should not be surprising, moreover, that new democracies have failed to establish themselves firmly in the developing world. Other types of political systems have not done much better. Unstable democracies have given rise to authoritarian regimes. Authoritarian regimes, in turn, often have been judged illegitimate. This has generated new pressures for democratization. Since regime fluctuation often has been the rule, there is no reason to hold that authoritarian regimes either are inevitable or deserve support because they are "necessary evils."

The argument of this essay is developed in two parts. First, it is shown that the developmental performance of Third World democratic regimes must be judged satisfactory. Although the links between regime type and economic performance may not always be easy to specify, there is enough evidence to suggest that democratic regimes tend to promote a broadly similar pattern of development. Countries as diverse as India, Malaysia, Sri Lanka, Venezuela, and

Costa Rica have achieved relatively impressive records. For the most part, their economies have grown at moderate but steady rates. Income inequalities within most of them have either remained stable or even narrowed, and their foreign debts have been kept within manageable limits. These countries contrast with a number of prominent cases steered by bureaucratic-authoritarian regimes. In the latter, growth rates may have been somewhat higher, but income inequalities widened, and foreign debts rose to staggering proportions. The case for democratic development is therefore relatively strong.

Despite this record, however, the transition to democracy in the Third World has been either slow to come or difficult to sustain. The second part of this essay delineates a number of "structural" obstacles that militate against the spread of democracy in developing countries. Third World states face competing imperatives that are not easy to reconcile. To facilitate socio-economic development, public authorities need to stand above and apart from the society. At the same time, to enhance regime legitimacy, they must incorporate the demands of diverse social groups. In addition, conditions of economic scarcity—in which political office provides a ready opportunity for rapid upward mobility—give a "zero-sum" quality to power struggles. The scope and intensity of elite competition thus tends to be fierce, undermining the possibilities of stable democratic rule.

It is important to recognize, however, that these sources of political strain militate not only against democracy, but against all forms of stable political rule. The validity of the old argument that authoritarianism is a natural alternative to failed democracies is highly questionable today, when many of the authoritarian regimes are themselves in tatters. Failed authoritarian experiments provide the strongest case for democratic development. Yet political instability and regime fluctuation are likely to continue to mar the Third World.

This essay argues that the conditions under which elites compete with one another for power are a political variable that is more amenable than others to "social engineering." And there is little to recommend a strategy that stifles political competition in the name of stability over one that aims to promote it.

The Impact of Democracy on Economic Development

The issue of which countries are or are not democratic is often a matter of degree. Assessing the degree of democracy involves evaluation of both formal and substantive criteria. The formal criteria involve such characteristics as adult suffrage, periodic elections, and legal freedoms of association and expression. When considering specific cases, however, one often needs to go beyond these formal indicators. Determining just how free a specific country's elections in fact are, what effective political choices exist, and how free socio-economic groups are to organize and press their demands are all difficult judgments. Such judgments concern the *substance* of democracy and usually require fairly detailed knowledge of a specific nation.

A formal, bare-bones definition of a democracy, then, clearly is no substitute for a more detailed analysis of the substance of democracy in specific cases—but it nevertheless is important for beginning to analyze the complex issues involved in the two-way relationship of democracy and development.

All democracies share at least two formal characteristics: They have periodic elections for national leadership in which rival elites compete freely for support; and most adults within them have legal rights to vote in elections. The substance of democracy varies; nevertheless, these two characteristics are widely recognized as the formal criteria defining democratic government.[1] Although governments satisfying these criteria are rare in the Third World, there are enough of them to give meaning to the following question: *What is the impact of democratic rule on economic growth, income distribution, and the management of foreign debt?*

Before analyzing this question, it should be noted that the causal link between regime type and economic development stipulated below is a weak one. Regimes choose policies from a number of available options. Similar regimes do not always pursue similar policies. Moreover, economic outcomes are influenced not only by a regime's policies, but also by such other factors as: conditions in the world economy, the level of economic development already achieved, natural resource endowment, and variables (such as management skills and work ethic) comprising an economy's "culture of efficiency."

Although regime type thus is only one of the many conditions influencing economic outcomes, most developmentalists agree that economic policies do influence economic development; and many further agree that the choice of economic policies in part reflects the political imperatives faced by leaders. It should therefore be possible to relate regime type systematically to patterns of economic development. How authority is structured limits the range of economic policies that a regime can ad,pt and implement. It is often politically naive to visualize clever decision makers as simply choosing among "rational" economic policy packages. Once governments get involved in economic issues—and in the contemporary Third World, they always do—economic and political "rationalities" compete for the attention of political authorities and, therefore, of development analysts.[2] The interaction of political and economic logic behind adopted development strategies thus adds meaning to the question of the impact of regime type on economic development.

The impact of democracy on economic development has been a much-debated subject. On the issue of economic growth, for example, many thoughtful observers have noted the "cruel choice between rapid (self-sustained) expansion and democratic processes."[3] The earlier growth models of the Harrod-Domar type upheld the "cruel choice" perception; it was felt that higher economic growth would result from higher rates of domestic savings and that, in turn, non-democratic governments would be relatively more likely to limit consumption and boost national savings. Others, in contrast, have argued that democracy lays the basis for successful long-term economic growth.[4] Systematic statistical evidence has failed to resolve the debate. Three cross-national studies have supported the "cruel choice" position by concluding that authoritarianism promotes economic growth, whereas one has found the reverse relationship to hold, and another has found the impact of authoritarianism on higher growth rates to be very weak.[5] Some scholars have even concluded that there may not be any systematic relationship between regime type and economic growth.[6]

The inconclusiveness of the debate makes it easy to sustain a more modest claim: *The economies of many democratic Third World countries have grown at satisfactory rates.* In Table 1, the countries in Group A were, over the period 1960–1982, generally more democratic than those in Group B. This mode of categorizing selected data poses a number of problems. First, some developing countries do not easily fit the dichotomous categories of democratic or authoritarian regime types. Second, authoritarianism is a residual regime type in the contemporary Third World; most countries are not democratic and, therefore, must be authoritarian. Fortunately, this is not seriously problematic for the general observations being made here, since these concern democratic regimes primarily and authoritarian ones only secondarily. Finally, selected countries cannot make a watertight case for anything. The countries listed are those for which data on change in income inequality were available. These data unfortunately are not available for a much larger set, in which countries that do not fit the generalizations probably could be found readily. Consequently, the data should be viewed only as broadly supportive of the argument presented.

Table 1. Development Indicators of Selected Developing Countries, 1960–1982

	Annual GDP Growth[a] (percentages)		Direction of Change in Income Inequality, 1960–1970[b]	External Debt Service as a Percentage of Exports, average[a] 1980–1982	Measure of Democracy[c] 1965
	1960–1970	1970–1982			
Group A					
Costa Rica	6.5	4.5	reduced	15.2	90.1
India	3.4	3.6	reduced	7.1	91.2
Malaysia	6.5	7.7	reduced	3.7	80.3
Sri Lanka	4.6	4.5	reduced	6.5	85.9
Venezuela	6.0	4.1	not available	13.8	73.4
Average	5.4	4.9		9.3	
Group B					
Argentina	4.3	1.5	not available	20.1	52.6
Bra.il	5.4	7.6	increased	36.7	60.9
Egypt	4.3	8.4	reduced	18.8	38.7
Morocco	4.4	5.0	increased	31.9	32.2
Republic of Korea	8.6	8.5	increased	12.5	53.0
Average	5.5	6.4		24.0	

[a] World Bank, *World Development Report, 1984*, pp. 220–21 and 248–49. The debt service figure for India is an average of 1980 and 1982; the figure for 1981 was not available. Costa Rica's debt problems have grown much worse since 1982.

[b] Direction of change in income inequality was dervied by subtracting income inequality in 1960 from income inequality in 1970. Income inequality was calculated as a ratio of income shares of the top 5 per cent to the bottom 20 percent. These figures are from various World Bank sources and have been brought together in Atul Kohli, et al., "Inequality in the Third World: An Assessment of Competing Explanations," *Comparative Political Studies*, Vol. 17, No. 3 (October 1984), Appendix A, p. 314.

[c] Figures from Kenneth Bollen, "Issues in the Comparative Measurement of Political Democracy," *American Sociological Review*, Vol. 45 (June 1980), pp. 370–90. The scores are on a scale of 0–100; the higher the score, the more democratic a country according to this measure.

Economic Growth

The data on economic growth suggest some important trends. During the 1960s, many of the democratic, Group A countries and the authoritarian, Group B countries grew at similar rates. Since 1970, however, the selected authoritarian countries grew faster. Yet the overall growth rates of the democratic Third World countries, though somewhat slower, were not much worse than those of the faster growing, harsh authoritarian ones: Over the two decades, the democracies grew at about 5 per cent annually, while the selected authoritarian countries grew at about 6 per cent.

Any fully adequate explanation of these trends of course would have to focus on a number of proximate economic *causes*. Two questions for macro political-economic analysis, however, are also posed by these trends: Why should democracies as a group have grown at a somewhat slower rate than a number of authoritarian regimes? And related to this, why should most of the cases of "hyper-growth" be authoritarian? There is a well-known hypothesis that an authoritarian regime is a necessary, though insufficient, condition for generating very high growth rates. However, the logic supporting this view has turned out to be a lot more complex than the older explanation—linking growth to rate of savings—would have suggested. A few comments on the two significant cases of Brazil and India may help clarify some of the complex factors relating regime type to economic growth.

The post-1964 military regime in Brazil successfully insulated the state from the society.[7] A specific type of authoritarian regime—some have called it a bureaucratic-authoritarian regime—achieved this insulating effect. It provided state authorities considerable room for policy maneuverability, and thus a capacity for restructuring an "inward-looking," low-growth economy into an "outward-oriented," high-growth one. This restructuring involved a variety of tasks: breaking the public's well-established inflationary expectations; repression of labor unions and imposition of a decline in real wages; reduction in business protection; increments in the cost of public services; tax increases; repudiation of economic nationalism, manifested in repeal of profit remittance laws, good relations with the IMF, and attempts to attract new foreign investment; and rigorous attempts to promote exports.[8]

Could this major shift in development strategy have been accomplished without a *prior political change*? Judgments differ, but a number of scholars have emphasized the necessity of an authoritarian regime for the "Brazilian miracle."[9] The high economic growth rates that resulted from "economic liberalization" in Brazil cannot be dismissed lightly. Yet this strategy had high costs: the loss of political liberties; widening income inequalities; growing dependency on foreign capital and finance, leading to some perceived loss of state sovereignty; failure to institutionalize legitimate authority; and even a slowing of the high growth rates.

This bureaucratic-authoritarian model of development contrasts sharply with the "nationalist-reformist" model adopted by India.[10] Within India's democratic framework, policy shifts can at best be incremental, and labor discipline is difficult to impose. Given a commitment to national sovereignty, explicit dependence on foreign economic resources is a political liability. And as organized groups compete for state resources, investable public resources are channeled into various forms of politically motivated economic support. The result has been sluggish and lackluster economic growth. Yet this pattern of development also has been accompanied by relatively stable income inequalities, democratic freedoms, and the maintenance of a degree of national pride.

India and Brazil may well be two extreme cases—highlighting the link between democracy and sluggish growth on the one hand and bureaucratic-authoritarianism and "hyper-growth" on the other hand. Clearly, as Table 1 indicates, other democracies have experienced higher growth rates than India's. The opposite relationship—that authoritarianism is responsible for higher growth rates—is neither being postulated nor likely to be sustainable against evidence. The claim made here is rather modest: Most cases of very high growth rates have involved authoritarian regimes, and authoritarianism may be a nearly necessary, though not a sufficient, condition for rapid economic growth.

Although no strong generalization linking regime type to economic growth is suggested here, when the growth rates of a set of democracies appear to be lower than those of a group of authoritarian regimes, the underlying dynamics may well be similar to the contrast noted in the cases of India and Brazil. Specific types of authoritarian regimes are capable of installing hyper-growth development strategies, whereas democracies tend to muddle through. Democracies worry about regime legitimacy and are often captured by competing interest groups. The capacity of democratic regimes to extricate themselves from social ties so as to restructure the economy is minimal. Generally, only incremental shifts are possible. Moreover, leaders in democracies concern themselves with what appears to be politically "rational"—namely, how to generate and enhance political support. Thus economic policies often are chosen because of the political benefits they may bring to the leaders. Policy incrementalism and the use of economic resources for sustaining political support generally tend to retard economic growth in democracies.

If democracy is a valued goal in the contemporary Third World, it may be necessary to settle for moderate growth rates. More value may need to be placed on the political rationality of economic policies that appear irrational from the standpoint of economic science. Nation-building is a long-term process in which the need to create viable political institutions has to be balanced against the demands of economic efficiency. This is not to suggest making a virtue out of economic irrationality.[11] Many Third World democracies, including India, could benefit from a "rational" policy shift toward lesser controls and a more open and competitive economy.[12] However, a South Korean or a Brazilian "miracle" is not likely in an India, and the reasons for this are in part the differences in respective political systems.[13] Policy advice that ignores such political realities is likely to be counterproductive.

Before moving on, it is important to reiterate the basic fact that the growth performance of many democratic regimes is not all that bad, especially when considered over two or more decades. If one leaves aside the few exceptional cases of "hyper-growth," where considerable political and other types of costs have been paid for rapid development, *Third World democracies clearly are capable of generating and sustaining moderate but satisfactory growth rates.*

Income Distribution

The dimension of economic development on which democracy clearly has a more desirable impact than do the many versions of authoritarian regimes is income distribution. Table 1 presents data on the direction of change in income inequality in selected countries during the 1960s.[14] The rather consistent pattern evident here suggests that, during the 1960s, income inequalities narrowed in democracies while they tended to widen in authoritarian countries attempting high-growth development. The magnitude by which income inequalities were reduced in democratic countries was often small, but the magnitude by which they increased in authoritarian countries was considerable. It seems then that democratic regimes provide conditions within which income inequalities tend to more or less stabilize, while authoritarian regimes pursuing rapid development exacerbate these inequalities.

Although this generalization is here derived from selected examples only, such a case has been made more systematically elsewhere.[15] Using cross-sectional, short-term longitudinal and case-study data, a group study in which the author participated concluded that short-term changes in income inequalities within the space of one or two decades are better explained by regime type and by the development strategies that governments adopt than either as a function of levels of development, as Simon Kuznets has argued, or as a function of levels of economic dependency, as many neo-Marxists postulate. More specifically, the data fit the argument that "authoritarian-exclusionary" regimes tend to worsen income inequalities, while democratic regimes stabilize them. The only major exceptions to this generalization are those cases—e.g., Taiwan—where early in the process of state-guided industrialization, unusual political circumstances facilitated significant land reforms.

Why should democratic development be associated with stable income inequalities? The reasons relate partly to the direct role of democratic governments, and partly to the role of organized groups and local institutions, which often are more active in democratic settings. To maintain legitimacy, democratic regimes find it difficult systematically to deprive specific social groups of their relative economic shares. Any systematic tendency toward increasing inequalities is therefore either preempted by suitable policies or vigorously opposed by the losers. Even if such redistributive policies as land reforms fail, which they often do, they tend to retard the process of rapid wealth concentration. Additionally, democratic regimes usually involve freedom of expression and of association. Organized groups such as labor unions fight hard to maintain their shares of the growing economic pie. Scholars doing micro-level research on rural development have also noted egalitarian consequences of local "self-help" institutions,[16] which one presumes are more likely to flourish in democratic than in centralized and authoritarian settings. While the dynamics of individual cases obviously varies, some combination of reform policies and interest group activism seems to help explain the benign consequences of democracy for income inequalities.[17]

Foreign Debt Management

The status of a third dimension of economic development—foreign debt management—recently has been raised to a potentially competing goal with growth and equity concerns. How effective are Third World democratic regimes likely to be in dealing with foreign debt problems? Prior to answering this question, a caveat should be noted: The problem of foreign debt, while serious, is a very serious problem for only a few Latin American countries. The international status of the foreign debt problem was raised in the aftermath of the panic of August 1982 in international banking circles. While the international concern is understandable, the long-term goal of growth with equity in the Third World certainly should not be subordinated to short-term problems of international liquidity.

When discussing the issue of Third World democracy in the context of the "debt crisis," the normal concern is: How well will fragile democratic regimes fare in implementing difficult adjustment programs? Other scholars are already writing on this and the related subject of stability in the context of adjustment.[18] A fact that has been virtually ignored, however, is that the worst debts within the Third World were accumulated not by democracies but by bureaucratic-authoritarian regimes. Table 1 documents this rather clearly. Whereas the average debt-service ratio for the democratic countries in 1982 was close to 10 per cent, the figure for the selected authoritarian countries was 24 per cent. The largest debtors are Latin American authoritarian countries. In contrast, the Asian democracies—India, Malaysia, and Sri Lanka—have borrowed less than their creditworthiness would have allowed; they have kept debt service to less than 10 per cent of export earnings—clearly a quite conservative borrowing pattern.

Why should democracies as a group have borrowed more cautiously than many an authoritarian country? The explanation is probably rooted in the differences between democratic and authoritarian countries in the perceived need for high economic growth as well as in the varying capacities for pursuing strategies of rapid development. Democracies do not rest their legitimacy exclusively on economic growth. Authoritarian regimes often do. Faced with the high oil prices and the generally difficult international economic conditions of the 1970s, most democratic governments accepted the prospect of somewhat slower growth rates. For non-democratic regimes, in contrast, the slowing of economic growth must have been a great deal more threatening. The legitimacy of military juntas, such as that in Brazil, is often dubious. The minimal legitimacy that they have enjoyed rests on restoring order and efficient management of the economy. For them, economic slowdown must have spelled political danger. Many bureaucratic-authoritarian governments therefore appear to have decided to pursue rapid economic growth, partly financed by foreign borrowing and foreign investment. The feasibility of this option was, of course, also influenced by the "supply" side of the equation: Banks and investors found bureaucratic-authoritarian regimes attractive risks that seemed to promise political stability and high, export-oriented economic growth.

In conclusion, when the developmental performance of Third World democratic regimes is assessed on the grounds of economic growth, income distribution, and debt management, the results must be judged satisfactory. The overall economic performance of democracies certainly has been no worse than that of many non-democratic regimes. The growth performance of democracies may sometimes appear lackluster in contrast to the slick authoritarian cases of "hyper-growth"; overall, however, democracies have grown at respectable rates. The clearest positive impact of democracies has been their ability to stabilize patterns of income distribution. In the case of foreign borrowing, many democracies borrowed conservatively in the 1970s and are not now experiencing the same international pressures as are the over-borrowed, authoritarian governments of Latin America. Although this essay does not dwell on the positive impact of democratic governments on preserving human rights and enhancing basic liberties of expression and association, this is a central if relatively obvious contribution of democracy. When one adds this dimension to the relatively satisfactory economic performance of a number of democratic regimes, the case for democratic development is strong.

The Dynamics of Third World Democracy

Although the handful of relatively stable Third World democracies have performed well economically, new stable democracies have been slow in coming. Other seemingly stable ones, such as Chile, have been replaced by harsh authoritarian regimes. Clearly, just because specific political systems can solve economic problems does not mean they will come into being or will be sustained.

Democracy has been tried, but has not succeeded in becoming stable, in many Third World countries. On the other hand, failed authoritarian regimes have often given rise to democratic experiments. There is no clear trend either toward, or away from, democracy in the developing world. As Samuel Huntington has recently noted, "It would be difficult to argue that the world was more or less democratic in 1984 than it had been in 1954."[19] If there has been any discernible political trend in the Third World, it is one of cyclical movements. Democratic experiments have been followed by periods of instability. This has often led to the installation of authoritarian regimes. Failure to institutionalize legitimate power, in turn, has been followed again by dissent, protest, and political pressures of various kinds. Thus, renewed attempts to introduce electoral politics have emerged. The question for analysis is: Are there any general factors that help explain such regime fluctuations? And for speculation, the question is: Is there a way out of this situation?

The question of why democracy has not taken root in much of the Third World draws attention to the more general issue of the conditions under which stable democracies come into being. This, in turn, forces one to choose from among the numerous theories of democracy available.

Theoretical Observations

Three theories have stood the test of time and continue to be relevant for understanding conditions for democracy. First, and probably most important, is the theory that perceives democracy as a form of government likely only in market or capitalist economies. A second, old, and interesting theory views democracy as more likely to be sustained in wealthy or economically developed societies. Finally, a third, more political theory posits that well-established political traditions of compromise politics and of checks and balances on central power help countries evolve into democracies. Taken together, these theories suggest that democracy is most likely to take firm hold in wealthy capitalist countries with traditions of proto-democracy. As these theories are generally based on Western experiences, they do not easily lend themselves to explaining why democracy has not taken root in the Third World. Nevertheless, an understanding of why capitalism, economic wealth, and traditions of compromise politics may generally be conducive to democratic government helps provide some insights into why democracy is such an uphill battle in the contemporary Third World.

Whatever the evaluation that liberals, conservatives, or Marxists give the democratic form of government, most of them readily admit the historical and the logical connections between capitalism and democracy. Contemporary scholars as diverse as Charles E. Lindbloom, Samuel Huntington, and Barrington Moore, Jr., have posited this link.[20] Why should this be so? Historical analysis of European democracies has often stressed the rise of a victorious bourgeoisie. According to this view, the rising business classes successfully tamed the monarchical state. They successfully challenged the aristocratic claim of government as a prerogative of birth and slowly replaced it with the principle that government is a natural domain of wealthy "commoners." Ultimately, however, especially under pressure from organized working classes, legitimacy in Western democracies came to rest on the notion that governmental representatives have to be elected by a legally equal citizenry.[21] This historical sequence in several countries led Barrington Moore to the succinct conclusion: "No bourgeois, no democracy."[22]

The logical links between democracy and capitalism are also suggested by this historical process. Capitalism, as an economic system based on private property, provides a fundamental check on state power. It generates a "private sphere" of social and economic activity separate from the "public sphere." And it is this separation between the public and the private realms that is an initial and necessary condition for the evolution of democracy as a form of limited government. Moreover, the division into the public and the private realms makes the sphere of legal and political equality somewhat separate from that of substantial social and economic inequalities. Separating political equality from economic inequalities not only lays the basis for legitimate elected governments in inegalitarian societies. It also opens up the hope and opportunity—though radical critics of democracy may with some legitimacy call it a false hope—of modifying inherited inequalities through the use of democratic state power.

The general statement that democracy is positively related to economic development[23] has over the years come under heavy criticism. Critics have noted not only that the process of economic development can as easily create "political decay,"[24] but also that many industrialized communist countries are not about to become democratic. A more limited version of the positive linkage between democracy and development nevertheless merits attention. The simple and overwhelming fact remains that most of the industrialized, capitalist countries of the world today are democratic. In many of these countries, democracy clearly has not been a "homegrown" affair. But once installed, industrialized capitalism has proved to be a hospitable environment for sustaining democracy. The possible link between capitalism and democracy already has been discussed. The remaining question for scrutiny is: Why should industrial society be more hospitable to democracy?

Political theorists have delineated a number of characteristics of industrial economies that may help democracy.[25] A factor that seems more important than others is the one that all industrial capitalist societies share: They are relatively wealthy. Economic wealth—absolute levels and rates of change—helps to ease both intra-elite and elite-mass political strains. In Western capitalist economies, prolonged periods of steady economic growth laid the basis for welfare states. The welfare state, in turn, helped ease and tame class conflict in early industrial capitalism. The fact that a prolonged economic recession has contributed to political and social polarization even in a democracy as well established as modern Britain provides evidence for this general historical point.

Wealthy capitalism, moreover, helps ease the intensity of intra-elite conflict. The stakes of the political game are lower when the losers have alternative channels of social and economic mobility. Under these conditions, access to the state is not necessarily viewed as the only route for upward mobility. The struggle for power also is not viewed as a zero-sum game. Losers in the power game are in these circumstances less likely to attempt destabilizing political mobilization such as organizing mass demonstrations, riots, or participation in underground terrorist activities. In other words, wealth helps to create boundaries within which elites choose to fight. Disruption of these boundaries damages the system that creates the wealth and thus curtails the opportunities for advancement. Yet bounded struggle is crucial for initiating and sustaining democracy.

Some political theorists have pointed out that democratic institutions often took hold prior to the age of capitalism and industrialization. With England in mind, German scholars have been especially struck by how a feudal past contributed to democratic evolution.[26] Feudalism in England bequeathed a legacy of power-sharing arrangements between the monarchs and the nobility. Thus, institutions rooted in the principles of political compromise, power sharing, and checks and balances existed prior to the rise of capitalism. The evolution of democracy in England was, of course, slow and often tortuous. Nevertheless, according to this influential line of thinking, the early establishment of proto-democratic institutions was critical. These institutions provided a framework for accommodating the demands of new social classes in a democratic manner. The generalization suggested by this historical argument is that the ruling traditions of a nation are important for understanding how authority gets organized during the process of significant socio-economic change. Countries with proto-democratic pasts are more likely to deal with political challenges in a democratic manner.

These three theories—about capitalism, high levels of economic development, and proto-democratic traditions—highlight some general factors that contribute to the evolution of democratic politics. They do not, however, say anything about how democracy actually has spread. Even in the West, the spread of democracy has been slow, uneven, and often marked by violence. A case can be made that the major democracies—England, France, and the United States—were born out of revolutionary upheavals.[27] Whether this is so or not, indigenous democracies in any case have been rare. Barring a handful of countries of Northwestern Europe and the United States, most of the democracies of the modern world have come into being either through "diffusion" or through "imposition." Diffusion of democracy has occurred either through immigrant cultures—as in Canada, Australia, and New Zealand—or through influences born of geographical and cultural links—as in modern Portugal and Spain. The imposition of democracy also has been of two types: that imposed by the victors of war (as in Germany and Japan) or that left over as a legacy of colonialism (as in India, Sri Lanka, and Malaysia).

This brief excursion into some theories of democracy and the process by which it spreads suggests that the forces that give birth to a democracy are not necessarily the same as those that help sustain it. Only a few democracies have indigenous roots. Most have been imported. What indigenous and imported democracies share, however, is the fact that democracies are born when, either due to virtue or necessity, the competing elites of a society decide to take a chance on their power prospects by agreeing to follow a set of rules in the conduct of their power struggles. The "glue" that has facilitated this minimum binding force upon competing elites historically has come from many diverse sources. These include colonial institutions, immigrant political cultures, constitutions imposed by war victors, traditions of political compromise, and the emulation of other systems deemed desirable.

Whatever the binding glue, before democracies can be born, elites must come to "agree to disagree" and be willing to put "rules above personal power." These relatively obvious points need emphasis because they provide insights into an issue explored later in this essay—namely, how democracies can be "engineered." The factors that help sustain democracy are not, however, easily engineered. If capitalism, economic development, and proto-democratic traditions indeed have been important to the development of democracy in the West, the question that needs to be discussed is: How relevant are such historical associations for the contemporary Third World?

Obstacles to Democracy in the Third World

Capitalism and self-sustained economic development have helped transform the proto-democracies of the West into modern democratic states. In the contemporary Third World, however, macro change takes place almost in the reverse order: State authorities have to generate capitalism and economic development. Sovereign states in the Third World have often been born of nationalist struggles against colonialism. It is these states that in turn support incipient capitalism so as to generate economic development. Even in Latin America, where direct colonialism is a dim memory, systematic economic development has only been stimulated by state intervention. Whereas in the West, democracy was historically supported by the rising entrepreneurial classes, in the contemporary Third World, generating and supporting capitalism is itself a political task. Where the state is in command of socio-economic change, the task of simultaneously making the state responsive to society is inherently difficult. State domination of society in the West historically was tamed only by dynamic and strong social forces. When socio-economic change itself needs to be generated by political means, who can tame the state? It is because of this historical sequencing that democracy in today's developing world is more likely to be a "gift" of the political elite to the society and less likely to be a political system that significant social forces—such as the middle class—create of their own volition.

Democracy in the contemporary Third World faces a number of "structural" obstacles in the form of political and economic conditions that do not change easily and that militate against stable democratic regimes. These barriers make democracy more difficult, but not impossible.

The most significant of these obstacles is the issue discussed above—namely, the commanding position that the state occupies in relation to the society in much of the Third World. This superior—and essentially anti-democratic—positioning of the state over society is not easily done away with because it is historically inherited. As economies develop, social forces are likely to be strengthened in relation to the state. This may increasingly be the situation in a handful of the newly industrializing countries (NICs). Even here, however, the relative political acquiescence in East Asian NICs compared to Latin American NICs suggests that economic development does not transform societies politically in any simple one-to-one relationship. For most Third World people—who, in any case, live in low- rather than middle-income economies—state domination over weak societies tends to be the rule.

The areas we now call the Third World were historically fragmented politically and often lacked economic dynamism. Brittle states and weak economies made them vulnerable to colonialism. The sovereign states that were later established came not so much at the behest of rising entrepreneurial classes as under the leadership of nationalist political movements. Thus politics has been a primary source of dynamism in these areas. Third World societies and economies are in need of "development," and state authorities often are responsible for facilitating such development. Yet even when Third World states are very weak, which often is the case, they nevertheless are in a position to dominate, control, and manipulate the societies they rule. Thus political movements and states, rather than organized social groups, have the greater capacity to build national coherence, mobilize resources, organize for task achievement, and provide support necessary for releasing economic dynamism within the Third World. This general characteristic of much of the Third World does not make it conducive to the creation of states responsive to societies.[28]

In state-dominated societies, democracy is likely to be primarily an affair of the elites. This is not to suggest that the large "unkempt masses" are irrelevant to the process of Third World democracy. However, elites in these settings often have the capacity to deliver or withdraw democratic rights. The "masses" often enter politics only when competing elites mobilize them for their own political purposes. "Mobilization" or "demobilization" of the masses thus is as much a product of elite behavior as it is an independent variable thrown up by ongoing economic development.

The more a society develops, the more likely it is to assert itself in relation to the state. Yet the process of organized social groups making demands on the state characterizes only a few of the more advanced Third World countries. The popular image that democracies disintegrate when they fail to meet the multiple demands of competing interest groups applies to only a handful of developing countries. Whether "pressures from below" are the wave of the future or not, socio-political conflict in many of the contemporary developing countries—especially in the low-income ones—often can be traced to intra-elite conflict. Thus, neither fearing nor romanticizing the "masses" will serve the purpose of Third World democracy.

The conditions that govern elite competition are important for understanding why Third World elites often find it difficult to work together. These conditions help explain why elites periodically undertake political mobilization of the type that can undermine democracies. They also help explain why, in other rare cases, competing elites fight for power through democratic means, opening up long-term possibilities of incorporating the "masses."

Born out of anti-colonial nationalism and into a world dominated by industrialized powers, political authorities in the Third World have inherited twin mandates: They are expected to create viable states and to generate economic development. The task of creating orderly, viable states involves, at minimum, establishing effective control over a territory and, at maximum, establishing a legitimate state perceived to be both sovereign and responsive to its citizens' needs. Similarly, economic development at minimum means initiating economic growth and, at maximum, reconciling growth with distributive concerns. These varying tasks have fostered a host of competing legitimacy formulas. Some elite groups are committed primarily to political order and economic growth. Others demand responsive states capable of coupling economic growth with more equitable distribution. Either set can appear legitimate—depending on who has failed most recently. Nationalism adds another complicating variable that competing elites of various ideological shades can manipulate to their advantage. Thus power competition does not revolve only around who can perform similar tasks more effectively. If this were its nature, it would be easier to accommodate within democratic bounds. But the power struggle can just as often be about defining and redefining which political tasks are important. Such struggles are more likely to be resolved by regime change—a change in the system of rule— than by a mere change of rulers.

Widely varying legitimacy formulas do not facilitate stable democratic politics. They give rise to competing elites with substantially different orders of political preference. Whenever governing elites with a given set of preferences appear to be weak performers, rival elites promising different priorities are always waiting in the wings. In any case, institutional arrangements for the transition of power are weak. Therefore, when political priorities change, this often brings new regimes and not only new rulers to power. Thus regime fluctuations in the contemporary Third World are structurally rooted in the broad mandate that the post-colonial states inherited: simultaneously to preserve sovereignty, create viable states, and generate economic development.

Conditions of economic scarcity further contribute to the intensity of elite competition for power. Access to the state often provides lucrative opportunities for economic advancement in Third World countries. This is partly a function of the significant involvement of Third World states in economic activities. It is also facilitated by the considerable opportunities for appropriating public resources for private use. A major reason why holding state office is so attractive a means of private aggrandizement is that alternative opportunities for upward mobility are scarce. Political office is sought not only as a vehicle for power and for influencing policies but also as a means of personal economic advancement. Political struggles can become struggles without issues. More important, they can take on a zero-sum quality. Those in power tend to divide up the state's "free" resources among themselves, while rival elites are often excluded from the patronage network and given few alternative economic opportunities. The struggle for power frequently takes on a vitriolic intensity that makes compromise and democratic accommodation between competing elites nearly impossible.

To summarize, the argument so far has suggested that Third World states are often in a position to direct their respective societies, and that this relatively "superior" positioning of the state over society makes the prospect of creating responsive states very difficult. Democracy is only likely to evolve under these conditions if competing political elites decide that power struggles can be carried out within democratic bounds. The fierceness of elite competition is exacerbated both by the widely varying tasks that Third World states are supposed to perform and by the intense personal political ambitions generated by conditions of economic scarcity. Elite fragmentation in state-dominated societies thus poses formidable challenges—not only to democratic politics, but to all forms of stable political rule. Various types of group and class conflicts add fuel to the political fire in the more economically advanced developing countries. Under these adverse circumstances, democracy can be sustained only if some force short of state repression exists to limit elite fragmentation and divisiveness.

The Cases of India and Brazil

The few Third World countries in which democracy has survived without interruption, notably the poor democracies of Asia, suggest that political institutions inherited from the colonial past have been the glue that has held elites together. In the case of India, for example, the British inadvertently helped the Indian National Congress, which had grown out of a movement opposed to colonial rule, to become one of the mature forebearers of democracy.[29] One has only to contrast the British role in India with that of the Dutch in Indonesia or the French in Indochina to realize how widespread repression forced the nationalist opposition in the latter two cases to be extremist. The extremism of the opposition in turn severely diminished the chances of democratic evolution in Indonesia and Vietnam. The British in India, moreover, left behind a functioning parliament, a cohesive and "apolitical" bureaucracy, and an independent judiciary and press. The tradition of civilian control over the military so far has proven to be especially important. The contributions of these institutions to a relatively stable democracy in India can hardly be minimized.

In India, proto-democratic institutions, especially the democratically inclined nationalist movement, have helped, at least so far, to keep elite fragmentation within limits. The role of a first-generation ruler like Nehru, whose very considerable political influence kept elite divisiveness within bounds, was also important. Nehru did not use his dominant position to undermine India's democracy. On the contrary, his commitment to democratic values led him to strengthen democratic institutions. The early nationalist consensus on two goals—"self-sufficiency" and a "socialist pattern of economic development"—also helped minimize elite divisiveness over the role of the state in socio-economic change.[30] The state remained in command, but it created a framework for slow but steady political incorporation of the society's "periphery."[31]

Many would argue that by contrast, Indira Gandhi, India's major political figure for nearly two decades—from the beginning of 1966 to her assassination in late 1984—weakened the country's democracy.[32] As the colonial and the nationalist legacy retreated into the background, her regime was increasingly marked by the emergence of elite divisiveness. In 1975, when faced with considerable challenge to her own power, Mrs. Gandhi temporarily suspended India's democracy. The relative ease with which she did away with democratic processes—only to reinstate them with similar ease two years later—is about as clear evidence as one needs to substantiate the point that elites can make or destroy Third World democracies.[33] If Mrs. Gandhi could play such a substantial role in a country with fairly well-developed institutions, is it not reasonable to conclude that the major obstacles to democracy in places like Chile or the Philippines are not only pressures from below but also over-ambitious leaders like Pinochet and Marcos?

The case of India further highlights how open political competition in low-income settings easily leads to destabilizing populism. Massive poverty cannot be alleviated in the short run. A large segment of the dissatisfied population can, therefore, readily be mobilized by politicians. When pressed politically, as well as for other welfare considerations, Mrs. Gandhi did indeed adopt the slogan "alleviate poverty," thus temporarily boosting her electoral popularity in India. However, the government's inability to make good on such slogans has lately led the Indian leadership slowly to disassociate itself from such seemingly radical commitments. It is not at all unlikely that another leader at another time will find poverty politically useful. Then, once again, in spite of the state's minimal capacities to alleviate poverty, another politician will make promises that cannot be fulfilled. There are other countries besides India in which such a drama has already unfolded. The destabilizing consequences of such populist tendencies highlight a cruel dilemma of democracy in underdeveloped settings.

Democracy, after all, promises political, not economic, equality. Establishing democratic legitimacy often means teaching the many to value institutions which, as far as economic rewards are concerned, essentially serve the few. That is why radical critics of democracy often label it as "bourgeois democracy" or as a system of "class hegemony." In advanced capitalist societies, the long tradition of a separation between the public and the private realms, and the relatively high standards of living even among the working classes, have made the establishment of democratic legitimacy possible. Where poverty remains massive, however, and where the state is involved in all manner of economic activities at very early stages of economic development, and where adult suffrage has come long before the capacity to feed the adults, democracy is much more difficult to establish and sustain.

Democracy thus remains a fragile affair even in those developing countries that inherited strong institutions from a colonial past. The fate of Chile and the Philippines highlights this fragility. In other countries, which either did not inherit such institutions or in which inherited institutions were destroyed by over-ambitious leaders, stable political systems have not taken root. Authoritarian regimes may have provided brief periods of order in highly fragmented situations, but the fact is that such regimes have as a rule failed to legitimize themselves. They have either been overthrown—often only to be replaced by similar regimes—or they have had to give way to more open systems of government. Brazil, one of the prominent contemporary bureaucratic-authoritarian experiments, exemplifies some of the typical strains.[34]

Brazil emerged as a sovereign state almost by default—when the Portuguese emperor escaped to South America after being defeated by Napoleon. Thus sovereignty was gained neither at the behest of new rising social classes nor under the leadership of a strong nationalist movement. The civilian consensus around the new state was weak from the beginning. It took nearly half a century after the declaration of the republic before a consolidated state finally did emerge in the 1930s; and even then, the armed forces played a critical role in generating political unity. This "original sin"—the failure of a civil consensus to develop around the nature and the role of the state, and the significant role of the armed forces in creating the state—has haunted Brazil ever since in its search for stable political institutions.

During the Vargas years, especially in the 1950s, differences among the fragmented political elite arose over two alternative "models" for the future of Brazil. To simplify a complicated historical process drastically, those favoring a "nationalist-reformist" approach generally argued for democratic institutions; an independent foreign policy; the political-economic incorporation of the lower classes through such varying means as labor unions, higher wages, and land reforms; and a reduced role for foreign investment. The competing group worried about the suitability of democratic institutions for Brazil; wanted to maintain close contacts with the West; were suspicious of criticisms of foreign investment; and felt that sympathetic attitudes toward the "laboring classes" revealed a leftward tilt. These major issues concerning the role and the nature of the state never really got resolved within Brazil's political elite. During the "populist" periods presided over by powerful leaders such as Vargas, these differences could be papered over. But when lesser leaders later sought to push the Brazilian political economy in a nationalist-reformist direction, the cleavages at the top became sharp and wide, precipitating the military coup of 1964.

The Western-supported military junta imposed a harsh authoritarian regime and severely curtailed all civil liberties. It also initiated a rapid development program, which has since become widely known as the "authoritarian-dependent" model of development.[35] The "authoritarian-dependent" path has meant that both the Brazilian state and foreign finance and capital have taken on much greater roles in generating high economic growth. It is possible that the military junta may have enjoyed a degree of legitimacy in its early years, as it restored political order and began to mastermind the rapid development strategy. Over the years, however, the inevitable pressures for *abertura*—a political opening—have mounted.

The more fundamental roots of these pressures penetrate the very nature of authoritarianism. Regimes that exclude a substantial segment of the politically active population—often the rival elites—from some form of active or anticipated role in government leave intact considerable forces of latent opposition. As long as this latent opposition exists, the regimes are not likely to become institutionalized—the leaders are not seen as legitimate by the people they rule. Those who have been excluded generally wait their turn. They can probably be excluded for a long time, but only through the continued use of tools of state repression. Exclusion becomes difficult, however, under certain circumstances: if the regime performance falters, if the opposition is willing to take greater and greater risks, and/or if factionalism develops within the ruling circles.

In the case of Brazil, the regime's performance had been faltering since the recession of the mid-1970s. The opposition of the Church and organized labor became more overt, and factionalism developed within the elite.[36] The pressures of the Carter administration for more "human rights" also contributed. Demands for the restoration of democracy inevitably mounted. The Brazilian experience highlights 1) how a weak civilian consensus on the nature and the role of the state makes stable political rule difficult, 2) how sharp cleavages among the political elites make democratic experiments vulnerable to military intervention, and 3) how bureaucratic-authoritarian regimes face difficulties in institutionalizing their hold on power.

In Brazil's experience, political conflicts tend to involve issues of both policy and regime legitimacy. This is often not so, however, in countries at lower levels of development. In many African countries, for example, coup after coup brings to power new governments that hardly differ from each other on the substance of policy. Even in Nigeria, the major commitment of the military junta that terminated the short-lived democratic experiment was less to a "new type of development" than to ridding the government of bickering, dishonesty, and corruption.[37] In such cases, also, elite fragmentation and unhampered pursuit of power and personal gain make the prospect of instituting a system of government premised on elite compromise very difficult.

Prospects of Democracy

The Third World countries with the best chances of establishing sustained democratic rule are those with historically inherited institutions that facilitate elite unity. The unfortunate political fate of many countries has been fluctuation back and forth between failed democratic experiments, unacceptable authoritarian regimes, and occasional rule by charismatic demagogues.

The question for speculation remains: Is there any way to move away from such regime fluctuations and toward more stable democratic rule in the Third World? Over the short run, the answer has to be: probably not. But it helps to recognize the sources of strain on democratic experiments. The argument presented here focuses on the conditions under which competing elites can accept democratic rules in their power struggles. In today's Third World, which consists mostly of the state-dominated societies described above, it is the elite that is likely to deliver or withdraw democratic rights from the masses. This is not because the masses are irrelevant to political outcomes, but because the extent and the mode of their political participation often reflect the nature of the elite's struggle for power.

The lower classes in the Third World do not enter the political arena merely as a consequence of economic development and the resulting social mobilization. The rate and the pattern of lower-class political participation in the Third World is profoundly influenced by the nature of the leadership. One set of the elite can choose to mobilize the disaffected masses because it suits their political needs. Another set can just as easily choose to demobilize the masses when the political situation seems too turbulent. The lower classes, of course, are not totally manipulable. Their roles also differ considerably in the more- and the less-developed of the developing countries.[38] Yet the lower classes are not as significant an independent political force as they sometimes are made out to be. In too many popular arguments, the "unruly" and the "over-demanding" masses are blamed for a nation's political instability. This then becomes an implicit justification for authoritarian rule. Such Burkean fear of the masses pounding on palace doors may well reflect a sound knowledge of the French Revolution. But it is not rooted in the realities of the contemporary Third World. If democracy is to have a chance in the developing world, it is not the masses but overly ambitious political elites that need to be tamed.

If democracies indeed come into being when rival elites are willing to "take a chance" on their power prospects and when they agree to compete for power according to rules such as free elections and universal suffrage, the question becomes: What circumstances or conditions typically enhance the possibility of such minimal elite unity? Five such conditions should be noted:

- When no single leader or political group is likely to usurp all power, the prospect is enhanced that rival elites will be willing to take a chance on democracy. Overly ambitious leaders who have little regard for institutional constraints are democracy's worst enemies.

- Even when power is concentrated in one leader or group, if a realistic prospect exists that the losers of today may have a chance to make a political comeback tomorrow, the competing elite are more likely to operate within democratic bounds.
- Even if the chances for a political comeback are not very good, the existence of significant non-political opportunities for social and economic mobility help tame the system-damaging political inclinations of those out of power.
- The aftermath of failed authoritarian experiments provides some of the most favorable circumstances for the establishment of new democracies. At that point, discarding what appears not to work and attempting something new—namely, a democracy—looks attractive.
- Democratic regimes typically attempt to reconcile the developmental goals of economic growth, decreasing income inequality, and management of external dependencies. Whatever their relative success in juggling these competing goals, the ideology of Third World democratic leaders tends to be characterized by nationalism (often expressed as "anti-imperialism") and a commitment to both state intervention in the economy and some redistributive goals (often expressed as "socialism" or "social democracy"). Those supportive of democracy in the developing world need to cultivate greater ideological tolerance of such political attitudes. These ideological goals should be understood for what they are: legitimizing devices that are necessary accompaniments for many Third World democratic regimes.

Conclusion

Democracy has proved to be an elusive goal in much of the Third World. The near future is not likely to be all that different from the recent past.

The reasons for the failure of new democracies to take root are not, however, to be found in the inability of democratic regimes to facilitate economic development. Wherever democratic regimes have survived, economic performance has not been any worse than in many non-democratic settings: The economies of democratic countries have grown at moderate rates, inequalities within them have been relatively stable, and democratic regimes have tended to be cautious in their foreign economic dealings.

The failure of democracy in the Third World has to be understood from the standpoint that these are state-dominated societies. Most of these countries, especially those in Asia and Africa, have been carved out as sovereign entities by post-colonial, nationalist elites. Even when these elites fail to create effective states, they often rule societies that do not possess autonomous and sufficient resources—economic, intellectual, and organizational—to control the political process. Thus, state domination of society is a common characteristic of Third World countries. The creation of a democratic state—a state responsive to demands of competing social groups—is an inherently uphill struggle in such a setting.

In state-dominated societies, democracy is likely to be, first and foremost, an affair of the elites. Third World democratic regimes are thus better understood as proto-democratic. This does not reduce the significance of democracy in a developing country. The economic performance of democratic regimes is still broader-based than that of many harsh authoritarian ones. And the human rights record of democracies is often superior. What the proto-democratic nature of Third World democracies clarifies, however, is the significance of elite consensus for the functioning of such regimes. This paper has argued that elite fragmentation is exacerbated both by the numerous competing functions that Third World political authorities are expected to perform and by the intensity of personal political ambitions generated within low-income economies. The resulting elite divisiveness has often become the motor force behind destabilizing social mobilization—ringing the death knell of many a Third World democratic experiment.

This analysis does not lead one to be too optimistic about the prospects of democracy in the developing world. It is worth recognizing, however, that: 1) established Third World democracies can facilitate satisfactory economic development, and 2) the disintegration of Third World democratic experiments (like that of authoritarian experiments) often is traceable back to a highly divisive political elite.

Any justification of non-democratic regimes that relies on their developmental capacities is, at best, weak. Moreover, the focus of many conservative and radical scholars on the elite-mass gap as the nemesis of democracy is exaggerated. Instead of coming from "over-demanding" or "over-deprived" masses, the threat is posed by elite behavior itself.

Therefore, if democracies are to be encouraged, conditions that facilitate elite consensus need to be both understood and created.

Greater awareness is also needed of the real, unexaggerated meaning of the ideologies of nationalism and redistribution that Third World democratic leaders often express to legitimize their rule.

Notes

Note: The author wishes to acknowledge that comments and criticisms by a number of individuals, especially Jagdish Bhagwati, Marie Gottschalk, Marc Levinson, John Lewis, and Joan Nelson—as well as the general discussion among participants at the ODC Conference on Development Strategies at Wingspread were very helpful in refining some of the issues presented in this paper.

[1] Robert Dahl, for example, holds two similar criteria, which he labels "contestation" and "participation," as central for defining a polyarchy (read democracy); see Robert A. Dahl, *Polyarchy: Participation and Opposition* (New Haven, Conn.: Yale University Press, 1971), pp. 4–9. Samuel Huntington has used a virtually identical definition of democracy in his latest published work, "Will More Countries Become Democratic?," *Political Science Quarterly*, Vol. 99, No. 2 (Summer 1984), p. 195. And Barrington Moore, although his emphasis is different, similarly treats elite contestation for ruling positions and public participation as central to his analysis of democratic government; see Barrington Moore, Jr., *Social Origins of Dictatorship and Democracy: Lord and Peasant in the Making of the Modern World* (Boston, Mass.: Beacon Press, 1966), especially p. 44.

[2] Albert Hirschman makes a similar point in a different and broader context: "Development economics started out as the spearhead of an effort that was to bring all-around emancipation from backwardness. If that effort is to fulfill its promise, the challenge posed by dismal politics must be met rather than avoided or evaded. By now it has become quite clear that this cannot be done by economics alone." Hirschman concludes his criticism of "development economics" for the neglect of political and distributional issues by suggesting that at its core was the mistaken assumption that developing countries have only *interests* and *no passions*. Albert O. Hirschman, "The Rise and Decline of Development Economics," in Albert O. Hirschman, *Essays in Trespassing: Economics to Politics and Beyond* (New York: Cambridge University Press, 1981), pp. 23–4. Jagdish Bhagwati makes a similar point: "Our optimistic assurance about how to generate steady growth has thus been moderated by a sense of the complexity of the developmental process. In turn, it has provided a significant stimulus to those who seek to integrate analytically the political processes with more orthodox economic-theoretical formulations." Jagdish Bhagwati, "Development Economics: What Have We Learned?," *Asian Development Review*, Vol. 2, No. 1 (1984), p. 32.

[3] Jagdish Bhagwati, *The Economics of Underdeveloped Countries* (New York: McGraw-Hill, 1966), p. 204.

[4] For example, see Robert Holt and John Turner, *The Political Basis of Economic Development* (Princeton, N.J.: Van Nostrand, 1966).

[5] Three studies that tend to support the "cruel choice" position are: Irma Adelman and Cynthia Morris, *Society, Politics, and Economic Development* (Baltimore, Md: Johns Hopkins University Press, 1967), p. 202; Samuel Huntington and Jorge Dominguez, "Political Development," in Fred Greenstein and Nelson Polsby, eds., *Handbook of Political Science*, Vol. 3 (Reading, Mass.: Addison-Wesley, 1975), p. 61; and Robert Marsh, "Does Democracy Hinder Economic Development in the Latecomer Developing Nations?," *Comparative Social Research*, Vol. 2 (1979), p. 240. The study that supports the reverse relationship is G. William Dick, "Authoritarian versus Nonauthoritarian Approaches to Economic Development," *Journal of Political Economy*, Vol. 82 (1974), pp. 823–4. And the study concluding that the positive impact of authoritarian government on economic growth in developing countries is very weak is Erich Weede, "The Impact of Democracy on Economic Growth: Some Evidence from Cross-National Analysis," *Kyklos*, Vol. 36 (1983), especially pp. 32 and 35.

[6] For example, see Joseph LaPalombara and Myron Weiner, "Political Parties and Political Development," *Items* 20 (March 1966), pp. 1–7.

[7] The view of the "Brazilian miracle" posited here in generally corroborated by a collection of essays in Alfred Stepan, ed., *Authoritarian Brazil* (New Haven, Conn.: Yale

University Press, 1973), especially those by Albert Fishlow, Fernando Cardoso, and Thomas Skidmore. For a more general and historical overview of the Brazilian political economy, see Peter Flynn, *Brazil: A Political Analysis* (Boulder, Colo.: Westview Press, 1983).

[8] See Skidmore in Stepan, *Authoritarian Brazil*, op. cit., especially pp. 19–28.

[9] In addition to Cardoso and Skidmore in Stepan, *Authoritarian Brazil*, op. cit., see a more recent argument along this line: Sylvia Ann Hewlett,*The Cruel Dilemmas of Development: Twentieth-Century Brazil* (New York: Basic Books, 1980), especially p. 4.

[10] Two useful recent volumes are Francine Frankel, *India's Political Economy, 1947–1977: The Gradual Revolution* (Princeton, N.J.: Princeton University Press, 1978); and Pranab Bardhan, *The Political Economy of India's Development* (Oxford: Basil-Blackwell, 1984). Two other volumes concerning earlier periods are John Lewis, *Quiet Crisis in India* (Washington, D.C.: Brookings, 1962); and George Rosen, *Democracy and Economic Change in India* (Berkeley, Cal.: University of California Press, 1968).

[11] Bhagwati, in another context, makes a similar point. While discussing export promotion (EP) strategies, he suggests that "paradoxically and unhappily, the authoritarian regimes may be more likely to adopt the superior EP strategy." He also immediately adds, however, that "it is simply a non-sequitur to count this as a shining point in favor of the import substitution strategy and as a dark blot in the EP book!" See Bhagwati, "Development Economics," op. cit., p. 30.

[12] The issue of what types of economic strategies may be compatible or even supportive of fragile democratic institutions is a subject that has not received enough scholarly attention. One interesting beginning along these lines has been made in John Mellor, *The Economics of Growth: A Strategy for India and the Developing World* (Ithaca, N.Y.: Cornell University Press, 1976), especially Ch. XI.

[13] A number of scholars continue to hold that the differences here may not be political systems but merely policy choices. The resulting debate between supporters of "export promotion" and "import substitution" is thus often both oversimplified and politically naive. The choice of growth strategies is a choice, and not all regimes are free to borrow policies from other seemingly successful cases. This point has already been made with reference to India and Brazil. For an interesting discussion of the case of South Korea, which has not been discussed here, see Leroy Jones and H. Sakong, *Government, Business and Entrepreneurship in Economic Development: The Korean Case* (Cambridge, Mass.: Harvard University Press, 1980). Those who continue to subscribe to the simple conclusion that East Asian cases corroborate the virtues of export promotion might well take note of Paul Streeten's succinct conclusion: ". . . the reasons for the success of South Korea and Taiwan are much more complex. The countries promoted labor-intensive import substitution as well as exports; early import substitution led to later exports; the labor force employed in exports was a small proportion of the total labor force; and government intervention as well as the public sector played a very important part. The singling out of export promotion through liberal trade policies is a false account of the success stories." Paul Streeten, "Development Dichotomies," Discussion Paper 17, Center for Asian Development Studies (Boston, Mass.: Boston University, November 1982), pp. 11–12. An interesting essay that reviews some of the new literature on "explaining the success of the NICs" is Stephen Haggard, "The Newly Industrializing Countries in the International System," *World Politics*, forthcoming.

[14] Systematic data for how income inequalities have changed over the 1970s are not yet available for many countries.

[15] Atul Kohli et al., "Inequality in The Third World: An Assessment of Competing Explanations," *Comparative Political Studies*, Vol. 17, No. 3 (1984), pp. 283–318.

[16] For example, see Norman Uphoff and Milton Esman, *Local Organization for Rural Development: Analysis of Asian Experiences*, Rural Development Committee (Ithaca, N.Y.: Cornell University Press, 1974).

[17] The opposite—whereby rising inequalities may threaten the stability of a democratic regime—is also possible. See Huntington, "Will More Countries Become Democratic?," op. cit., especially pp. 198–202.

[18] In a recent, insightful essay, Robert Kaufman suggests that democratic governments, such as that of President Alfonsin in Argentina, may well be as suited, if not better suited, to deal with the debt issue in novel, left-of-center ways than the more authoritarian right-of-center governments of Mexico and Brazil. See Robert Kaufman, "Democratic and Authoritarian Responses to the Debt Issue: Argentina, Brazil, Mexico," presented at the 1984 Annual Meeting of the American Political Science Association, Washington, D.C., August 30–September 2, 1984. For two other, more general, discussions of the potential destabilizing impact of cutting state expenditures, see Henry Bienen and Mark Gersovitz, "Economic Stabilization, Conditionality, and Political Sta-

bility," *International Organization*, forthcoming; and Joan M. Nelson, "The Politics of Stabilization," in Richard E. Feinberg and Valeriana Kallab, eds., *Adjustment Crisis in the Third World* (New Brunswick, N.J.: Transaction Books, for the Overseas Development Council, 1984), pp. 99–118.

[19] See Huntington, "Will More Countries Become Democratic?," op. cit., p. 197.

[20] See Charles Lindbloom, *Politics and Markets: The World's Political-Economic System* (New York: Basic Books, 1977), especially Part V; Huntington, "Will More Countries Become Democratic?," op. cit., pp. 203–5; and Moore, *Social Origins of Dictatorship and Democracy*, op. cit., especially Ch. 7.

[21] For example, see Moore, *Social Origins of Dictatorship and Democracy*, op. cit., Ch. 7; Reinhard Bendix, *Nation-Building and Citizenship* (Berkeley: University of California Press, 1977), especially Ch. 3; and T. H. Marshall, *Class Citizenship and Social Development* (New York: Doubleday and Co., 1964).

[22] Moore, *Social Origins of Dictatorship and Democracy*, op. cit., p. 418.

[23] For one of the most influential and systematic statements relating economic development to democracy, see Seymour Martin Lipset, "Some Social Requisites of Democracy: Economic Development and Political Legitimacy," *American Political Science Review*, Vol. 53 (1959), pp. 69–105.

[24] See Samuel Huntington, *Political Order in Changing Societies* (New Haven, Conn.: Yale University Press, 1968), especially Ch. I.

[25] In addition to Lipset, "Some Social Requisites of Democracy," op. cit., see Karl Deutsch, "Social Mobilization and Political Development," *American Political Science Review* (September 1961), pp. 493–514; and Alex Inkles, "Participant Citizenship in Six Developing Countries," *American Political Science Review* (December 1969), pp. 1120–41.

[26] These scholars generally build on the work of Max Weber. For example, see Felix Gilbert, ed., *The Historical Essays of Otto Hintze* (New York: Oxford University Press, 1975), Ch. 8; and Reinhard Bendix, *Kings or People: Power and the Mandate to Rule* (Berkeley: University of California Press, 1978), especially Chs. 6 and 9.

[27] See Moore, *Social Origins of Dictatorship and Democracy*, op. cit., Ch. VII.

[28] A realization of this sort seems to have engendered a wave of concern with "self-help" local institutions. Scholarly concern with such institutions is now also flourishing. See the work of Norman Uphoff and Milton Esman (in a broad comparative context), Michael Bratton (with interest in Zimbabwe), Albert Hirschman (with an interest in select Latin American countries), and Rajni Kothari (or the "Lokayan" group in India).

[29] For a lengthier development of this line of argumentation on India, see Atul Kohli, *The State and Poverty in India: The Politics of Reform* (Cambridge: Cambridge University Press, 1986), Ch. 2.

[30] In India, as elsewhere, "socialism" has always been an ambiguous word. It has certainly never been perceived as a system of economic organization that is capable of replacing capitalism. Rather, it has been understood as a way to humanize capitalism by making it more egalitarian. In practice, it has often meant no more than a significant role of the state in the economy and repeated ideological commitment to the poor and the "downtrodden."

[31] See, for example, Rajni Kothari, *Politics in India* (Boston, Mass.: Little, Brown and Co., 1970), especially Chs. 3–8.

[32] See, for example, Rajni Kothari, "Crisis and Decline of Democracy," in Peter Lyon and James Manor, eds., *Transfer and Transformation: Political Institutions in the New Commonwealth* (Leicester: Leicester University Press, 1983), especially pp. 42–3; and James Manor, "India and After: The Decay of Party Organization in India," *The Round Table*, October 1978, pp. 315–24.

[33] Commenting on Mrs. Gandhi's role, Myron Weiner was thus led to an eloquent generalization: "Societies do not destroy their democratic institutions. States do." Myron Weiner, "The Wounded Tiger: Maintaining India's Democratic Institutions," in Lyon and Manor, *Transfer and Transformation*, op. cit.

[34] The following brief account of Brazil draws heavily on Flynn, *Brazil*, op. cit.

[35] See Peter Evans, *Dependent Development: The Alliance of Multinational, State, and Local Capital in Brazil* (Princeton, N.J.: Princeton University Press, 1979).

[36] The role of the Church is examined in Thomas C. Bruneau, *The Church in Brazil: The Politics of Religion* (Austin: University of Texas Press, 1982); that of labor, in John Humphrey, *Capitalist Control and Worker's Struggle in the Brazilian Auto Industry* (Princeton, N.J.: Princeton University Press, 1982); and the focus on elite factionalism, especially the opposition of business groups to the military, in Peter McDonough, *Power and Ideology in Brazil* (Princeton, N.J.: Princeton University Press, 1981), especially p. 199.

[37] See Larry Diamond, "Nigeria in Search of Democracy," *Foreign Affairs* (Spring 1984), pp. 905-27. For an attempt to generalize this type of argument to other African cases, see Gerald A. Heeger, *The Politics of Underdevelopment* (New York: St. Martin's Press, 1974).

[38] Joan Nelson quite rightly made such a point while commenting on an earlier version of this paper at the ODC Conference on Development Strategies: "Surely an authoritarian Pinochet in Chile faces different problems than the ruler of Chad."

About the Overseas Development Council and the Contributors

The Overseas Development Council is a private, non-profit organization established in 1969 for the purpose of increasing American understanding of the economic and social problems confronting the developing countries and of how their development progress is related to U.S. interests. Toward this end, the Council functions as a center for policy research and analysis, a forum for the exchange of ideas, and a resource for public education. The Council's current program of work encompasses four major issue areas: trade and industrial policy, international finance and investment, development strategies and development cooperation, and U.S. foreign policy and the developing countries. ODC's work is used by policy makers in the Executive Branch and the Congress, journalists, and those concerned about U.S.-Third World relations in corporate and bank management, international and non-governmental organizations, universities, and educational and action groups focusing on specific development issues. ODC's program is funded by foundations, corporations, and private individuals; its policies are determined by a governing Board and Council. In selecting issues and shaping its work program, ODC is also assisted by a standing Program Advisory Committee.

Victor H. Palmieri is Chairman of the ODC, and J. Wayne Fredericks is Vice Chairman. The Council's President is John W. Sewell.

The Editors

Development Strategies Reconsidered is the fifth volume in the Overseas Development Council's new series of policy books, U.S.-Third World Policy Perspectives. The co-editors of the series—sometimes jointly and sometimes alternately, collaborating with guest editors contributing to the series—are Richard E. Feinberg and Valeriana Kallab. John P. Lewis is guest editor of this volume.

John P. Lewis, is professor of economics and international affairs at Princeton University's Woodrow Wilson School of Public and International Affairs. He is simultaneously senior advisor to the Overseas Development Council and chairman of its Program Advisory Committee. From 1979 to 1981, Dr. Lewis was chairman of the OECD's Development Assistance Committee (DAC). From 1982 to 1985, he was chairman of the three-year Task Force on Concessional Flows established by the World Bank/IMF "Development Committee" (formally the Joint Ministerial Committee of the Boards of Governors of the Bank and Fund on the Transfer of Real Resources to Developing Countries). He has served as a member of the U.N. Committee for Development Planning, of which he was also rapporteur from 1972 to 1978. For many years, he has alternated between academia and government posts (as Member of the Council of Economic Advisors, 1963–64, and Director of the U.S. AID Mission to India, 1964–69), with collateral periods of association with The Brookings Institution, the Ford Foundation, and the World Bank.

Valeriana Kallab, is vice president and director of publications of the Overseas Development Council and series co-editor of the ODC's U.S.-Third World Policy Perspectives series. Before joining ODC in 1972 to head its publications program, she was a research editor and writer on international economic issues at the Carnegie Endowment for International Peace in New York. She was co-editor (with John P. Lewis) of *U.S. Foreign Policy and the Third World: Agenda 1983* and (with Guy F. Erb) of *Beyond Dependency: The Third World Speaks Out.*

Richard E. Feinberg is vice president of the Overseas Development Council and co-editor of the Policy Perspectives series. Before joining ODC in 1981, he served as the Latin American specialist on the Policy Planning Staff of the U.S. Department of State, and as an international economist in the Treasury Department and with the House Banking Committee. Dr. Feinberg is the author of numerous books as well as journal and newspaper articles on U.S. foreign policy, Latin American politics, and international and economic and financial issues. His most recent book is *The Intemperate Zone: The Third World Challenge to U.S. Foreign Policy* (1983).

Contributing Authors

Irma Adelman is professor of economics and agricultural economics at the University of California at Berkeley. Previously, she taught at the University of Maryland, Northwestern University, Johns Hopkins University, and Stanford University. From 1964 to 1971, Dr. Adelman served as a major advisor to the government of the Republic of Korea on the economic plan that launched the country on its export-led growth strategy. For this contribution, she received the Order of Bronze Tower from the Korean government in 1971. Dr. Adelman has been a consultant to the International Labour Organisation (ILO), the World Bank, and the U.S. Agency for International Development. Her many published works in the development field include *Economic Growth and Social Equity in Developing Countries* (with Cynthia Taft Morris, 1973) and *Income Distribution Policy in Developing Countries* (with Sherman Robinson, 1978). Dr. Adelman is a Fellow of the American Academy of Arts and Sciences; she is one of a hundred economists worldwide listed in *Great Economists Since Keynes.*

John W. Mellor is director of the International Food Policy Research Institute (IFPRI). Prior to joining IFPRI, he was professor of agricultural economics and Asian studies at Cornell University, and then chief economist of the United States Agency for International Development. John Mellor is the recipient of the Wihuri Foundation International Prize for 1985, and is a Fellow of the American Academy of Arts and Sciences and of the American Agricultural Economics Association. In 1978, his book, *The Economics of Agricultural Development,* won the award for publication of enduring value from the American Agricultural Economics Association, and in 1967, his article "Toward A Theory of Agricultural Development" won that Association's award for quality of published research. His more recent books include *Agricultural Growth and Rural Poverty,* and *The New Economics of Growth.* Dr. Mellor has served on the board of directors of the International Voluntary Services, and he is a member of both the ODC Council and the ODC Program Advisory Committee.

Jagdish N. Bhagwati became Arthur Lehman Professor of Economics at Columbia University in 1981. Professor Bhagwati first came to Columbia University as visiting professor of economics from Delhi University in 1966. From 1968 to 1980, when he returned to Columbia University, he taught at the Massachusetts Institute of Technology—with the exception of 1973–74, when he was visiting professor at the University of California at Berkeley. Over the past twenty years, he has served many times as an expert consultant to major international organizations, including UNCTAD, UNIDO, ILO, OECD, and has been a member or chairman of expert groups convened by these and other agencies. Dr. Bhagwati is a former Guggenheim Fellow and the recipient of numerous international honors, prizes, and grants, including several from the Ford and Rockefeller Foundations. He is a Fellow of the American Academy of Arts and Sciences. The most recent of his many books on international trade, aid, and development are his two-volume *Essays in Development Economics* (M.I.T., 1985).

Leopoldo Solis is Chairman of the Presidential Council of Economic Advisors of Mexico and a Member of Mexico's El Colegio Nacional. In 1977, he served as Under-Secretary of Commercial Planning of the Secretariat of Commerce, and from 1977 to 1984, he was Deputy Director of the Central Bank of Mexico. He was the director of the General Coordinating Bureau of Economic and Social Programming at the Secretariat of the Presidency from 1970 to 1975. Dr. Solis is a trustee of the International Food Policy Research Institute (Washington, D.C.) and serves on the board of the Latin American Institute of Economic and Social Planning in Santiago, Chile. His many publications on economic development include *Economic Policy Reform in Mexico* (1981), *Mexican Financial Development* (1966), *Alternativas para el Desarrollo* (1980), and *La Realidad Economica Mexicana* (1970).

Aurelio Montemayor is currently a member of the staff of the economic research department at the Central Bank of Mexico. He is also professor of project appraisal and industrial organization at the Technological Institute of Mexico and at the Pan-American University, both in Mexico City. He is the author of numerous articles on investment in human capital, internal commerce, public finance, and monetary policy in Mexico. His current work focuses on the areas of subsidies, cost-benefit analysis, and financing of education.

Colin I. Bradford, Jr. teaches international economics at Yale University, where he directs a two-year Masters Program in International Relations and is associate director of the Yale Center for International and Area Studies. He also holds a research appointment at the National Bureau of Economic Research. Dr. Bradford previously was economic and foreign policy advisor to U.S. Senator Lawton Chiles, director of the Office of Multilateral Development Banks in the U.S. Treasury Department during the Carter Administration, and an associate fellow of the Overseas Development Council. Since taking up his duties at Yale, he has participated in several research projects focusing on the NICs, leading to numerous articles on the subject, and has been a consultant to the OECD Development Centre, UNCTAD, and the United Nations Association's East Asian program. He is the editor of two books on related issues: *Trade and Structural Change in Pacific Asia* (with William H. Branson), to be published by the University of Chicago Press, and *Europe and Latin America in the World Economy,* published by the Yale Center for International and Area Studies.

Alex Duncan is a research associate at Queen Elizabeth House, Oxford, and a consultant on agricultural issues. He has worked for the U.N. Food and Agriculture Organization (1975–76) and for the World Bank's Agricultural Development Service (1976–80). His research interests include food production and marketing policies, smallholder farming, and pastoralism. He took part in a recent study of aid effectiveness, to be published in 1986 as *Does Aid Work?*, the Independent Consultants' Study of Aid-Effectiveness—the report prepared by R. H. Cassen and associates for the Task Force on Concessional Flows (1982–85), established by the Joint Ministerial Committee of the Boards of Governors of the Bank and Fund on the Transfer of Real Resources to Developing Countries.

Atul Kohli is assistant professor of politics and international affairs at Princeton University. He is the author of *The State and Poverty in India: The Politics and Reform* (Cambridge University Press, forthcoming) and the editor of *The State and Development in the Third World* (Princeton University Press, forthcoming). His research has also appeared in such journals as *World Politics, Asian Survey, Pacific Affairs, Comparative Political Studies,* and *The Journal of Commonwealth and Comparative Politics.* He is the review article editor of *World Politics.*

Overseas Development Council

Board of Directors*

Chairman: Victor H. Palmieri
Chairman, The Palmieri Company
Vice Chairman: J. Wayne Fredericks
Ford Motor Company

Marjorie C. Benton
Chairman of the Board
Save the Children Federation

William H. Bolin
San Francisco, California

Thornton F. Bradshaw
Chairman of the Board
RCA Corporation

William D. Eberle
President
Manchester Associates, Ltd.

Thomas L. Farmer**
Prather, Seeger, Doolittle and Farmer

Roger Fisher
Harvard Law School

Stephen J. Friedman
Debevoise & Plimpton

John J. Gilligan
Chairman, Institute for Public Policy
University of Notre Dame

Edward K. Hamilton
President
Hamilton, Rabinovitz, Szanton,
and Alschuler, Inc.

Frederick Heldring
Deputy Chairman
Philadelphia National Bank

Susan Herter
Santa Fe, New Mexico

Ruth J. Hinerfeld
Former President, The League
of Women Voters of the USA

Joan Holmes
Executive Director
The Hunger Project

Robert D. Hormats
Vice President
International Corporate Finance
Goldman, Sachs & Co.

Jerome Jacobson
President
Economic Studies, Inc.

William J. Lawless
President
Cognitronics Corporation

C. Payne Lucas
Executive Director
Africare

Paul F. McCleary
Associate General Secretary
General Council on Ministries of the
United Methodist Church

Robert S. McNamara

Lawrence C. McQuade
Executive Vice President
W. R. Grace & Co.

William G. Milliken
Former Governor
State of Michigan

Alfred F. Miossi
Executive Vice President
Continental Illinois National Bank
and Trust Company of Chicago

Merlin E. Nelson
Kleinwort, Benson (International)

Jane Cahill Pfeiffer
Former Chairman, NBC, Inc.

John W. Sewell**
President
Overseas Development Council

Daniel A. Sharp
Director, International Relations
and Public Affairs
Xerox Corporation

Board members are also members of the Council.
**Ex Officio.*

William McSweeny
Occidental International

John W. Mellor
International Food Policy Research Institute

Robert R. Nathan
Robert Nathan Associates

Rev. Randolph Nugent
General Board of Global Ministries United Methodist Church

Joseph S. Nye
John F. Kennedy School of Government Harvard University

Richard Ottinger
Pace University Law School

Daniel S. Parker
Charleston, South Carolina

James A. Perkins
International Council for Educational Development

John Petty
Chairman and Chief Executive Officer Marine-Midland Bank, N.A.

James J. Phelan
The Chase Manhattan Bank, N.A.

Samuel D. Proctor
Rutgers University

Charles W. Robinson
Energy Transition Corporation

William D. Rogers, Esq.
Arnold & Porter

J. Robert Schaetzel
Washington, DC

David H. Shepard
Cognitronics Corporation

Eugene Skolnikoff
Massachusetts Institute of Technology

Davidson Sommers, Esq.
Webster & Sheffield

Joan E. Spero
American Express Company

Stephen Stamas
Exxon Corporation

C. M. van Vlierden
San Francisco, California

Alan N. Weeden
Investment Banker

Clifton R. Wharton, Jr.
State University of New York

Thomas H. Wyman
CBS, Inc.

Andrew Young
Mayor, Atlanta, Georgia

George Zeidenstein
The Population Council

Barry Zorthian
Senior Vice President Alcade, Henderson, O'Bannon & Rousselot

ODC Program Advisory Committee

A New Series from the Overseas Development Council

U.S.-THIRD WORLD POLICY PERSPECTIVES

Series Editors: Richard E. Feinberg and Valeriana Kallab

This new ODC policy series expands and diversifies the issue coverage provided by the ODC in its respected *Agenda* policy assessments, *U.S. Foreign Policy and the Third World*—now published every other year as part of this series. In the new series, the Overseas Development Council singles out for policy analysis issues that merit priority attention on the U.S.-Third World policy agenda. Each volume offers a variety of perspectives by prominent policy analysts on different facets of a single policy theme. The series addresses itself to all who take an interest in U.S.-Third World relations and U.S. participation in international development cooperation—in the U.S. government, Congress, international institutions, U.S. corporations and banks, private U.S. education and action organizations, and academic institutions.

Series Editors:

Richard E. Feinberg is vice president of the Overseas Development Council. He previously served as the Latin American specialist on the Policy Planning Staff of the U.S. Department of State, and as an international economist in the Treasury Department and with the House Banking Committee. His most recent book is *The Intemperate Zone: The Third World Challenge to U.S. Foreign Policy* (1983).

Valeriana Kallab is vice president and director of publications of the Overseas Development Council. Before joining ODC in 1972, she was a research editor and writer on international economic issues with the Carnegie Endowment for International Peace in New York.

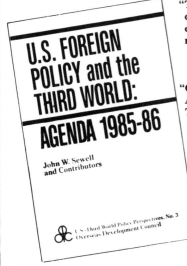

"These volumes have the virtue of combining cogent and comprehensive analysis with constructive and practical policy recommendations."
—Lawrence A. Veit
Brown Brothers Harriman & Co.

"ODC continues its important contribution to American understanding of U.S. interests in the Third World's economic and social progress."
—Governor Richard F. Celeste
(Peace Corps Director, 1979-81)

ODC's Agenda— now part of this new series

INVESTING IN DEVELOPMENT: NEW ROLES FOR PRIVATE CAPITAL?

Theodore H. Moran and contributors

The tone of the debate about foreign direct investment in Third World development has changed dramatically since the 1970s. There are expectations in both North and South that multinational corporations can play a key role in restoring growth, replacing aid, providing capital to relieve the burden on commercial bank lending, and (together with the private sectors in the local economies) lead to an era of healthier and more balanced growth.

To what extent are these expectations justified? This volume provides a reassessment of the impact of multinational corporate operations on Third World development. It covers not only direct equity investment in natural resources and manufacturing, but non-equity arrangements extending to agriculture and other sectors as well. It examines whether the efforts of less developed countries to attract and control multinational corporations have constituted a serious "distortion" of trade that threatens jobs in the home nations. It analyzes the link between international companies and the "umbrella" of World Bank co-financing as a mechanism to reduce risk. Finally, it attempts to estimate how much of the "gap" in commercial bank lending might plausibly be filled by direct corporate investment over the next decade.

In each case, it draws policy conclusions for host governments, for home governments (focused particularly on the United States), for multilateral institutions such as the World Bank and the agencies of the United Nations, and for the multinational firms themselves.

Contents:

Theodore H. Moran—Overview: The Future of Foreign Direct Investment in the Third World

Joseph M. Grieco—Foreign Direct Investment and Third World Development: Theories and Evidence

Dennis J. Encarnation and Louis T. Wells, Jr.—Evaluating Foreign Investment

Stephen Guisinger—Host-Country Policies to Attract and Control Foreign Investment

David J. Goldsbrough—Past Trends and Prospects for Foreign Direct Investment in Developing Countries: The Link with Bank Lending

David J. Glover—Multinational Corporations and Third World Agriculture

Charles P. Oman—New Forms of Investment in Developing Countries

Vincent Cable and Bishakha Mukherjee—Foreign Investment and Low-Income Developing Countries

Theodore H. Moran is director of Georgetown University's Landegger Program in International Business Diplomacy as well as professor and member of the Executive Council of the Georgetown University School of Business Administration. A former member of the Policy Planning Staff of the Department of State with responsibilities including investment issues, Dr. Moran has since 1971 been a consultant to corporations, governments, and multilateral agencies on investment strategy, international negotiations, and political risk assessment. His publications include many articles and five major books on the issues explored in this new volume. He is a member of the ODC Program Advisory Committee.

ISBN: 0-88738-074-3 (cloth)   **$19.95**
ISBN: 0-87855-644-X (paper)   **$12.95**
April 1986   **224 pp.**

BETWEEN TWO WORLDS:
THE WORLD BANK IN THE COMING DECADE

Richard E. Feinberg and contributors

In the midst of the global debt and adjustment crises, the World Bank has been challenged to become the leading agency in North-South finance and development. The many dimensions of this challenge—which must be comprehensively addressed by the Bank's new president assuming office in mid-1986—are the subject of this important volume.

As mediator between international capital markets and developing countries, the World Bank will be searching for ways to renew the flow of private credit and investment to Latin America and Africa. And as the world's premier development agency, the Bank can help formulate growth strategies appropriate to the 1990s.

The Bank's ability to design and implement a comprehensive response to these global needs is threatened by competing objectives and uncertain priorities. Can the Bank design programs attractive to private investors that also serve the very poor? Can it emphasize efficiency while transferring technologies that maximize labor absorption? Can it more aggressively condition loans on policy reforms without attracting the criticism that has accompanied IMF programs?

The contributors to this volume assess the role that the World Bank can play in the period ahead. They argue for new financial and policy initiatives and for new conceptual approaches to development, as well as for a restructuring of the Bank, as it takes on new, systemic responsibilities in the next decade.

Contents:

Richard E. Feinberg—Overview: The Future of the World Bank
Gerald K. Helleiner—The Changing Content of Conditionality
Joan M. Nelson—The Diplomacy of the Policy-Based Lending:
  Leverage or Dialogue?
Sheldon Annis—The Shifting Ground of Poverty Lending
Howard Pack—Employment Generation Through Changing Technology
John F. H. Purcell—The World Bank and Private International Capital
Charles R. Blitzer—Financing the IBRD and IDA

Richard E. Feinberg is vice president of the Overseas Development Council and co-editor of the U.S.-Third World Policy Perspectives series. From 1977 to 1979, Feinberg was Latin American specialist on the policy planning staff of the U.S. Department of State. He has also served as an international economist in the U.S. Treasury Department and with the House Banking Committee. He is currently also adjunct professor of international finance at the Georgetown University School of Foreign Service. Feinberg is the author of numerous books as well as journal and newspaper articles on U.S. foreign policy, Latin American politics, and international economics. His most recent book is *The Intemperate Zone: The Third World Challenge to U.S. Foreign Policy* (1983).

ISBN: 0-88738-123-5 (cloth)
ISBN: 0-88738-665-2 (paper)
June 1986

$19.95
$12.95
208 pp.

THE UNITED STATES AND MEXICO: FACE TO FACE WITH NEW TECHNOLOGY

Cathryn L. Thorup and contributors

Rapid technological advance is fast changing the nature of the relationship between the industrial countries and the advanced developing countries. This volume explores the meanings of this change close to home— as it affects the U.S.-Mexican relationship.

What is the impact of the new technology on trade, investment, and labor flows between the United States and Mexico? Will development of a stronger Mexican industrial sector constitute an aid or a threat to specific U.S. industries? While demand for the middle-technology goods that countries such as Mexico can produce is growing in the United States, the debt crisis and the high dollar make procuring the high-technology capital goods necessary for this effort difficult and expensive.

An overview essay explores the impact of technological change upon conflicts between the economic and political objectives of the two countries and ways in which the coordination of national policies might be maximized. The authors—representing a mix of government and business experience in both countries—offer specific recommendations on improving the efficiency of bilateral economic interaction, reducing the adjustment costs of technological change, and avoiding diplomatic tensions between the two nations.

Contents:

Cathryn L. Thorup is director of the Overseas Development Council's U.S.-Mexico Project, a policy-oriented, Washington-based forum for the exchange of ideas among key actors in the bilateral relationship. She is the author of many articles on conflict management in the U.S.-Mexican relationship, on Mexico's attempts to diversify its foreign investments, on the Reagan administration and Mexico, and on U.S.-Mexican policies toward Central America.

ISBN: 0-88738-120-0 (cloth)   **$19.95**
ISBN: 0-87855-663-6 (paper)   **$12.95**
October 1986   **224 pp.**

ADJUSTMENT CRISIS IN THE THIRD WORLD

Richard E. Feinberg and Valeriana Kallab, editors

**"major contribution to the literature on the
adjustment crisis"**
—B. T. G. Chidzero
Minister of Finance, Economic Planning
and Development Government of Zimbabwe

**"The adjustment crisis book has really stirred
up some excitement here"**
—Peter P. Waller
German Development Institute (Berlin)

"good collection of papers"
—*Foreign Affairs*

Just how the debt and adjustment crisis of Third World countries is handled, by them and by international agencies and banks, can make a big difference in the pace and quality of *global* recovery.

Stagnating international trade, sharp swings in the prices of key commodities, worsened terms of trade, high interest rates, and reduced access to commercial bank credits have slowed and even reversed growth in many Third World countries. Together, these trends make "adjustment" of both demand and supply a central problem confronting policy makers in most countries in the mid-1980s. Countries must bring expenditures into line with shrinking resources in the short run, but they also need to alter prices and take other longer-range steps to expand the resource base in the future—to stimulate investment, production, and employment. Already low living standards make this an especially formidable agenda in most Third World nations.

What can be done to forestall the more conflictive phase of the debt crisis that now looms ahead? How can developing countries achieve adjustment *with growth?* The contributors to this volume share the belief that more constructive change is possible and necessary.

Contents:

ISBN: 0-88738-040-9 (cloth)   **$19.95**
ISBN: 0-87855-988-4 (paper)   **$12.95**
1984   **220 pp.**

UNCERTAIN FUTURE: COMMERCIAL BANKS AND THE THIRD WORLD

Richard E. Feinberg and Valeriana Kallab, editors

"useful short papers by people of differing backgrounds who make quite different kinds of suggestions about how banks, governments and international bodies ought to behave in the face of the continuing debt difficulties"
—*Foreign Affairs*

"the very best available to academia and the general public . . . on the criteria of reader interest, clarity of writing, quality of the research, and on that extra something special that sets a work apart from others of similar content"
—James A. Cox, Editor
The Midwest Book Review

The future of international commercial lending to the Third World has become highly uncertain just when the stakes seem greatest for the banks themselves, the developing countries, and the international financial system. Having become the main channel for the transfer of capital from the North to the South in the 1970s, how will the banks respond in the period ahead, when financing will be urgently needed?

The debt crisis that burst onto the world stage in 1982 is a long-term problem. New bank lending to many developing countries has slowed to a trickle. The combination of high interest rates and the retrenchment in bank lending is draining many developing countries of badly needed development finance. While major outright defaults now seem improbable, heightened conflict between creditors and debtors is possible unless bold actions are taken soon.

New approaches must take into account the interests of both the banks and developing-country borrowers. No single solution can by itself resolve the crisis. A battery of measures is needed—reforms in macroeconomic management, in the policies of the multilateral financial institutions, in bank lending practices as well as information gathering and analysis, and in regulation.

Contents:

Richard E. Feinberg—Overview: Restoring Confidence in International Credit Markets
Lawrence J. Brainard—More Lending to the Third World? A Banker's View
Karin Lissakers—Bank Regulation and International Debt
Christine A. Bogdanowicz-Bindert and Paul M. Sacks—The Role of Information: Closing the Barn Door?
George J. Clark—Foreign Banks in the Domestic Markets of Developing Countries
Catherine Gwin—The IMF and the World Bank: Measures to Improve the System
Benjamin J. Cohen—High Finance, High Politics

ISBN: 0-88738-041-7 (cloth) $19.95
ISBN: 0-87855-989-2 (paper) $12.95
1984   144 pp.

U.S. FOREIGN POLICY AND THE THIRD WORLD: AGENDA 1985-86

John W. Sewell, Richard E. Feinberg, and Valeriana Kallab, editors

"high-quality analysis ... has made the ODC's *Agenda* series necessary reading for anyone interested in American foreign policy or development issues"
—Joseph S. Nye
Professor of Government and Public Policy
John F. Kennedy School of Government
Harvard University

"This year's volume begins with an interesting balance sheet of the Reagan administration's 'reassertionist' approach ... All [chapters] are full of ideas ... for policy-making."
—*Foreign Affairs*

The Overseas Development Council's 1985-86 *Agenda*—the tenth of its well-known annual assessments of U.S. policy toward the developing countries—analyzes the record of the Reagan administration's first term and identifies the main issues currently looming in this area of U.S. foreign policy. The losses and gains of the administration's "reassertionist" approach are tallied both in terms of its own expressed objectives and in terms of broader, longer-term criteria for advancing U.S. economic, security, and humanitarian interests in the Third World.

Contents:

Overview: Testing U.S. Reassertionism: The Reagan Approach to the Third World
Paul R. Krugman—U.S. Macro-Economic Policy and the Developing Countries
Richard E. Feinberg—International Finance and Investment: A Surging Public Sector
Steve Lande and Craig VanGrasstek—Trade with the Developing Countries: The Reagan Record and Prospects
John W. Sewell and Christine E. Contee—U.S. Foreign Aid in the 1980s: Reordering Priorities
Anthony Lake—Wrestling with Third World Radical Regimes: Theory and Practice
Stuart Tucker—Statistical Annexes

John W. Sewell has been president of the Overseas Development Council since January 1980. From 1977 to 1979, he was the Council's executive vice president, directing ODC's program of research and public education. Prior to joining ODC in 1971, he was with the Brookings Institution, and served in the U.S. Foreign Service. A contributor to several of ODC's past *Agenda* assessments of U.S. policies and performance in U.S.-Third World relations, he was also recently a co-author of *Rich Country Interests and Third World Development* and of *The Ties That Bind: U.S. Interests in Third World Development*

ISBN: 0-88738-042-5 (cloth)
ISBN: 0-87855-990-6 (paper)
1985

$19.95
$12.95
242 pp.

HARD BARGAINING AHEAD: U.S. TRADE POLICY AND DEVELOPING COUNTRIES

Ernest H. Preeg and contributors.

U.S.-Third World trade relations are at a critical juncture. Trade conflicts are exploding as subsidies, import quotas, and "voluntary" export restraints have become commonplace. The United States is struggling with record trade and budget deficits. Developing countries, faced with unprecedented debt problems, continue to restrain imports and stimulate exports.

For both national policies and future multilateral negotiations, the current state of the North-South trade relationship presents a profound dilemma. Existing problems of debt and unemployment cannot be solved without growth in world trade. While many developing countries would prefer an export-oriented development strategy, access to industrialized-country markets will be in serious doubt if adjustment policies are not implemented. Consequently, there is an urgent need for more clearly defined mutual objectives and a strengthened policy framework for trade between the industrialized and the developing countries.

In this volume, distinguished practitioners and academics identify specific policy objectives for the United States on issues that will be prominent in the new round of GATT negotiations.

Contents:

Ernest H. Preeg—Overview: An Agenda for U.S. Trade Policy Toward Developing Countries
William E. Brock—Statement: U.S. Trade Policy Toward Developing Countries
Anne O. Krueger and Constantine Michalopoulos—Developing-Country Trade Policies and the International Economic System
Henry R. Nau—The NICs in a New Trade Round
C. Michael Aho—U.S. Labor-Market Adjustment and Import Restrictions
John D. A. Cuddy—Commodity Trade
Adebayo Adedeji—Special Measures for the Least Developed and Other Low-Income Countries
Sidney Weintraub—Selective Trade Liberalization and Restriction
Stuart K. Tucker—Statistical Annexes

Ernest H. Preeg, a career foreign service officer and recent visiting fellow at the Overseas Development Council, has had long experience in trade policy and North-South economic relations. He was a member of the U.S. delegation to the GATT Kennedy Round of negotiations and later wrote a history and analysis of those negotiations, *Traders and Diplomats* (The Brookings Institution, 1969). Prior to serving as American ambassador to Haiti (1981-82), he was deputy chief of mission in Lima, Peru (1977-80), and deputy secretary of state for international finance and development (1976-77).

ISBN: 0-88738-043-3 (cloth)   **$19.95**
ISBN: 0-87855-987-6 (paper)   **$12.95**
1985   **220 pp.**